TRAIL
OF
WORTH

SHANNON COLMAN

Trail of Worth

Tellwell Talent
www.tellwell.ca

ISBN
978-0-2288-5544-6 (Paperback)
978-0-2288-5787-7 (eBook)

ACKNOWLEDGEMENTS

I acknowledge with respect the Lekwungen, T'Sou-ke, W̱SÁNEĆ, Coast Salish, and Syilx peoples, on whose unceded territory I am fortunate to live and work, and on whose traditional lands this story is based.

A special thanks to my mum and dad for giving me a childhood that inspired imagination and adventure, and for encouraging me to be my authentic self.

*

This story is based on actual events as I remember them. Identities have been changed.

PROLOGUE

After a glance over his shoulder, the cab driver pulls onto the road leading away from the airport.

"So, what are your plans for Kelowna, Sara?" he asks with a faint Indian accent. "Are you visiting family?"

I cast my eyes up at the snow-dusted hills before letting them fall onto the department stores and car dealerships on the side of the highway.

"No, I'm just going to wander around," I reply absent-mindedly.

In the mirror, I notice the driver's eyebrows furrow with puzzlement. He proceeds to drive in silence. Just the way I like it.

Fifteen minutes later, we pull up outside the Airbnb motel I've booked for three nights. Fresh flakes of snow are starting to fall as I step out of the car. The driver flashes me a look of concern as I head towards a set of narrow steps and find my room with a lockbox attached to the door. A glance behind me shows him still parked with the engine running. I give him a wave in hopes he'll leave and turn to unlock the door.

A box room with a queen-size bed, wooden desk, and door to a small bathroom greets me. It's all I need. I lock the door behind me, dump my holdall on the floor, kick off my boots, and collapse onto the bed. A quick check of my phone reveals that he hasn't messaged me.

A cloud of exhaustion suddenly surrounds me. I close my heavy eyelids and run my fingers through my hair, recollecting how I came to be in this situation.

PART ONE

ONE

"Ladies and gentlemen, as we are going through an area of turbulence, we ask that you return to your seats and fasten your seatbelts. Thank you."

The bumpy motion of the plane distracted me from my thoughts. I was remembering how Dad had concealed his small digital camera in his pocket when walking me to the platform. Perhaps I should have suggested taking a picture together before I boarded the train.

I glanced out of the window to notice the white peaks of the Canadian Rockies peeping above thick clouds. The journey from England to Canada was one I had become familiar with over the past few years. The only difference was that this journey had no return date.

An hour later, I sat up in anticipation as the twinkling Christmas lights on Sidney's houses became sharper in focus through the plane window. I was so close to what I'd spent months waiting for.

The immigration officer at Victoria International Airport stapled my two-year work permit into my passport with a friendly smile. "Welcome to Vancouver Island. Have fun!"

I hitched my backpack up higher and dragged my other suitcase towards the arrival doors, an expectant smile already forming at the corner of my lips.

He wasn't there.

I glanced around the room in case he was playing a trick on me, but there was no sign of him. I took a seat in the lounge with an accepting sigh and reminded myself I wasn't the type of girlfriend that needed big gestures.

Ten minutes later, Harry walked into the lounge. He had one hand tucked into the pocket of an unrecognizable pair of tight, burgundy pants, and the other he ran through his dark hair that had grown much longer. As he stopped to scan the room, something prevented me from running to him. He looked so different from the boy I'd met over five years ago.

I waited a few seconds longer to see a sign of worry on his face, only for impatience to persuade me to gather my things and walk over to him. At the sight of me, his face broke into a smile.

"What are those pants?" I asked teasingly as he wrapped me in a long hug.

"I just bought them. Brendan thought they would suit me."

I ignored the reference to Harry's professor-turned-friend and looked up at his face with a tired smile. He looked down at me with his warm brown eyes, and I found comfort in their familiarity after so long apart. On the drive to his family home, I studied his side profile and held his right hand, reminding myself of the slight coarseness of his fingers from years of guitar playing.

"Did you want to do anything for New Year's Eve tomorrow?" he asked.

"I don't mind what we do. I'm just happy to finally be here."

"In a few days, we'll be cat sitting at Frank and Theresa's again."

I smiled as my mind flashed back to looking at the moon from a veranda that wrapped around a large wooden house surrounded by tall trees. "Great, I love their place."

"You brought your DSLR, right?" he asked. "I've decided that I want to start making more memories this next year."

I looked at him with pleasant surprise. Normally, I was the one more interested in taking photos of our times together.

"It will be nice to have some more space to ourselves, now that the barn is finished," I said.

Harry nodded as he turned off onto a smaller road. "Mom's booked a night in a hotel suite for all of us on the 1st. She got it using credit card points or something."

I shifted in my seat. "That'll be nice."

"And she confirmed that for the few months you were planning to stay here, she'd be okay with you not paying any rent in return for helping out a bit."

"That's kind of her. I'll of course help out, though I will need some time to look for jobs as well," I said.

I knew full well that "helping out a bit" meant something different to Ruth.

"I was thinking you should try to find a job in the government," said Harry. "That way, it should be easier for you to get permanent residency."

A warm feeling brewed inside me, and I squeezed his hand reassuringly. "I'll do my best."

We pulled up on the property that Harry's family had moved into the previous autumn during one of my visits. As I stepped out of the car, the cold winter breeze wafted a familiar fusion of pine and hay into my nostrils. I looked around at the tall trees and Swedish-style barns and smiled at the knowledge they would not be short-term sights.

To provide more room for him to play music, Harry's parents had converted one of the small barns into a living space. I had helped out with the initial cleaning stage, back when it was difficult to imagine the abandoned building being inhabited. It had gone on to become a beautiful space with an authentic, rustic character.

A wooden staircase led up to the mezzanine that formed Harry's bedroom. It was just how I remembered: random socks strewn here and there, pens and guitar picks lying around on different surfaces, various half-open math books spilling over his desk, the same faint smell of apricot-scented deodorant on the sweater that hung off his chair.

Harry nodded at the corner where a few wrapped presents waited. I opened them with surprise to find a woolly hat ("We call it a toque here," he said teasingly), matching gloves, and a yoga mat.

"I'm sorry, I didn't bring you any presents," I said shame-facedly.

"That's okay, you being here is my present," said Harry.

I gazed at him gratefully and sat down on the bed. The sheets were still warm from the dryer.

"It would be nice to lie down for a bit before seeing everyone else," I said.

We shared a knowing smile.

Jetlag woke me in the early hours of the morning as the wind howled through the small cracks in the timber frames above the bed. I slipped quietly out of the covers and tiptoed over to Harry's desk. Along with the math books was his notepad, on which were scribbled math equations, chords, quotes, and mini to-do lists. *Read two chapters of Math 400 book, work on website, jam with Jake, call Brendan.*

Beneath one of the textbooks on the side of the desk was a card I'd sent Harry for his birthday in the summer. Now crumpled at the edges, it contained photos of him and me that I'd taken over the years. I smiled fondly at the one of us taken on the beach the summer we met in 2011. We looked so much younger: my bashful smile on a nineteen-year-old face tanned during five weeks of backpacking through Canada; his bare, smooth skin and cheeky seventeen-year-old grin.

I had arrived at Harry's family's home on the final leg of my trip. With a week left until I flew home, I'd come to them as a WWOOFer—someone who did a few hours of work on a farm each day in exchange for food and accommodation. When reading the family description on the website, I'd liked that there were horses, a vineyard, and two kids who were interested in sports. I hadn't expected to develop feelings for the eldest.

For the few days that we kept our romance secret, part of me had felt embarrassed about the circumstances. But Harry had seemed mature and intelligent, and there was something exciting about the way his eyes followed me curiously through the vines. He had that appealing teenage West Coast confidence in the way he rode his longboard or ran through the waves, but he was also sensitive; he cared about his sister, listened intently to my stories, asked thoughtful questions, and shared his insecurities. With him, in this beautiful part of the world with its endless sunsets and ocean views, I could experience the freedom and excitement of a teenage summer romance that I'd never really had before. I wasn't sure one could love someone after such a short time, but it was the closest I'd felt to what I assumed love was supposed to feel like.

When I returned to England and moved to London to start university, I assumed I'd form relationships that were even better, but realistically, nobody quite matched up the same. Nobody seemed to have Harry's depth, emotional maturity, and loyalty. Boys that were set on joining London's stock market and making lots of money in the corporate world didn't appeal to me. When

Harry and I reunited three summers later to go on a road trip through the western United States, our compatibility seemed to be confirmed. And after touring various national parks, hiking mountains, and exploring canyons, I pictured a life of outdoor adventures that London couldn't offer.

Harry was the one who suggested we be friends once I returned to England again. Long-distance would ruin us, he said. It wasn't sustainable. I left Canada crushed. In the end, it was he who initiated the video calls and started the email threads.

Being in a long-distance relationship brought many challenges, but something convinced me to persevere. I used my time between work contracts to visit, but it wasn't enough. City life seemed to sap my energy and drive, and I felt disillusioned with England's culture. Both Harry and Canada seemed to be my calling, and that was why I applied for my working holiday visa in February 2016.

I spent New Year's Eve in the barn watching Harry play music with his younger cousin, Jake. Harry's sister sat next to me with her head on my shoulder.

"I can't believe you're finishing high school this year," I said. "It seems like only yesterday you were twelve, obsessed with boys and singing country ballads all the time."

Hannah smiled. "My music tastes have expanded since then, but I still don't have a boyfriend."

"I didn't when I was seventeen, either."

"And now here you are, with my brother," she said fondly. "Just like I thought would happen."

I remembered the smell of ocean water and how it had felt when I ran my fingers over it, the heat of the sun on my back as Harry and I exchanged glances, the way Hannah grinned and whispered "I think he likes you" as we walked along the pebbled beach.

"Do you know what you want to do when you graduate?" I asked.

"I'm going to take a gap year," she said brightly. "I want to WWOOF like you did, and I want to do something that raises awareness of plastic pollution."

Alongside her passion for music, Hannah had grown increasingly interested in the environment and sustainability over the past few years. Unlike many other girls her age, she wore no makeup, cared little for fashion trends, and had only just got a phone. She seemed comfortable being herself, and I liked to think I had had some influence over it. From the beginning, Hannah had viewed me as a sister, and I had viewed her the same. She was as much a part of my life as Harry was.

The night in the hotel suite on the following evening seemed to reinforce how much a part of Harry's family I had become. It was an evening of comfortability with card games, toilet jokes, old movies, and laughter in an outdoor hot tub. With all the exchange students and travellers that they hosted, it was rare for the family to spend a night alone together. There was something touching about the fact that Harry's mother had planned this evening to include me.

And yet, the magic never seemed to last long. The next morning, Ruth's mood changed when it was established that going out for breakfast was preferred over her cooking. As she criticized the café's food, I looked away uncomfortably, reluctant to be a witness as the positive energy from the prior evening disappeared faster than a plate of eggs. Something always seemed to happen that instantly brought the mood of the room down.

From the time I first met her over five years ago, I knew I would find Ruth difficult to be around. We had completely different personalities. I valued tact, whereas she was abrupt. She was quick to criticize and slow to apologize. She was nitpicky and would fault the smallest things, to the point where chopping vegetables around her seemed like a daunting task. At times, it felt like nothing I did would be good enough for her. But she also had a generous side to her that made me feel guilty for my thoughts. I always reminded myself of the necklace she had given me at the airport when we said our first goodbye. I tried to convince myself that the gesture signified she thought highly of me, that she was the type of person who expressed her feelings through actions versus words.

In recent years, I had become more confident in challenging Ruth's opinions and approaches, but with the snap of a finger, she had the ability to make me feel inadequate again. I told myself it wasn't personal and that she did it to everyone. However, I had concluded a while ago that the easiest way to handle her was in small doses.

TWO

After breakfast, Harry and I left the family to start our week of cat sitting. I was grateful for a period of complete privacy. I wanted to enjoy some quality time with Harry before he became busy with his next semester of classes.

We stopped in the downtown mall to buy a SIM card for my Canadian phone. The sales assistant was a friendly man in his twenties who blushed with bafflement when I told him my mother's maiden name to create an account security question. As I spelled the name for him, Harry approached.

"That seems a little misleading," he said with a smirk to the assistant, nodding at a poster advertising a deal on two-year plans.

I looked up curiously to see the man smile nervously. "That's something the head management drew up."

"I just love marketing," Harry continued sarcastically. "Conning customers is awesome."

The sales assistant swallowed uncomfortably and looked away. I glanced down at the paperwork in front of me, feeling my face burn with an unfamiliar sense of shame. I handed my signed form back to him with a thank you, and he said bye without looking up.

I jogged after Harry with a lingering feeling of embarrassment. "It was quite rude of you to talk to him like that, Harry."

Harry looked at me with confusion. "But the math doesn't make sense. You're not getting more value from buying two at that price."

"Okay, but he obviously doesn't decide the sales strategy. It's probably just a part-time job he took to fund himself through university. He's probably not thrilled about working there."

"Well, in that case, maybe he shouldn't choose to work for such a greedy corporation."

"Maybe it was the only job available at the time. Not everyone is lucky enough to live at home rent-free and drive an electric car bought for them by their parents," I said pointedly. "It was unnecessary to confront him like that."

"I disagree," said Harry with calm confidence.

Not wanting to argue, I crossed my arms, and we walked to the parkade in silence. Christmas decorations still hung from buildings and street lamps, but their lights were switched off. There was something deflating about the way they no longer glowed.

The cat house, as we called it, was nestled in a forested area at the top of a steep driveway leading from a quiet road in the Highlands. The living room had high ceilings and was surrounded by large windows. The house looked much the same as it had when I last stayed in 2014.

After tending to the ailing cats, I sat on the sofa and reopened my phone package, only to groan with annoyance.

"It's not there!"

"What isn't?" asked Harry from the kitchen.

"The SIM card, it's missing."

"Are you sure? I can have a look."

"Yes, I'm sure. I have eyes!"

"I never said you didn't," said Harry calmly as he approached. "Was it definitely there when you first got it?"

"I assume so. They wouldn't have given it to me without one."

Harry shrugged. "I guess you'll just have to go get a new one."

I slumped further down the couch with an irritated sigh. "How am I supposed to do that? There are no buses on this road."

"Maybe you could come to school with me tomorrow and then drive downtown?" he suggested.

I regarded him with skepticism. "Drive downtown by myself? I haven't driven on the right in ages, and I hardly know the roads."

Harry looked at me with a mixture of surprise and disapproval. "Why are you getting cross with me? I'm just trying to help."

"How am I supposed to start applying for jobs when I don't have a working phone?"

"You can just start looking another time," he said.

I shook my head adamantly. "No, my plan was to start tomorrow. I don't want to be just sitting around here doing nothing."

"Just take the bus from campus tomorrow then."

"You said your last class finishes at five o'clock tomorrow. I don't want to wait all that time for a ride back."

Harry regarded me collectedly. "Then I don't know what else you want me to suggest."

"I don't want you to suggest anything." I rose from the sofa and stormed upstairs to the bedroom.

As it slowly grew darker outside, I lay on the bed and chewed my lip with remorse. It had only been a few days since I arrived; it wasn't supposed to be like this. Minutes later, I returned sheepishly downstairs. Harry was typing on his laptop and didn't look up. I sat down opposite him.

"I'm sorry," I said quietly. "I shouldn't have lost my temper with you. It's not your fault."

Harry closed his laptop and rested his hands on the table with a contemplative expression. "I'm quite confused right now. Your reasons for complaining about things, they confuse me. I don't understand the reasoning behind them."

I fiddled with my hands. "I just want to find a job as soon as possible."

"I understand that," he said. "But for you to just lose your temper with me like that is a little concerning."

My stomach began to twist into uncomfortable knots. "I never said I was perfect."

"I don't expect you to be perfect, but your behaviour seems unnecessary to me. I'm a pretty happy person, and I find it difficult to understand where that mood switch comes from."

Suddenly, I found myself growing defensive. "I could say the same about your behaviour in the phone store earlier. I've never seen that side of you before, nor did I get why it was necessary."

"Questioning the morality of a service someone sells is different than being hostile towards someone over an incident they aren't connected with," he said steadily.

Taking in Harry's calm, collected gaze, I resented his self-assurance. I didn't want him to think he was right.

I folded my arms. "I suppose we're bound to have changed a little in the time we've been apart."

Harry nodded, deep in thought.

"And we just have to get used to each other again," I continued. "We've gone from one extreme of not seeing each other for six months to living with each other."

"Yes, it takes time to adjust."

His eyes lingered on mine, and I wondered if we were both thinking the same thing. Unwilling to raise the subject, I cleared my throat.

"Once I have more of a routine, it will be better," I said. "When I have a job and more friends, we'll be less on top of each other."

I stepped towards him. In the warmth of his embrace, I cursed myself for having let us get to this moment.

"I sometimes think I work better alone," I said with a mild laugh. "That way, nobody else has to deal with the effects of my mistakes."

Harry stroked my hair. "I know what you mean."

Harry set off for school early the next day, and the house was suddenly filled with silence. After feeding the cats and collecting the hen's eggs, I went for a walk. My boots crunched over frosty soil, and my cheeks tingled from the hint of an arctic breeze as sun rays danced between the tall fir trees.

In the calm whisper of the wind between the leaves, it finally seemed to hit me that I was in a completely different world from the one I'd been living in in London for the past few years. This wasn't just a holiday like it was before. For a moment, I felt a surge of trepidation about the reality of it and the prospect of challenges ahead. But I had put myself out of my comfort zone many times before, and everything had worked out.

Harry brought home another SIM card package and told me about his day as I spooned our dinner onto plates.

"I like my analysis teacher a lot, but the class is going to be really hard. He said he'll give us an A+ for simply getting through the whole semester."

"I'm sure you'll cope," I said. "I swear you say this at the start of every semester, that it's going to be really hard. You always end up doing well."

Harry grinned. "I'm not sure about this one."

As I went to get a glass of water, he piped up behind me. "Oh yeah, there was a notice today looking for a nanny."

I turned off the tap indifferently. "Oh?"

"Well, I wondered if you'd be interested?"

My hand paused in midair, caught by surprise. "You mean, in working as a nanny?"

"Yeah."

My grasp on the glass tightened. I slowly lowered it on the counter and closed my eyes in an effort to sound calm.

"Why would I be interested in that job, Harry?"

"I don't know. I wasn't sure if you were just looking for any kind of job."

I exhaled slowly before turning around to face him. "Why would I be looking for any kind of job when I spent the past two years in a professional one?"

"Well, I figured your priority might be earning some money."

"My priority is finding a job in my line of work. I purposely saved money to get me through in the meantime."

"Oh, okay then." Harry shrugged and continued eating.

I watched him with bemusement, debating whether it was worth risking another argument. His eyes focused on his plate, unaware I was watching him.

I looked at the floor and swallowed. "I don't really understand why you would think I'd want to work as a nanny when we've previously talked about me applying for permanent residence."

"You worked as an au pair in Switzerland a couple of years ago," he said matter-of-factly.

My hands gripped the counter behind me to restrain myself.

"Yes, and I didn't enjoy it at all. Do you not remember how miserable my messages were at that time? If I have the option, I'm of course going to apply for something that helps develop my career."

"I understand. I just thought I'd check."

I watched, stunned, as he continued eating. *Surely he knows me better than that?*

"I just have this aspiration to get to my twenty-fifth birthday and be able to look back on my life and feel like I've accomplished what I hoped to," I explained. "And having a job that challenges and fulfils me comes into that."

"I get that," said Harry. "I'm just aware that Victoria may have fewer opportunities than London when it comes to your preferred field of work."

My stomach flipped at the reminder of a previous worry, but I forced a smile. "I know, but I'm sure I'll find something I like."

Harry nodded. "I guess Vancouver is always an option too."

I looked up at him in mild surprise. "True, but ideally, I'd stay here for the first few months to, you know, see how things go and spend time with you."

Harry smiled. "I know, just so long as you're doing what's best for you."

He got up to put his plate in the dishwasher, and then he pulled a textbook from his bag and turned on his laptop, his attention now completely elsewhere.

He made it seem like he was looking out for my interests, but I wondered if he worried having me around would get in the way of his own.

THREE

The arrival of snow provided some excitement to compensate for an uninspiring job search during my week at the cat house. I'd spent the past two years handling recruitment and staffing for what was considered one of the world's most iconic sports venues. Aware there wouldn't be as many opportunities in that area, I had broadened my search to general administrative opportunities. I found two interesting openings and laboured over my cover letter, tailoring it to the job specifications and making sure my spelling matched Canadian versions. I submitted my application with confidence but didn't hear back. One position was at the University of Victoria, where Harry studied. I told myself to see it as practice and stay positive.

My close friend Amy, who I had met at my old job, was working in Australia on a one-year visa. She suggested I register with a staffing agency, so I searched online and sent a locally owned business my resume. I had an interview scheduled the next week.

At the sound of Harry arriving home from school, I turned off my laptop for the day. Relations between us had improved over the course of the week as we adjusted to being in one another's presence again. The time together in a private setting had also exposed our different habits—some that were known and others that were less familiar.

Snowfall increased on the day we were due to leave the house. The steep driveway was covered with thick snow that concealed layers of black ice, and the car didn't have four-wheel drive or winter tires. Harry began boiling huge pans of water to pour onto the ice in hopes it would melt it. As a country girl who had grown up in the rural valleys of the North Yorkshire Moors, this method made no sense to me. I grabbed a shovel from the shed and tossed any bits of soil and gravel I could find onto the ice for grip.

We arrived back at the family property and went to greet everyone in the main house.

"I'm going to buy a horse!" Ruth exclaimed before I'd even taken off my shoes.

"You are?" I asked in surprise. "But you already have two."

I had known Ruth long enough to know that her purchases were often spontaneous and ill-thought-out.

Ruth waved her hand dismissively. "Yes, but Hannah rides Teddy and Jacob isn't safe. He bolts off unexpectedly."

"Maybe it's because he isn't getting enough exercise," I suggested. "Some horses play up because of that."

"Well, I just know that he's bucked off the last three people that rode him."

I opened my mouth to ask how experienced the riders had been but decided it wasn't worth it. Once Ruth was set on her opinion, it was difficult to change it. She proceeded to show me a photo of the cob she was looking at.

"So cute and totally bombproof," she said with an adoring smile.

"When would you have time to ride it?" asked Hannah skeptically from the table. Ruth ignored her.

I struggled to see how this plan would work out but, as always, while living on her property, I felt pressed to support Ruth's idea as a form of courtesy. And so, while Ruth's children departed the kitchen, I listened and smiled and made enthusiastic sounds at the right time.

"I'd be careful with encouraging my mom," said Harry later as we made our bed. "I know you're trying to get in her good books, but once she thinks she has someone on her side, she tries to take advantage."

"I know, but I feel sorry for her when none of you listen to her. She does a lot for you. I wonder if she's happy."

"I'd imagine she isn't very happy, but she doesn't help herself."

I stuffed the pillowcase in thought. While Ruth's ideas often lacked rationality, I couldn't help but feel a sense of pity for her at times. She had devoted most of her life to work in order to pay off mortgages, provide for the kids, and care for animals. She rarely received equal gratitude and reward in return for her endeavours.

The next morning, Ruth entered the barn and asked me for some help with a job outside. Caught off guard, I saved the cover letter I had just started writing. I spent the morning refilling water buckets, mucking out stables, cleaning duck houses, and sifting through messy trash cans to separate plastics, paper, and tins. As cold, dirty water from a plastic bag splashed down my leg and into my boots, Harry's warning came back to me. Realistically, I knew that Ruth would take advantage of my support by getting me to do her dirty jobs. I always seemed to fall for the trap.

I got out of helping Ruth the next morning by getting a ride into Victoria with Harry. I'd arranged a meeting with a bank to set up an account.

"So, what brought you to Victoria, Sara?" asked an advisor named Greg as I sat in his office.

"I really like it here, and my boyfriend's here."

"Okay, and what does he do?"

"He's a math student at UVic."

"Nice, and what about you? Are you working?"

"No," I said with a small sigh. "Still looking."

"Victoria is very much a government and tech town."

"So it seems. Are you from here?"

"No, I grew up near Vancouver. We'll likely stay here though, as we've bought a couple of properties on the island."

I noticed a ring on his hand. "Have you always wanted to work in finance?"

"Yes, I graduated from UVic's Commerce program a few years ago," he said. "I'm actually only a year older than you."

Married with houses and a full-time job at the age of twenty-five, I thought with a pinch of insecurity. *Our lives couldn't be more different.*

Greg asked if I was planning to buy a credit card. I told him I had never had one in England but that I understood fewer places in Canada accepted payment by debit.

"I'd recommend getting one," said Greg. "That way, you can start earning a credit score which will help you and your boyfriend get a mortgage to buy a house."

I broke into a short burst of laughter. "Oh, I think we're a long way off being in that position."

A quizzical look briefly crossed Greg's face before he began to explain various cards available and the associated fees. Banking in Canada had more differences from England than I'd expected, and he patiently listened to my questions.

As I put on my coat, I found myself feeling disappointed my interaction with another human being was coming to a close. While waiting outside to be picked up, a daydream entered my mind of Harry and me going for dinner with Greg and his wife.

On the way home, Harry stopped outside a small, shabby building to buy lunch from his favourite deli that had been recommended by Brendan.

"Do you ever feel like trying a new place?" I joked as he bit into his curry.

"This place is so cheap and so good; why would I want to eat anywhere else?" he replied.

Unsure if he wanted an answer, I changed the subject. "I got a credit card today. The advisor I met with was really nice and helpful."

Harry wrinkled his nose. "Personally, I'm hesitant to trust people who work in banks. He was probably being nice because he gets a cut from selling you one."

I sat back in my seat, and the daydream of going for dinner together quickly dissolved.

Raindrops pattered off the pavement as I stepped off the bus the next day. I instinctively fumbled inside my bag only to remember that Harry had borrowed my umbrella. Pulling my hood up, I walked towards the employment agency for my interview, coughing repeatedly to clear my throat. I wasn't sure what to expect, and my voice had a tendency to come out squeaky when I was nervous.

The door jingled as I walked in. The office had exposed brick on the sides, with a set of stairs leading up to a spacious area where paintings hung from the walls. A smiley brunette named Jenna greeted me from behind the front desk and invited me to take a seat. I straightened my shirt collar and rubbed my hands together. My interviewer came down wearing a woolly sweater and tight, black pants, and I immediately felt overdressed. Our hands fumbled together awkwardly in a handshake before

I followed her upstairs to her office. I spoke fluently about my experience but wondered if I came across too formal.

"And what sort of salary expectations did you have?" asked Paige as she took notes.

"Well, I'm aware it's a different economy here, and I know I might not make as much as I did in my last job..." My voice trailed off, embarrassed that I might have sounded snooty. "Ultimately, I'm looking for Canadian experience more than anything," I continued hastily.

Paige handed me a bunch of registration forms to complete. I read over the tax forms with confusion, unsure what some of the terms meant. Every day, I was learning new things and realizing how many differences there were between Canada and England.

I handed over my reference letters, and Paige told me she would send me an email when a suitable opportunity came up. Many of their requests were temporary placements, she said. I told her I was available immediately.

Harry's car was nowhere to be seen when I stepped off the bus in Sidney later that afternoon. I walked up to the grocery store and waited under the covered entrance as it started to rain heavily. Shoppers dashed towards their cars, trying to avoid the puddles. Feeling a shiver run through my exposed feet, I went into the store where Valentine's Day chocolates were already on display. This year would be the first one I had spent with Harry in person. He had hinted before I arrived that he had plans for us during his reading break in February, perhaps a trip up island.

A call went straight to his voicemail, so I called the home phone. Ruth said she would send Hannah to collect me.

"Your brother needs to learn to pick up his phone," I remarked as I got in the car ten minutes later. I flopped my head back against the rest with a sigh of relief. "How's your day been?"

"Pretty good. I'm just working on my university application," said Hannah as we pulled away. "UBC has a really interesting environmental conservation program. The application deadline is in a couple of days, though, and I have a school project due this week."

"I'm happy to help if you'd like?" I offered.

Hannah smiled at me appreciatively. "I was going to ask if you could. Thanks."

We went up to her room, and I spent a couple of hours with her, helping her think of some responses to the application questions. I could sense Hannah's excitement growing as she got closer to the end of the application. After the last question, I followed her as she ran downstairs to the kitchen where Ruth was rolling dough.

"Hey, Mom, I've almost finished my UBC application," she said brightly. "Could I have your credit card to pay the submission fee?"

Ruth made a disapproving face. "UBC? Why do you want to go to Vancouver?"

"They have a really interesting conservation course there. I'd learn a lot."

"You don't want to go to Vancouver; there are gangs there." Ruth shook her head and continued rolling. "Go to UVic. Then you can live here and help out."

"But UVic doesn't offer that course."

Ruth shrugged. "Well, to be honest, you'd be better off staying here and getting your own business going in the garden."

Hannah's shoulders sank. "Mom, I've told you I want to go to university."

"Why? I didn't go, and I've done fine."

I watched the scenario from the corner of the room, inclined to step in and defend Hannah but wary of offending Ruth. Her outlook on the situation couldn't be more different from the approach my parents had taken with my siblings and me regarding our educational goals. Unsure of what to say, I surrendered and slipped quietly out of the house.

Harry was in the barn on his computer.

"Ah, there you are!" he said, pulling me down for a kiss.

"I've been helping Hannah with her UBC application."

"That's great, just as long as you haven't been writing it all for her. I know you have a tendency to take over on things like that," he said with a teasing expression.

"I've just been giving her some support, which is more than your mum has," I said sourly.

"That's not surprising. I do think Hannah should go to UBC, though. So she can escape here."

"You want Hannah to escape here, yet you don't want to yourself?"

Harry sat back slowly in his chair like a wise old man preparing to make a profound statement. "Hannah would be more likely to stay here her whole life, whereas I know that I won't do that."

"Maybe," I replied as Harry turned his attention back to a page of code. I cleared my throat. "My interview seemed to go okay."

"Oh, right! Awesome." Harry flashed me a smile before his eyes drifted back to the screen.

"I'll start dinner, then."

"Let's just eat with the others."

"But we've done that the past two nights," I said in protest. "I feel bad having your mum cook for me when we have a kitchen here."

"I'll be there too," he said with a shrug.

"I know, but I feel rude. It's not like I've bought any of the food, and I'm not paying rent."

Harry reached across and rubbed my arm. "Okay, don't worry about it. Make something you want."

An hour later, Ruth came by to let us know dinner was ready.

"Thanks, but I actually just made some food for Harry and me," I said as I wiped my hands on the kitchen towel.

Ruth looked at me with an insulted expression. "You weren't planning on eating with us?"

I swallowed and looked to Harry for help, but he wasn't in sight. "Well, I guess we could eat with you and keep this for lunch."

I consciously put small portions of food on my plate as Hannah told her dad about her UBC application.

"I just wonder if they'll let me defer, so I can take a gap year," she said ponderingly.

"Who are you planning to go travelling with?" asked Ruth with a frown.

Hannah shrugged. "I figured I'd just go on my own."

"Good for you!"

The words left my mouth just as Ruth exclaimed, "You can't go on your own!"

A silence followed. I broke it.

"Sure she can. I have."

Ruth's eyes flashed me what appeared to be a look of contempt. "But you did homestays, not backpacking."

"Actually, I've done both," I said, sitting up higher in my chair. "In Canada, before I came to BC, and in Europe too."

Ruth ignored me and turned back towards Hannah. "How would you get around?"

"I don't know," she replied sheepishly. "Bus?"

"Hitchhike?" pitched in Peter playfully.

Ruth's mouth dropped open. "Hitchhike? Of course not! That's totally unsafe, Peter."

I cleared my throat. "Carpooling is quite popular in Europe. It's cheap, and there are regulated sites you can use, so it's pretty safe."

"You mean, you get in a car with strangers?" asked Ruth incredulously.

"Well, yes. I did it in Germany, and it was fine. It was actually a really fun, memorable experience." I sipped some water, feeling my face start to flush in anticipation of a heated debate.

"I think it's a crazy idea for young girls to get in cars with strangers," said Ruth.

"If there's anything I've learned from travelling alone, it's that strangers can be extremely kind," I said.

"But why would you trust someone you've never met? What about all those kidnapping stories you hear on the news?"

I rested my cutlery on my plate. "It's no different from inviting strangers to stay in your home."

Ruth closed her mouth abruptly, only to scowl at Peter as he said "exactly" in a quiet voice.

"But WWOOFers are vetted," she said. "They have profiles so we can see who they are before we meet them."

"So do the carpooling drivers. Either way, it doesn't necessarily mean any of these people can be trusted," I replied.

"Doesn't mean anything," agreed Peter.

"They could all be thieves for all you know," I joked.

Ruth locked her eyes sharply onto mine. I held her gaze but could feel my face growing redder. Suddenly, I remembered that I was in her kitchen eating her food that she had cooked for me. I had taken it too far.

When everyone finished, I proceeded to load the dishwasher and clean the cooking pots like usual.

"Feel free to cook for us sometime, Harry," called Ruth dryly over her shoulder as he headed towards the door. I focused on the dishes, knowing full well that the sentence was actually directed at me.

I lay in bed unsettled. In the weeks before the barn was completed, Harry had made it seem like he would be buying groceries and cooking his own meals, living a more independent lifestyle. In reality, nothing had changed. Even though we now slept under a different roof, I hadn't escaped his mother.

FOUR

Over the next few days, I got into a routine of feeding the animals and mucking out the stables in the morning. I would then return to the barn, hoping I wouldn't be disturbed for the rest of the day so I could focus on my job searches. I applied to another clerical posting with UVic. I knew I could do the job, and I had a good feeling about my application. Aside from that, few opportunities caught my eye, and I hadn't heard anything from the agency.

I looked forward to when Harry would come home, partly because his presence could be a protective shield from Ruth. When he asked if I wanted to do Victoria's annual 10k run in April, I enthusiastically agreed. We went for a run later on the same day and took a circular five-kilometre route that led us past Patricia Bay, where herons perched on rocks to gaze out across the ocean and seals popped their heads up out of the water.

"Damn, Sara, you're fast!" panted Harry as we stopped by the driveway. "You destroyed me."

I laughed and instinctively shook off the praise. "A lot of people are fast runners; it would be more impressive if it was a sport that hardly anybody did."

Harry straightened up, frowning thoughtfully. "Actually, I'd say the fact that so many people run makes being good at it more impressive."

His words stuck with me as I walked up the driveway. Feeling a boost of motivation, I suspended my job search for the evening to focus on creating a training schedule for the two of us.

Having this newfound motivation, however, could only compensate for my lack of job application success for so long. When Harry asked how things were going, I felt too embarrassed to tell him that I'd applied for a job at his university. The idea of having to admit I hadn't even been invited for an interview filled me with shame. I had worked in recruitment; I was supposed to know what hiring managers looked for.

One afternoon, as I sat scrolling a job site, there was a knock on the barn door. I groaned in protest, only to sit up in relief when Hannah appeared in the doorway.

"I finished school early and was wondering if you wanted to go for a ride?" she asked.

After a moment's thought, I nodded enthusiastically. "That would be great."

She asked how I'd feel about riding Jacob and noted he was quite strong. I told her it was fine; I had ridden many forward-going horses growing up. I put on a scruffy pair of jeans and borrowed a pair of yard boots, one size too big for me. Hannah leant me a hat and handed me Jacob's tack. The smell of leather brought back a rush of childhood memories, and my excitement increased.

Ruth passed us on our way to the stables and dropped the wheelbarrow she was pushing. "You're going for a ride?"

"Yes, Sara's going to ride Jacob," said Hannah.

Ruth looked me up and down skeptically. "Careful, he has no brakes."

I smiled at her reassuringly. "I'll be fine."

But as I walked away, the nerves started to appear. I hadn't ridden a horse in three years. *Maybe I'm wrong to be so confident; maybe I won't be able to control him.*

Jacob stood still as I put my foot in the stirrup, only to shoot forwards when I landed in the saddle. I clutched the reins tighter and brought him to a stop, bracing myself for a warning comment to come from out of the shadows.

It turned out I had no reason to feel concerned. The entire ride went smoothly, aside from a brief moment when Jacob shied away from a piece of plastic on the trail. I regained control quickly and found myself wondering what had caused the experience of others to be so different.

The ride was short, and on my return to the property, I decided to take Jacob into the grass ring to do some more work. He broke reluctantly into a trot when asked, barely lifting his hooves over the grass. Getting him to maintain a canter for more than a few metres was a challenge. It was clear that he was extremely unfit.

As I changed rein, I heard a rummaging from inside the horse barn. Then I saw the flash of a figure. Instinct told me it was Ruth spying on me. I ignored the thought and focused on Jacob, sitting down in the saddle to ask him to canter again. He obliged, only to let out a few bucks in objection. I braced my core and pulled up his head while nudging him on with my legs, and he stopped within a few seconds. I smiled in amusement, reminded of my younger days battling naughty ponies at the local riding school.

Ruth was sweeping by the barn door as I led a sweating Jacob back to his stable. She kept her head down and said nothing, and I did the same.

Back in the barn, I checked my emails to find a message from UVic. My chest flooded with hope, only to sink in disappointment. *I had all the experience they were looking for.* The sound of my phone ringing spooked me back to reality. Unknown number. Another leap of hope. It was the bank, calling to do a quality control check. I hung up in frustration.

A few minutes later, Ruth opened the door without knocking.

"You have a letter," she said curtly.

She tossed it on the kitchen counter and turned sharply on her heel before I could thank her. I watched her through the window as she walked back to the house. Her face seemed surly, and I couldn't help but feel that it was because of my positive experience riding Jacob.

"What was she hoping—that I would fall off and break my back?" I muttered as I turned away from the window.

I turned on the stove and poured some oil into a pan. The letter was from the UK's student loans company, confirming that I wouldn't have to pay back any of my tuition loan until I was working full-time again. One less burden off my back, though it did little to ease my mood. An array of questions ran through my mind. *Why am I not getting interviews? What am I doing wrong? Why doesn't Ruth like me?*

I was growing more discouraged by the day, but I didn't seem to have anyone close by that I could talk to about my feelings. Frequently complaining about his mum would be unfair to Harry, and I didn't want to validate his concern that finding a job in Victoria would be too challenging. I also didn't want to worry my mum by venting about Ruth and my job search in every email to her.

The sound of the door opening brought me back to the present. Upon seeing Harry, I forced a smile.

He looked over my shoulder warily. "Uh—you realize those onions are burning, right?"

"Oh, crap." I turned in alarm and pushed the pan off the heat. "Sorry."

Harry looked at me in concern. "Is everything okay?"

I nodded quickly but felt my mouth starting to wobble. "Yeah, I just…" With a defeated sigh, my elbows dropped onto the counter, and I burst into sobs. "I didn't realize it would be this hard."

Harry gently took my hand and led me upstairs.

"I think back to what I was doing this time last year, and I feel so useless," I moaned as Harry stroked my back.

In my mind I had flashbacks to attending meetings and taking interviews, making decisions and solving problems. I pictured getting on a train to meet friends, cooking dinner for myself in a quiet kitchen, dancing to my favourite songs during an evening home alone. Responsibilities and independence that seemed to have been lost.

As my tears subsided, Harry knelt on the rug by the bed and rested his arms on my lap. "Hey, will you go on a date with me?"

I looked down at him in confusion.

"I'd like to take you on a date," he said. "Will you go with me?"

I broke into a goofy smile like a teenage girl. "Of course."

An hour later, we drove into Sidney and had dinner. After he paid the bill at the restaurant, Harry took my hand and led me in the direction of the local theatre, where we watched a biographical movie that made my challenges seem minuscule. We left the theatre arm in arm, snuggling against the January cold.

My shoulders sagged as we approached the car. I didn't want to go back. Here, alone in this moment, it felt like we had the relationship most others I knew had. One where the couple had their own place to live and having dinner with the parents was just a monthly or bi-weekly event.

"I almost forgot," said Harry as we drove back. "My nana texted me today. She's going on vacation in February and would like us to cat sit for the month."

My head filled with optimism. "That sounds wonderful."

FIVE

Harry's grandma's house had a special serenity to it. Oil paintings of ocean scenes decorated the walls, and French windows looked out over a quiet bay where boats bobbed gently up and down. On some days, the water sparkled in the sun; on others, a moody fog hung over the dense forest ahead. Two days after we arrived, we were treated to a light dusting of snow, and the view outside the window looked like a painting on a postcard.

I welcomed the independence and privacy offered by the house. I could walk across the polished hardwood floors without worrying about stepping on eggshells.

And yet, despite my beautiful surroundings, I was feeling restless. It had been a month since I arrived in Canada, and my job search was still proving unsuccessful. Applications were either followed by a rejection email or by no email at all.

Harry's reading break took place during the first week at the house. Any plans he had had for us to take a trip away appeared to have dissolved. His grandma had asked that we keep a special eye on the elderly cat, Harold, who had shown less appetite in the week before she was due to leave for her holiday. As Harry studied upstairs, I sat in the chair by the French windows and watched Harold's skinny frame walk daintily across the floor. He stopped and looked out of the window despondently, as if waiting for something.

Harry had a few social events planned during the week, to which he invited me to join him. Two of his closest friends from childhood, Joey and Nathan, were people I had connected with quickly upon meeting in 2014. Then there was Liz, who I had met in 2011 when she arrived at Harry's house as an exchange student. She had ended up staying in Canada to study at the University of Victoria, and we had kept in touch over the years.

Harry's math friends were harder to connect with, and I agreed with silent reluctance to go to a board game night one evening. I didn't find strategic board games particularly enjoyable. There always seemed to be one extremely competitive player who took it too seriously. Sure enough, I found myself in a game with four socially awkward individuals, wishing the ground would swallow me up after they explained the rules to me again with a hint of impatience. When I somehow ended up winning, one of them scoffed and folded his arms before saying with a cool manner, "You know, it's often down to luck."

On another evening, we went to a birthday party for Harry's childhood friend, Helena. A talented artist, she had a friendly and welcoming nature I had always appreciated. We pulled up outside a wooden house in the quiet neighbourhood of Fernwood. The surrounding houses were painted with pastel colours and had a charming, cozy look to them. I made a mental note to check this area when looking for a new residence in the spring.

"Are you studying at UVic too?" asked the organizer of the party after Helena introduced us.

"No, I work," I said. "I mean, I'm not currently working, but I'm job hunting."

"Has anything come up yet?" asked Helena sympathetically.

"Not yet."

"Do you have a degree?" asked the other girl.

"Yeah, I graduated in 2014 and have worked in recruiting since then."

"Well, I'm sure there will be cafés hiring in the meantime," she said with an encouraging smile.

I nodded and smiled politely. I had already decided that I didn't want to take a hospitality job. It would distract from my job search and potentially get me into a commitment that would affect my availability to take on immediate contract work more relevant to my field. Then there was the fact that I didn't even have waitressing experience. Perhaps I wouldn't be hired for that either.

I took a seat and sipped my drink quietly as I observed the room. One of the couples in attendance was engaged and due to marry in the summer. The girl had light brown hair and a shy demeanour, while her fiancé was louder and seemed more confident. He would rest his hand on her lap in a way that seemed both affectionate and possessive. I watched the girl smile quietly at his jokes and wondered how happy she was in her relationship.

As the evening went on, I grew more comfortable and began to contribute more to conversations. Harry and I sat apart, and I chipped in comments as he told the story of how we met, upon being asked. Guests gushed at the story in a way that made me squirm inside, and yet, the context of our meeting seemed to carry so many unique and romantic elements.

I left the house with a mixture of gratitude and disappointment. I had enjoyed the evening, but I wasn't sure I could see myself fitting into the dynamic of the tight group of friends.

"That was fun," remarked Harry as we drove away.

"It was; everyone was nice."

"You know that engaged couple?" he said brightly. "I found out that they're in a polyamorous relationship."

I looked at him in surprise. "Really? That seems hard to believe."

"It's true, the guy was actually telling me."

"I would never have suspected that," I said. "The girl seemed quite dependent."

"Apparently, it was her idea. They have a written contract and everything, stating the rules in place."

My nose wrinkled at the thought of it. "That's weird."

"Is it?"

I crossed my arms. "I just don't understand the point of getting married if you want to sleep with other people. The whole idea behind a marriage is commitment."

"They obviously still love each other," said Harry with a shrug. "I think that if they've both discussed it and want to do it, it's up to them."

"Even so, I don't think it's sustainable. One person is bound to get jealous."

"Not necessarily," said Harry confidently. "Look at Brendan and his partner. They've been poly for years and are still going strong."

I frowned with skepticism. "Do you really think his partner is okay with that arrangement? Brendan is obviously the more dominant personality in their relationship. For all we know, his partner is unhappy but too loyal to say anything."

"He's allowed to see other people too. He just chooses not to."

"It doesn't seem very fair, that's all. It's like Brendan is taking advantage of his devotion. It just seems like—"

I stopped myself, conscious of where this might lead.

"Like what?"

"Nothing, it doesn't matter," I muttered. "Polyamorous relationships are just something I personally don't understand the appeal of, that's all."

I turned on the radio and looked out of the window, hoping this would end the conversation.

I was fortunate to get along with most of Harry's close friends, but Brendan was someone I was reluctant to connect with. The context of his friendship with Harry had always made me uneasy. Having been a student in Brendan's class in his first year at university, Harry had soon become his protégé. Within a few months, they had begun meeting outside of the classroom. The idea of developing a personal friendship with a teacher was alien to me and my own university experience, and when Brendan later admitted that his interest in Harry had partly been influenced by a physical attraction, my reservations only increased.

It was difficult to see Harry and Brendan become closer emotionally while Harry and I were far apart physically. When Harry would video call and Brendan would appear in the background, my stomach would sink in disappointment at the knowledge that our conversation was no longer private. And when Brendan placed a hand on Harry's shoulder and smiled at me, my skin would prickle with suspicion.

When speaking with Brendan, questions about my relationship with Harry weren't uncommon. He was a confident individual whose approach to talking about relationships and intimacy differed from my own. Questions that I found intrusive and insensitive were questions he regarded as reasonable and valuable. A true advocate of open communication, Brendan encouraged difficult conversations about topics that made the speaker emotionally vulnerable.

Brendan's personality and communication style had rubbed off on Harry over the past couple of years. I noticed it in the way Harry would use the expressions Brendan used or say statements in the same manner as him, the way he would change the mood at a family dinner by asking complex emotional questions that caught the diners by surprise. I noticed Brendan in Harry's mannerisms and lifestyle choices: the way he had decided to swap his contact lenses for glasses, the way he pushed them up his nose like Brendan did, the way he motioned with his hands when explaining something. Brendan was teetotal, and I found it ironic that Harry had started looking down on regular bar-goers and spoke critically of his parents for having a drink with dinner most nights.

In witnessing Harry's changes, I couldn't help but feel like Brendan was a puppet master pulling the strings in Harry's mind that controlled how he thought and acted. But Harry was always quick to defend Brendan's behaviour. He seemed to regard him as a mentor worthy of full admiration. Harry's increasing receptiveness towards polyamorous relationships made me nervous, and I held Brendan to blame.

SIX

On the Monday after Harry's reading break ended, the employment agency contacted me about a temporary assignment with a provincial government ministry. The duties seemed quite dull, but the prospect of some work outweighed any cons, so I promptly replied to express my interest. Two hours later, I received confirmation that the client had approved my resume and requested that I start the next day. After so many instances of rejection, I felt my spirits lift at the gesture of acceptance.

At the sound of my alarm the next morning, I sat up with a flutter of butterflies. I walked up the road to the bus stop where other workers stood, blowing out puffs of breath into the cold air. As the bus approached downtown Victoria, I glanced at my phone and realized I was thirty minutes early. Butterflies began to flutter once more. I stepped off the bus and proceeded to walk in the opposite direction from the government building and along the wharf. Boats docked quietly in the harbour under a grey sky. Some snow remained on the ground, and I navigated the piles clumsily in my suede-heeled ankle boots.

After arriving at the building and reporting to security, a woman named Cindy came down to meet me before giving me a tour of a large office filled with cubicle spaces. My role involved going through a large number of boxes packed with folders, organizing confidential correspondence from each folder into different departments, scanning the documents, and uploading them to the government database.

I took in the chaotic piles of paper in front of me, some of them letters to the Minister or Premier from angry members of the public, others internal correspondence between departments across various ministries. Many people would long to have the opportunity to be sat where I was in a government building, but sitting in a cubicle where I couldn't see anyone else within the room where nobody seemed to speak was not my preferred work environment.

A voice of encouragement reminded me that the placement would enhance my resume and open doors, and so I worked diligently through the folders, smiling whenever Cindy came over to check on me. I took my breaks as assigned, eating my sandwich in the communal kitchen while reading an interior design magazine someone had left, so it wasn't obvious that I was being ignored by the permanent staff.

By four-thirty, I had a headache from the mundane repetition of reading over pieces of paper and ticking off a sheet. I left to catch my bus, grateful for the fresh air.

The journey home took almost an hour. I closed my eyes, waiting for the ache to subside. It was dark as we approached my destination. I squinted through the window to see where we were. Nothing looked familiar. I waited a few minutes longer. Still nothing looked recognizable. I walked up to the driver and bashfully asked when we would be at my road.

"This bus doesn't go that way. You needed to take the 75X," he explained. "If you get off at this next stop, you can cross the road and get the 75 going the other way."

At the stop, I stood shivering as I tried to decipher between Canadian coins in the dark. London's Oyster card system suddenly seemed more deserving of praise than I had ever considered. Twenty minutes later, I walked into the house with a rumbling stomach. A faint murmur of noise from upstairs led me to assume Harry was on a video call with Brendan. I stayed silent and scanned the kitchen surfaces, bare of any food or cooking tools.

"Guess what?" asked Harry cheerfully as he skipped downstairs a few minutes later. "I got an A on my first analysis assignment!"

I looked up from chopping vegetables. "That's great, well done."

Harry took a seat and rested his elbows on the counter. "There was one question my professor marked me down for that I was pretty upset about, so I asked if he would look at it again."

I opened my mouth to tell Harry that employers wouldn't care what precise percentage he'd received on an assignment, but a reluctance to seem like I was undermining his efforts stopped me.

"An A is still really good. Does it matter that much?"

Harry looked at me blankly. "Of course it matters, Sara."

I looked down and picked up the knife again. "Could you get me the eggs?"

"How was your day?" he asked as he opened the fridge. "How's the job?"

"It's okay. The work isn't super exciting, but it's better than doing nothing." I glanced up at his back. "I got the wrong bus back, which is why I wasn't home sooner."

"Oh, really? You should have called. I would have collected you."

"That would have required you to actually pick up your phone."

"Fair point," said Harry with a chuckle. "Well, anyway, back to studying. I have another assignment due on Tuesday."

He jogged back upstairs as I continued to cook dinner.

Cooking had never been a particular passion of mine, perhaps because it wasn't one of my mum's. Constantly busy as a homemaker with tasks like feeding and cleaning after animals, washing and ironing clothes, and collecting her five children from various after-school activities, her meals were tasty and nourishing but not extravagant in their culinary depth and detail. "I eat to live, I don't live to eat," she would say, and I had inherited the same outlook. I accepted my new de facto position of evening cook in this house because I didn't have the excuse of having to study. With Ruth not around, I could at least do it without the sense someone was looking over my shoulder, scrutinizing my every move.

"Dinner's ready!" I called upstairs twenty minutes later.

"Coming!" replied Harry.

A minute passed.

"It's going to get cold," I said pointedly.

A few minutes later, I stomped upstairs impatiently. Harry swivelled around in his chair and smiled sheepishly at me. "Sorry, I just had one last equation to solve."

His computer screen showed he had a social media page open. He closed the page as I approached, but not before I had seen the name of his ex-girlfriend on a message tab.

In that inexplicable way commonly felt by many towards a partner's ex, I had always felt a slight resentment towards Lauren. An academic achiever with a natural beauty, she had started dating Harry the summer after he and I met. From the beginning, she had been skeptical of me and the feelings Harry and I had developed for each other in a short space of time. Part of me envied the fact that during their year-long relationship, Lauren and Harry had had the opportunity to date properly—the fact that he had been able to have dinner with her parents, to throw her a surprise birthday party, to buy her flowers on Valentine's Day, to be with her at Christmas.

Lauren and I had met at a house party Harry hosted after we returned from our road trip in 2014. She confidently held her hand out to shake mine, but her eyes looked away in embarrassment. The house party had mostly been attended by Harry's high school friends, and I had found it difficult to mingle with a group whose shared stories I couldn't relate to and nostalgic jokes I didn't understand. Instead, I had sat by myself on the outskirts of the group, pretending to examine a pebble in my hands as I contemplated my impending departure. Then I had looked up to see Harry and Lauren sitting next to each other, laughing at a joke. I observed how at ease they seemed around each other, the way they exchanged amused looks, the way they looked like the couple. And with a building sense of discomfiture, I had quietly retreated, unnoticed, into the house.

Now I sat in the kitchen eating in absorbed silence, wondering what had been said in the messages.

"Thanks, Sara," said Harry as he put his plate in the dishwasher. "I'm going to take a shower."

At the sound of running water, I seized my chance and jogged upstairs. Harry never logged out of his profile when using his computer. A sudden sense of paranoia pushed me to do the unreasonable. I opened the conversation tab with a thumping in my chest and scrolled through the messages.

> I hope you had a great Christmas. Happy New Year!

> Thanks, you too. How was your Christmas?

> It was nice, thanks. Sara arrived before New Year's for two years, so it's great having her around and not having to worry about a departure date.

I sank back in the chair with relief before the feelings of guilt began to swarm. I had no reason to worry about Harry's commitment.

SEVEN

My pace of work at the Ministry began to increase. Suspecting that I would finish the project quicker than expected, I let Cindy know that I was available to help with anything else she needed. But as a temp, there were only so many tasks I had permission to perform. On Friday afternoon, I watched the hands of the clock tick tauntingly towards four-thirty, then I left the office and caught the bus to the university.

On the way, I thought about a conversation I'd had with Liz the evening prior. I had felt hesitant to ask her whether she found Harry to have developed arrogant tendencies, but I had felt relieved when she said yes. There was something reassuring about knowing I wasn't the only one who felt he took school too seriously and wasn't independent enough.

But as the bus approached the campus, I began to question myself. I admired Harry's talents and his work ethic. *Perhaps I'm being too harsh and confusing arrogance with passion.*

Students filtered out of buildings in excited groups, chatting about their plans for meeting up on the weekend. I wondered how long it would be before I found myself making similar plans with new friends.

Harry was finishing up his shift in the math centre where he tutored younger students a couple of times a week. I watched through the window as he sat next to a shy-looking male. He pushed his glasses up his nose before motioning with his hands as he explained something. His eyes lit up with genuine interest as he spoke, and he wore a smile that wasn't reciprocated by the student. I could see Harry was in his element.

Ten minutes later, we left the building and followed the tree-lined path out of campus towards the residential street where Harry parked his car.

"How was your shift?" I asked, linking my arm with his.

Harry sighed. "There was one girl who basically just wanted me to tell her the answer to each question instead of learning how to work it out herself."

"I'd probably do the same for anything math-related," I joked. "But I can see why that would be frustrating."

"I'm pretty sure she was a psychology major," he said.

"What makes you think that?"

"Because she was obviously only used to doing basic assignments. Psychology students here are all the same, all ditsy and 'I'm just really interested in people.'" His voice mocked that of a female before he shook his head with an expression of disappointment.

"That doesn't mean they don't work hard," I replied with a hint of defensiveness.

"No, but I don't think you can compare a psychology degree with a math degree when it comes to difficulty," said Harry scornfully. "Anyway, how was your day?"

I looked at the ground. "Fine. It's just a very different office environment from my old job. Nobody really talks."

"That's a shame. My healthy sexuality teacher is always getting everyone in the class to talk to each other. She's so great."

"Isn't Healthy Sexuality what you'd consider a pretty basic class?" I impulsively asked.

Harry smirked. "Of course it is, but I think I deserve to take a fairly light elective given how demanding my other classes are. Plus, it means I get to have a laugh with Tim." He pushed his glasses up his nose with a smile. "Actually, today's class was really interesting. We had to take a questionnaire where we rated out of ten the importance of certain relationships in our life. What rating do you think I gave ours?"

I looked up into the dark sky musingly. "I'm going to say a five."

"Actually, I gave it a two."

I looked at him in surprise, waiting for the sign he was joking. The light from a towering street lamp revealed that his facial expression remained unchanged. A punching hand twisted its way through my gut. I pulled my arm out of his in disapproval and came to a halt.

"Are you serious?"

Harry looked puzzled. "Yes. Is that…do you…" his voice trailed off uncertainly.

"You gave our relationship a two out of ten in importance?"

Harry shrugged, the puzzled look still on his face. "Yeah."

I scoffed and walked a few steps ahead of him before stopping in bewilderment to face him again. "Why would you rate it so low?"

There was a pause before Harry spoke. "Well, school and music are more of a priority to me right now than a relationship. I think you know that."

"Okay, but to give it so little as a two out of ten? I don't understand."

"I gave my relationship with Tim a two as well," he replied optimistically.

I snorted in offence. "You've only known Tim a year."

Harry sighed. "I think you're interpreting this rating wrong. I—"

"Wrong?" I said irritably. "It's two out of ten, Harry. What exactly am I interpreting wrong?"

"I just mean that you're interpreting the rating system differently from how I have. I always rate things lower than the average."

"You're really making me feel better."

"Hear me out," said Harry calmly. "To rate something higher than a seven would be unreasonable. Generally speaking, rating something out of ten is a silly way of measuring something."

"Why are you focusing on the damn rating system? This isn't a mathematical question, Harry. This is about your feelings towards me and our relationship." I studied his face searchingly as hurt began to build inside. "After all we've been through together, you rate me that low? And the same as Tim?"

"Having the same rating as Tim doesn't mean I value him more than you. It's just that in general, my friendships and relationships aren't as important right now in comparison to school and music."

"Then give me a five and them a seven. Don't rate me a bloody two! This is humiliating."

I stormed towards the car as tears pricked my eyes. The silence between us was filled by the roaring of the heater. A rush of questions whirled around my head as car lights and bright storefronts flashed by in a blur. Nothing seemed to make sense.

We walked into the house without uttering a word. I sat down at the kitchen counter and ran my hands over the smooth wooden surface.

"I don't understand why you're with me. If our relationship means so little to you right now, why do you want to be with me?"

"Because I'm happy with you." Harry reached out to touch my arm. "Just because school and music are my main focus doesn't mean I don't want a relationship with you."

I looked down sadly at his hand. "I'm starting to wonder if you're only with me out of pity, because you feel sorry for me not having many of my own friends here."

"That's not true."

"Then why am I here?"

"You're here because you wanted to live in Canada," he said matter-of-factly.

"I mean in this room with you," I said impatiently. "Yes, there were other reasons I wanted to move to Canada, but a big reason was because I wanted to be closer to you. I thought we both wanted that?"

Harry looked at me with his lips slightly parted, as if unsure what to say.

"Am I an inconvenience to you?" I asked.

"Of course not."

"Well, it seems like I am."

"When have I ever suggested that?" asked Harry calmly.

"You don't have to suggest it; it's obvious from the way we hardly ever do things together," I said bitterly. "We've gone out for dinner once since I arrived here. You asked if I wanted to run the 10k with you in April, and we haven't run together since the first time. There's always something else that's more important than spending time with me."

A faint smirk formed on Harry's lips. "I mean, I am a full-time math student taking some really intense courses."

I scoffed. "Lots of full-time students are able to make time for a relationship, Harry."

"You've said before that during your degree, you felt like you didn't have time for a relationship."

"Yes, and I was transparent about it. I didn't lead people on."

"How am I leading you on?" he asked steadily. "I made it clear before you arrived that I was going to be busy studying. And you told me you wanted to have your independence as well, to move to Victoria after a few months and meet new people."

"I still want that, but I don't think it's impossible to have a relationship at the same time." My face felt flushed. I stared at my hands and took a deep breath. "If you feel like you don't have time for our relationship, you should just tell me."

A brief silence surrounded us.

"I really like being with you, Sara," came a weak voice.

I looked up at Harry questioningly. "Do you even see a future with me?"

Harry stepped back with a sigh. As I waited for him to speak, an unnerving mob began banging on the doors to my stomach, waiting to get out.

"I hadn't planned to tell you this yet, but I've decided I would like to go to grad school in Ontario or Quebec after I finish my undergrad. And…" he hesitated. "Well, the truth is, I'd like to go alone."

I looked at him with confusion. "You'd want to do long-distance again?"

Harry looked down. "No. What I mean is, I'd like to be single when I go."

The doors to my stomach finally buckled under pressure, and the mob of panic charged through, spreading to all corners of my body. The room seemed to go blurry for a moment.

"You want to break up?" I asked breathlessly.

"Not right now," he said. "But next summer, yes, I will want to break up."

I looked down at the counter in shock. "I don't understand. I just got here. I thought you just said you were happy to be with me."

"I am happy, Sara. This isn't an easy decision to make."

He came forward to place his arms around me. At his touch, I began to cry.

"I'm sorry," continued Harry. "I didn't plan to bring this up until closer to the time, but now we're here…"

"How long have you felt this way?" I asked shakily.

Harry hesitated. "For the past few months."

A stab of betrayal sunk inside my skin. "And you didn't say anything?"

"I wanted to enjoy the time with you. I didn't want to spoil things by saying something."

"But we've hardly had any time *to* enjoy together! I only just got here. How can you be sure you want this?"

"There are days when I'm not sure, but ultimately, I think it's the best decision for myself," he said. "I want to have more independence; I want to move away from the island and live in a bigger city for a few years. And the schools in those provinces are really good for math."

I shook my head in a daze. "I can't believe this is happening."

"I really hate to hurt you like this."

He sounded so composed, so prepared. Why wasn't he more emotional? Anger suddenly rose up inside me, and I stood up and pushed his arms away.

"You don't give a damn how I feel! All you care about is yourself."

"That's not true." Harry reached for my arm pathetically.

"How can you do this?" I asked furiously. "I've been here just over a month, and now you're telling me you want to break up with me in a year's time?"

"I know, I know it seems awful," he sighed. "But I actually think that saying it now is fairer than closer to the time. It's easier that way."

I breathed unevenly, incensed by his insensitivity. And then a lightbulb flashed in my mind.

"You're punishing me. You're punishing me for what happened."

"I don't—what do you mean?"

"For what happened two years ago. You're punishing me, even though you know how lonely and unhappy I was."

Harry shook his head calmly. "I'm not punishing you, Sara. This has nothing to do with that."

He stepped towards me, but I moved away, so the counter was between us. A strained look appeared on his face.

"Please try to understand," he said imploringly. "I just want to have more of the life experiences that others my age have. I want to have the kind of independence you had when you were at university."

"Why don't you just cut right to it and admit that you want to sleep with other people?" I hissed. "It's pretty clear. You've been going on about polyamorous relationships for months now."

Harry sighed and shrugged his shoulders. "I mean, yes, I am interested in the idea of other relationships, but that's not the main reason for my decision."

"Then why don't you just go ahead and dump me? Just get it over with now."

I looked into his eyes daringly. They met mine with sadness.

"I don't want to do that, Sara."

We looked at each other helplessly, sharing a palette of emotions but unsure of the picture we should paint.

Harry cleared his throat. "It's not guaranteed that I'll still feel this way in eighteen months' time, but I do think this would be good for me. And who knows, maybe we'd get together again after some time apart."

I shook my head skeptically. "It's not as simple as that. You're just saying that to make me feel better."

I sat down at the counter and rubbed my forehead. Harry placed his hands soothingly on my back.

"Please, let's just go upstairs and lie down."

I opened my eyes. "I don't get it. You've had the opportunity to move out and be independent, and you haven't taken it. You could have moved away to study somewhere else for your undergrad, or you could have rented a place in Victoria instead of living at home."

Harry nodded. "I know that, but you have to understand that I didn't have much guidance from anyone. Mom and Dad didn't go to university; they didn't know much about it and weren't exactly encouraging. UVic just seemed like the obvious option." He shrugged and looked at me helplessly. "Plus, I wasn't as ambitious back then. I had no idea what I wanted to do with my life."

An ounce of pity grew inside me. I wiped my nose and sighed grudgingly. "I understand. I just feel stupid."

"Please don't feel like that. This isn't a reflection on you or how I feel about you." Harry stroked my back gently. "We're talking about something that's ages away. I want to make the most of this long time we'll have together and have fun."

In the bedroom, he held me tightly. I looked into the dark as tears silently traced my face.

EIGHT

I rose early the next morning and went for a walk. The snow had mostly all melted now, and with its disappearance, it seemed the honeymoon period of my arrival in Canada had also officially evaporated. My boots crunched over the pebbles on the small beach below the house. I joined a path to a grassy bank where I sat by an arbutus tree and looked out at the ocean and the distant sight of snow-capped mountains.

From a rational perspective, I could completely understand Harry's way of thinking. It was unfair for me to have had the life experiences I had and restrict him from having the same.

But despite my sympathy, the frustration over him not having taken this initiative years earlier refused to subside. To know he had felt this way for a few months made me wince with shame. I felt like the fool that wasn't in on the joke. I thought of the message he had written to his ex about me, his encouragement about applying for permanent residency, his expressed desire to capture more memories on camera. Suddenly, they seemed like meaningless statements. I had been blindsided, deluded in assuring myself of his commitment. And now, he had initiated a countdown on our relationship. To do so so soon into my arrival, after the compromises I had made to be closer to him, seemed cruel in nature. It seemed so unlike the Harry I knew.

But who is Harry? asked a voice in my head. *Is he the same person you met six years ago?*

I brought my knees up to my body and wrapped my arms around them comfortingly. I couldn't deny that in the months we had been apart, I had experienced occasional feelings of doubt, questions of whether we were still right for each other. I had pushed these feelings away by blaming them on long-distance and reassuring myself things would be different once we were together again.

A different voice now began to speak, firm and defiant in its tone. *You should take control of this situation and end the relationship.*

A shiver of trepidation ran through me at the very prospect. The reality of looking for a new place to live while still trying to find a job and make friends seemed too stressful to consider. In these unstable times, it was difficult to picture being happier as a single person. Harry was a security blanket I couldn't remove so easily.

I looked out over the water with a sigh, wondering if I had made a mistake. I had dreamed of living an exciting life in another country, developing my relationship with my boyfriend, working a job I loved, and adventuring every other weekend with new friends. The reality seemed far from the dream.

I knew that my family would be furious if I told them what had happened, so I decided not to. I resolved to stay with Harry and make the most of his companionship over the next year.

There was a note on the kitchen counter from Harry when I returned to the house. Joey wanted to go for a hike with us. We climbed into his truck twenty minutes later and arrived at an empty parking lot in Gowlland Tod Provincial Park before commencing the steep climb up to Mount Work. I walked quietly behind the two of them and kept my eyes on the snow-covered trail, following the treads of what looked suspiciously like cougar footprints.

The sun was beginning to set as we neared the summit. We stopped in a small clearing and watched the tall fir trees form a silhouette against the orange sky. Cold air pricked the skin underneath my thin leggings. Harry joked around with Joey like usual, like everything was normal. As we walked back down the trail under the guide of Joey's flashlight, I felt my resentment grow.

The trail was slippery and uneven, and as I stepped down on a ledge, my feet slid beneath me. I let out a gasp as I fell backwards and landed on my forearms.

Harry spun around in alarm. "Are you okay?"

"I'm fine." I stood up briskly and brushed myself off.

I studied the trail beneath me, and suddenly my mind flashed back to six years earlier. A longboard speeding away under my feet, squeals of uncertainty, a precarious tumble onto the grass, embarrassed laughter, hands parting from a blushing face to see Harry leaning over me with concern in his eyes.

The squawk of a crow brought me back to reality. I wiped my nose and continued down the trail.

"Sorry I can't hang out longer," said Harry as the truck pulled up outside his grandma's house. "I need to get back to my assignment."

"You go ahead," I said as he unbuckled his seatbelt. "I'm going to chat for a bit longer."

I watched Harry walk inside and close the front door.

When I told him about Harry's plan, Joey was skeptical.

"Harry has a lot of ideas, and he often doesn't follow through with them," he said. "He's talking about something that's ages away. I wouldn't worry too much."

"But he mentioned being interested in dating other people," I said.

Joey shook his head. "To be honest, I can't imagine Harry actively going out of his way to date people, not if he's busy doing a master's. He's just aware that he's young, and he finds the idea of committing to one person at this age quite daunting."

I let out a feeble laugh. "I'm not even sure anymore if he actually likes me."

"He's crazy about you, Sara. He's always talking about you."

He said the words so earnestly that I felt a brief surge of optimism. Harry had changed his mind before; what was to say he wouldn't do so again?

Heart-shaped balloons and red roses decorated desks as I walked into the Ministry on Valentine's Day. I had never cared too much for flowers and romantic gifts, and the potential fate of my relationship with Harry only made me more apathetic to the sight of them. The girl who sat across from me on the bus home had a box on her lap, wrapped with a red bow. I hadn't bought anything for Harry, nor did I expect anything from him.

Jazz music played as I stepped through the front door. In the kitchen, I found Harry in a nice shirt chopping vegetables. He gave me a quick glance as I came in.

"Hey, dinner will be ready in fifteen."

I observed the scene with surprise. "Thanks."

"I wasn't sure if you wanted wine," he hastily said as he poured the vegetables into the wok.

He worked hurriedly, as if he had a deadline to reach or a conflicting task on his mind. I watched with discomfort, wishing it didn't look so forced. He looked like someone who was outside his comfort zone being romantic.

And yet, I knew that Harry knew how to be romantic. I had seen it before—the tenderness in his eyes before a sunset, the softness in his voice on a walk in the moonlight, the warmth of his hand under a star-filled sky.

Something told me that if Harry was pulling back, I should too. If he was looking out for his own interests, I would focus on mine. I spent the next couple of days looking for available rooms on rental sites in preparation for my departure from Harry's family home.

At the knock on the door on Friday evening, I closed my laptop and stood up to greet Joey and Nathan.

"It must be really nice living together after so long," said Nathan, glancing between Harry and me warmly as we sat at the kitchen table.

"Yeah, it's nice." I looked down and cleared my throat. "I'm actually going to view a suite on Wednesday, though."

"You are?" asked Harry in surprise. "I didn't know that."

"It's in Cadboro Bay. You were busy studying earlier. I didn't want to interrupt."

As if sensing an awkwardness, Joey stood up. "What board games do you have here, Harry?" He looked over the pile in the corner and held up a box. "What's this one?"

Harry squinted over at the box before smiling. "Oh, Brendan got me that one."

"How is Brendan?" asked Nathan with interest.

"He's good. We've been chatting a lot. He applied for a teaching job at the University of Waterloo, and he's just waiting to hear back."

I looked up sharply. Nathan's response was muffled by the thoughts racing through my head. *Is this why Harry wants to go to an Ontario school?*

"He's told me about some of its graduate math courses," said Harry. "Sounds super interesting."

Why would he talk about this in front of me when he knows how I feel about it?

Nathan smiled innocently as he rubbed his chin ponderingly. "It would be weird if one of us moved away. We've always lived so close to each other."

I thought back to all the goodbyes I'd said over the years. Exchange students met at university, friends made during travels, family members. It had become a familiar routine.

Harry shrugged. "I'd still see you during summers."

My jaw tightened at the sight of his casual manner. I couldn't help myself.

"Not me, since you're going to dump me."

The room fell silent. Out of the corner of my eye, I noticed Nathan look between us in confusion.

"That's a bold statement to make," said Harry with an uneasy laugh.

I shrugged and held my cool gaze. "But it's basically the case, isn't it?"

I rose from my chair and left the room in its uncomfortable silence.

Footsteps sounded up the stairs as I sat on the bed scribbling furiously on a notepad. Harry appeared in the doorway, his face holding a look of pensive sadness. The pity I felt at the sight of him was quickly replaced by a feeling of triumph.

Harry sat down and touched my arm. "You're a fantastic girlfriend, Sara. I'd be crazy to break up with you."

"But that's what you said you want to do."

He lay back on the bed and sighed. "I don't know what I want to do. I just know that the idea of being attached to someone is something I find scary."

"You do realize how it feels to hear that, don't you?"

"It's not about you, Sara. You check all the boxes."

"It doesn't feel like that," I said sullenly. "I'm struggling to understand where I fit into your life. I feel disposable."

"You're not disposable to me." He sat up and shook his head with a shrug. "I just sometimes have these moments when I think, 'If I hadn't spent the evening hanging out with Sara, I would have got more work done.'"

"So, I am an inconvenience."

"No, because I really enjoy those times," he said insistently. "I'd rather be living with you than be living apart."

I frowned with confusion. "I don't understand what the issue is, then."

"I'll see how well my friends are doing in math and how dedicated they are, and I'll think to myself, I should be like that. But I don't want to sacrifice my other interests as much as they have. And so, I'll realize that those initial thoughts are just silly and irrational."

I looked down, running my hands over the soft bed sheets we shared together. With their touch came a dull ache in my stomach.

"It's hard to hear that I tick all the boxes when I know you want to date other people."

Harry rubbed my leg. "Please don't think that's my main motive. I really can't see myself actively pursuing other relationships, and I don't want to imagine being with anyone else right now."

I looked up at his face, searching his brown eyes for the sincerity I needed.

"Have you talked to your dad about all this?" I asked after a pause.

"No, but I know he'd call me an idiot," he said with a sheepish grin.

His words brought a faint smile to my lips. I chewed my lip in thought, then looked him squarely in the eye. "You definitely still want to carry on?"

"Yes. I do."

"Okay." I looked down before meeting his eyes again. "Please don't take me for granted."

"I won't."

I moved forward with a more positive outlook, reassured by a greater understanding of Harry's motives. The prospect of him moving away slowly became easier to digest. As I sat on the bus on the way to my house viewing, I told myself I would be more settled by next summer and more independent. I told myself that any future relationships Harry had with other girls wouldn't take away from our time together. And I told myself I would be a hypocrite to feel upset about him pursuing other relationships.

It was 2015. I was lonely and miserable, living with a troubled roommate in a grungy apartment on a loud street in central London. Police and ambulance sirens seemed to sound incessantly from outside the window of my tiny room. I spent my evenings browsing social media aimlessly, seeing photo evidence of my peers from university finding new friends in their jobs while I struggled to meet people my own age at mine. The effort to maintain a long-distance relationship in which I was questioning the commitment of someone whose personality seemed to be changing was making me exhausted. First, there were Harry's light-hearted comments about girls on campus wearing short dresses as the weather changed. Then began casual references to a girl in his class. When Harry nonchalantly mentioned that she'd invited him to hang out with her one weekend, I filled with apprehension. I told him I wouldn't want to know if anything happened between them.

In the midst of all this uncertainty, someone new appeared who was completely different from Harry. We'd shaken hands across a table at the start of a meeting at work, and I'd detected his foreign accent. He was a few years older than me, and his maturity and confidence seemed to show through the way he walked into a room, ordered a drink, and delivered a briefing. He seemed effortlessly cool and collected, a grown man with life experience and a promising career. There was something esteem-boosting about the fact that a recent graduate who had just turned twenty-three caught his interest over the other females in the organization.

When the man first initiated doing something together after work, I didn't intend for things to turn romantic. I envisioned fun platonic company with occasional sprinkles of harmless affection. I was naïve to think that feelings wouldn't intensify with each meeting, each lingering look, each playful touch. I was too distracted by my newfound happiness to think about the consequences. Caught in a moment, I let myself slip.

Things swiftly changed. I became confused, and the man became distant. His walks past my window no longer included the smile and wave I'd come to anticipate each day. Instead, there was a glance at his phone, reading a message that didn't exist. Any future conversations carried a stiff awkwardness. In my quest for company, all I had ended up finding was disappointment.

I tried to compensate for my guilt by convincing myself that if I wouldn't want to know, Harry wouldn't either. I told myself that a confession would bring nothing of value. I kept the secret from him for several months until the guilt grew too big. Both surprising and admirable, Harry's reaction highlighted our different views on communication. Through long and difficult virtual conversations, we started to rebuild. As part of my efforts to make amends, I booked a week off work to fly to Victoria to surprise him, only to feel disappointed with what felt like a lack of appreciation. On the flight home, I wondered if I would always be paying for my sins, if Harry would always be silently vindictive and wishing to punish me in some way.

The sound of an automated voice woke me from my daydream, and I quickly pressed the bell. The bus stopped in a small village situated a couple of hundred metres up from a beach. I walked up a hill to a quiet cul-de-sac and spotted the right house number. A pretty girl with big brown eyes and cheek dimples answered the door at the back. Lucy was a humanities student at UVic. Her roommate was doing a summer co-op overseas and subletting her room for four months from May 1st. This date worked perfectly, as Ruth had asked me to look after her animals in April while she and Peter went on vacation.

The suite was cozy and clean and opened onto a backyard. Lucy seemed a lot more girly and sociable than me. I laughed at the right times as she chatted about her hangover that morning, not bothering to share that I had lost interest in going to nightclubs a few years ago. I had always thought my priority was to find a like-minded roommate and a long-term option, but the location and price of this suite drew me in. I expressed my interest, and Lucy emailed me the landlord's paperwork later that evening. I felt a fraction of weight leave my shoulders. Progress towards independence had been made.

NINE

My assignment at the Ministry finished on the second Friday of March. In the afternoon, my supervisor hosted a mini tea party for me, which I received with bashful gratitude. The agency had emailed me details of another administrative assignment with a large investment management company. The job seemed to carry more responsibilities and was set to last four months, but it didn't fill me with excitement. I replied on my lunch break to say I could start next Wednesday if chosen. The consultant replied to inform me that the hiring manager was impressed with my resume but hoped for an earlier start date. A desire for a few days off stopped me from changing my availability, and the role ended up going to someone else. Although it was a reputable organization, something stopped me from regretting my decision.

The faces on my bus had become familiar. There was the bald, bearded man that nodded his head while listening to his iPod, the young First Nations woman whose eyes remained focused outside the window for the entire journey, and the older lady who wore long skirts and read romance novels. I took a seat among them, feeling relieved that I could sleep in for the next few days. But the feeling of relief wouldn't last long, as all too soon, the pressure of finding another job would return.

Harry was emptying the dishwasher when I arrived at his grandma's house.

"I brought home some curry for dinner," he said as he gave me a hug. "Would you like to watch a movie?"

I walked upstairs to change, noticing how much tidier the room seemed from the morning. Harry sat behind me on the couch and massaged my shoulders as I rested my head on his stomach. I sipped my wine, and it didn't take long for the alcohol to take effect. As my mind became hazy with welcome relaxation, I stood up to play some music and moved to the rhythm with my eyes closed.

A hand wrapped tenderly around my waist, and I opened my eyes to see Harry looking down at me with a warm smile. The beat of a Motown song kicked in, and I pulled away, spinning around and clicking my fingers. Then a swing song came on, and I spun into Harry's hold, tapping my toes behind me. He looked at his feet in concentration, listening to the music for the right beat.

"Don't worry about being on time," I laughed, twirling myself around. "Just dance!"

He grinned and started to loosen up his hips. Suddenly, we were moving. We were on the road again, diving into the clear waters of Lake MacDonald in Glacier National Park, splashing each other with shrieks of glee. We were jumping into the desert in Arches National Park, climbing up sandy stones and hiding behind red rocks. We were young and carefree again.

All too soon, the music changed, and I was jolted back to reality in a daze as a man's calming voice filled the room. I looked at Harry, mind spinning, and he came towards me, his smile slowly fading into a look of sorrow. He gently took my hand and placed his other on my back. I felt his heart beat against my chest as I moved closer into him. We danced slowly in silence with our eyes closed, bound by shared knowledge. Now we were in a dimly lit room with nothing and nobody else around us.

As the lyrics sank in, I let a tear slowly roll down my cheek and looked up into Harry's eyes. He looked back at me with the same pained acceptance I saw in his seventeen-year-old self when we said our first goodbye. The same boy that would later set the timer on the relationship. I wondered if the memories we had created together would ever fade. We held a kiss for a long time, as if too scared to let go.

While it was clear that Harry's plan to run the annual 10k in Victoria had fallen through, I wanted to continue. I had competed in running since I was eleven years old—through athletics and cross country at school and through my participation in modern pentathlon outside of school. While most girls in the changing room groaned at the announcement that we would be running the 1500 metres, I felt a rush of excited adrenaline and thrived off the prospect of crossing the finish line first. My accomplishments helped compensate for the insecurities I felt when I stood among certain girls. Girls who wore the fashionable brands, who knew how to do makeup, who were popular with boys. Girls who made sweet comments with cunning smiles and nasty glints in their eyes.

Over the years, running had brought me friendships, relationships, injuries, tears of frustration, and smiles of pride. On some days, it was a burden, and on others, it was empowering. Sometimes I struggled to run farther or maintain the same pace and relied on mental resilience to push through to the end. On other days, I didn't have to push myself; everything came together and going faster and farther felt easy and comfortable.

Saturday's run fell into the latter. I strode up the hill that left the bay and continued along an undulating road. My legs felt strong, my breathing felt stable, and my stomach felt relaxed. I ran farther and farther, constantly extending my turnaround points—past that gate, past that tree, past that road sign, past that house—running farther away, as if trying to delay something.

When I returned to the house, I had a text from Hannah asking me if I'd like to go shopping with her for a prom dress. I hated shopping but had no other plans for the day.

"So, there's this boy I like," she said shortly after I got in the car.

"Oh?" I said with intrigue.

"He's called Jonas. He's a WWOOFer from Austria." She smiled. "He's been flirting with me."

"That's exciting! How long is he staying for?"

"I'm not sure. A couple of months?"

I paused, wondering how to phrase myself. "Well, it would be nice to have some fun, but I guess you wouldn't want to get really attached before he left."

"I suppose." Hannah's shoulders slumped, only for her to perk up. "Then again, look what ended up happening with you and Harry."

I opened my mouth but didn't know what to say. She looked so optimistic, and I couldn't bring myself to burst her bubble.

"True, but I wouldn't use us a benchmark," I said carefully. "Everyone's circumstances are different. Your brother and I got lucky."

We pulled up outside a small middle school in Saanichton, where an elderly lady with bright pink lipstick was renting out graduation dresses.

"Are you the mother?" she asked me in her slow, dainty voice.

I suppressed a laugh. "No, I'm a friend that's come to help her find a dress."

We sifted through a rail of tacky gowns encrusted with gemstones. Finally, I found a strapless burgundy dress with one solid colour and no extra details.

"Oh, yes!" the lady whispered encouragingly as I suggested it to Hannah.

I went to the changing room with her to help tie the back. As I looped the straps through each hole, I had a flashback to the playful twelve-year-old I first met with puppy fat and a goofy grin.

Now the seventeen-year-old stepped in front of the mirror and smiled. "I love it!"

A different assistant popped her head through the door and gave a smiling compliment before turning to me. "And have you got your graduation dress yet, sweetheart?"

I looked at her in amazement before nodding politely to avoid embarrassing her.

As we drove out of the parking lot, Hannah asked when Harry and I would be returning from her grandma's house. I tried not to sound too disappointed when I told her it would be the following weekend.

Everyone seemed excited for our return except me. Despite the difficult conversations I would now associate with Harry's grandma's house, staying there had given me an experience of the independence and routine I aspired to have for myself.

The following Saturday came round quickly. I looked wistfully out of the French windows at the scenic view I was about to leave behind while Harry packed his bag, chatting enthusiastically about being able to play music in the barn again. As I grudgingly stepped through its creaking doors an hour later, the barn felt cold and claustrophobic.

Ruth had organized a dinner with some of the relatives. I walked into her kitchen to find Hannah and Jonas setting the table. He was a handsome young man with broad shoulders and calloused hands from a few years of working in construction. Hannah looked down with a blushing smile as he gently touched her waist while squeezing behind her. I remembered Harry doing the same thing days after we met. We had snuck around, daring little smiles and touches here and there, enjoying our little secret with the false belief that nobody on the outside recognized what was happening. I took a seat and wondered if I should have warned Hannah about the challenges that would lie ahead. But deep down, I knew it was something she should experience and learn herself.

Harry's uncle and aunt arrived first. With his relaxed demeanour and sense of humour, Ted couldn't be more different from his older sister. An accountant in a government municipality, his wife Julie was down to earth and epitomized the cool but caring aunt figure. Ruth's mother, Jean, showed up last, mildly tanned from her time in Florida.

"How has your job search been going, Sara?" asked Julie.

I forced a smile at the question I had grown to despise. "It's been okay. I did a temp job at a ministry for a month. It wasn't the most exciting job, but it's good to at least have some Canadian experience on my resume now."

"Absolutely," she said encouragingly.

"Now I'm on the job hunt again, though." I laughed in self-deprecation, but it came out dry.

"You're not going to be working for the next while, are you?" Ruth cut in sharply. "We need you to look after the animals while we're away, remember?"

I felt my throat tighten up under her hard gaze. "No, I can be here."

"And what have you been up to, Hannah?" asked Julie.

"Well, I applied to UBC, but I didn't get an offer." Hannah quickly glanced at Jonas and then looked away with a smile. "But it's okay, I want to take a gap year to travel, so I can always reapply next year."

Ted spoke up before Ruth could begin to complain. "I can't believe you're already graduating this year. I swear you were only ten yesterday."

"Speaking of graduating, I got a prom dress last weekend!"

"You got a prom dress?" asked Ruth with a frown. "Why? I already brought one home for you from the thrift store."

Hannah hesitated. "Yeah, but..."

"What's the dress you got like?" asked Julie.

"It's strapless, and it's kind of like a..." Hannah turned to me quizzically. "What colour would you say it is, Sara?"

"It's like a plum or burgundy type of colour."

"Did you help her choose it, Sara?" asked Julie with a smile.

"She picked it," said Hannah before I had a chance.

"Let's see it, Hannah!" piped up Jean in excitement, almost spilling the wine from her glass.

Hannah ran upstairs and returned a few minutes later to sighs of admiration from the group. I glanced at Jonas to see him look down at the table with a swallow of surprise.

"Oh, Hannah, that's beautiful," gushed Jean.

"That's crimson, not burgundy," said Ruth with a look of disdain.

"That's not crimson!" interjected Ted, shaking his head.

"It looks great on you, Hannah," said Julie. "Very classy."

"It does. The colour really suits you," said Peter with a proud smile.

"It's nice," said Ruth unconvincingly, "but I think you'd look better in green. Hey, go try on the one I got you."

"Mom…" Hannah's voice trailed off with a look of protest. I looked down and pretended to examine my nails.

"Go on. You'll look lovely in it."

Hannah reluctantly turned back upstairs, and the competition commenced. At the sound of footsteps, Ruth waited expectantly. Wearing a lime green dress with the top half studded with gemstones, Hannah stood in front of us uncomfortably as the room succumbed to a silence that seemed to last a lifetime.

"I prefer the other one," said Ted.

"Yes, me too," agreed Jean as Peter nodded quietly.

"They're both very nice, but I think the other colour suits her more," said Julie tactfully.

"Really?" Ruth's face stiffened in offence before she shrugged with a sullen look. "Okay, fine."

Without another word, she rose from her chair. I watched her walk to the sink with the stance of someone whose pride had been bruised, and once more, the sense of guilt ensued.

TEN

With the return to the family property came the resumption of my previous routine. Once the morning chores were complete, it was back to hoping Ruth wouldn't call me while I looked for jobs and wrote cover letters. The sense of pressure to find a job had returned, and my cover letting writing extended into evenings and coincided with Harry's studying.

If Harry finished his work before I went to bed, we would sometimes watch a show on his laptop. Other times, he would play music with Jake, who would occasionally sleep over. Sometimes they would carry on playing around the time I went to bed, and Harry would lend me his noise-cancelling headphones. Finding a block of time to devote completely to myself was difficult, but I remained mindful of the otherwise fortunate state of my living situation.

A few evenings after our return, I stared tiredly at my laptop, lacking the inspiration to perfect another cover letter. I had almost nothing original left to say. My creativity had been used on so many applications that had amounted to nothing.

With a defeated sigh, I opened my music playlist and began to play an album by one of my favourite Canadian musicians. One song sang about a young adult unfulfilled in life and love. It reminded me of my first time on Vancouver Island, of an evening when Harry and I had sat watching the sun sink lower into the ocean. With nothing to hear but the gentle sound of buzzing mosquitoes and boats bobbing on the water, I'd started singing the song quietly to myself. Harry had proceeded to look at me with an admiring gaze I hadn't received from a boy before. I had always felt comfortable singing around him. He had often suggested that we record something, but nothing had transpired from it. There never seemed to be a right time.

A glance to my left showed that Harry was still engrossed in his studies. Unwilling to work any longer, I closed the document I had been working on and logged onto social media. Pictures of friends having brunch, travelling with their partner or going for drinks with colleagues made me glum. What was I doing in comparison? I was supposedly the one living the exciting new adventure, but that didn't seem to be the reality. My life seemed to be going backwards rather than forwards.

Listening to the album made me think of my mum. I had inherited many of my varied musical tastes from her—classic rock, soul, Motown, reggae. I pictured her in the kitchen, singing as she washed dishes. Then I felt a twinge of guilt at the thought that I hadn't had a video call with my parents since my arrival almost three months earlier.

My family home in North Yorkshire lacked mobile phone reception and wireless internet. The home phone didn't receive texts from Canada, and calling the landline from a mobile was expensive. With all these restrictions, email and video calls were the easiest options for keeping in touch. But the lack of privacy made video calls challenging. Peter's workshop was attached to the barn, and I didn't want to risk him or Ruth hearing me complain about a generous living situation. Plus, since hearing about Harry's plans, I had felt reluctant to show my face. Email had seemed like a preferable channel of communication to a visual one that risked exposing my pessimistic outlook on my new life overseas. I wanted to prevent my parents from worrying and prevent a conversation that would remind me of my lack of progress.

Knowing that Mother's Day was approaching in the UK, I decided to drop the excuses and schedule a call with my parents.

Dad and I chatted first. I kept the conversation focused on him. Where was Manchester United in the Premier League table? How were the bees? Had he been swimming much? When he asked after me, I wished I could give more than a brief response. After a few minutes, he left to finish cooking dinner, and mum's face filled the screen.

"How is everything?" she asked.

I gave a nonchalant shrug. "It's fine. Ruth can just be... difficult."

"Yes, I see that from your emails."

"The other day she—" I stopped at the sound of a door opening downstairs. Peter had been in the workshop all morning. The door closed again.

"She was just a little funny," I continued, lowering my voice. "But it's fine. I can handle it. She's like that with everyone."

Mum nodded slowly. I could tell she knew I had more to say.

"And how's Harry?" she asked.

I looked down and fiddled with the keyboard. "He's good, busy with school, but he seems to be doing really well in his courses."

"Hopefully not too busy that you can't get out and have fun," she said with a smile.

"Yeah, we sometimes go for dinner or go climbing at the indoor gym."

"Do you go down to Victoria that much? Or to the local pub?"

"Nah, Harry isn't really into drinking," I replied. "But it's fine, neither am I, really."

Mum nodded slowly. "You can always go with someone else, I suppose."

"Mmhmm." I rested my chin in my hand and nodded.

"And are there any upcoming jobs that look promising?" she asked hopefully.

"Not at the moment." I crossed my arms on top of the desk. "But it's okay because in a couple of weeks, I'm going to be looking after the place while Peter and Ruth are in California."

"Oh, right. And are you happy to do that? You won't miss out on a good job because of it?"

"It's fine."

"I suppose you could do some blogging during that time," she said encouragingly. "I've noticed you haven't written much since you arrived."

"I haven't really been exploring that much. I mean, we've done a couple of hikes but, you know, with the weather and all…"

"Right." Mum's brow furrowed slightly.

"I'll do more exploring in the summer," I said hastily. "The new place I emailed you about, it's in a really nice area, down from the university and close to the beach."

"Yes, it sounds nice," said Mum. "I expect Harry will stay with you quite often if it's so close to his campus."

"Maybe." I cleared my throat. "Anyway, how are you and Dad?"

"Oh, we're fine. I slipped in the yard last week when it was really icy, and my ankle has been bruised since, but I can walk on it okay, just a bit slower than usual."

I regarded her with concern. "Are you sure it's all right?"

"Oh, yeah." She smiled and shrugged.

I pictured her hobbling across the snow-covered fields with heavy buckets of water for the sheep and felt a tremor of worry in my chest.

A few minutes later, Dad's voice could faintly be heard calling her name.

"Well, it sounds like tea's ready, so I'd better leave you to it," she said.

"It's nice that Dad is cooking," I said with a smile.

"Yes, he loves cooking now that he has the time to. He's been trying to cut down on red meat."

"That's good." My face grew serious. "I hope your ankle feels better soon."

"Don't worry about me." She smiled before narrowing her gaze. "Now, are you sure you're all right?"

I could feel the intensity of her gaze through the screen, as if she were here in person, looking right through me.

"Yeah, I'm fine. It's just an adjustment."

Mum smiled with a flicker of sadness in her eyes. "Okay, then. Well, feel free to call whenever. You can just leave two rings, then hang up, and we'll call back. It only costs five pence an hour to call Canada with this new provider Dad found."

"I will. I wish the phone would receive texts from here."

"Yes, I miss your texts." Mum peered searchingly at the screen. "Now, I have to work out how to end this call."

"I can do it." A lump formed in my throat as I spoke.

"Okay, well, lots of love, my darling," she said.

I waved to her with a smile before clicking the red phone icon, but nothing happened.

"Go on, then," laughed Mum gently, giving me a wave. "Bye-bye."

"Bye." I clicked again, and the picture briefly froze to Mum's face with its sad smile before the call dropped and the screen went black.

I closed the laptop and burst into tears.

ELEVEN

As the clocks changed to daylight saving time and Peter and Ruth left for their vacation, life on the property became more enjoyable. My spirits were lifted by the arrival of a Belgian WWOOFer my age named Veronique. Having travelled across Canada by train, her plan was to stay on the island for six weeks before returning to Europe. We connected quickly, and in my gratitude for her company, I found myself loosening off my job search to spend time with her and do chores together.

With Veronique's arrival came sunnier skies and a sprouting of daffodils that brought a welcome change of colour to the land. We would take the dogs for walks, bus down to Victoria to have brunch, and bike to the local hot yoga studio for classes. I finally had a new friend to do things with away from the property. I finally had someone I could relate to and confide in. But through all the excitement of this novelty, a clock ticked away in my head, reminding me that all too soon, we would have to say goodbye.

"Veronique and I are going to go for a hike," I told Harry as I got dressed one morning. "Want to come?"

"I need to study and finish my application," he said. "My analysis teacher is looking for someone to help him with a summer research project."

During our walk, I decided to tell Veronique about Harry's plan for next summer. Aside from Amy, my friend in Australia, she was the only girlfriend I had told.

"And you are going to stay together until that time?" asked Veronique.

"That's the plan."

"Wow, you are loyal," she said, shaking her head with amazement. "It seems very selfish of him to tell you this so early."

I gave an acknowledging nod. "I know."

"Do you think he will go? To Ontario?"

"I don't know. He's very ambitious academically, but he's also quite...a home-boy. Do you know what I mean? He seems very comfortable and settled here."

"Yes, but I think that's because he is spoiled. He's been given too much by his parents."

The way Veronique communicated the English language had a tendency to come off blunt, but I liked it. I needed the honesty.

We walked on quietly, taking in the view.

"Would you really be happy staying in a relationship with someone who is not committed?" Veronique suddenly asked.

"It's not that he's not committed. It's just that he has bigger priorities than a relationship." I shrugged. "It's possible he'll change his mind. He has before."

"Is that what you are hoping for?" she asked astutely. "For him to change his mind?"

I looked at her in surprise. It always amazed me how having a different native language was not a barrier to understanding human emotions.

"I'm not sure." I looked at the ground musingly. "I guess there is a part of me that hopes he'll change his mind, but that's selfish of me."

"It's natural to feel this way when you care about someone."

"I suppose."

"I hope you won't be taken for granted," she said after a moment.

"You should be a counsellor," I said with a chuckle.

Veronique smiled and winked. "I did my degree in psychology."

I swallowed uncomfortably at the memory of Harry's mocking words. Then I pushed them away and smiled appreciatively at my new friend. "You're good to talk to."

I returned to the barn two hours later to find Harry still in his pyjamas with greasy hair, playing video games.

"It's really nice and sunny outside, you know," I said as I pulled off my sweaty t-shirt behind him.

"That's good. I'm just about to call Brendan. I need his help with my application." His voice brightened. "You could chat with him as well; it's been a while since you spoke."

I pulled a face at the wall as I undressed. "I'm going to shower." *Maybe you should too.*

"Maybe you could speak with him after? I'm sure he'd like to catch up."

"Can't. Veronique and I are going to yoga soon," I said. "Say hi for me."

I left him watching me go as I skipped down the stairs in my towel. Through the window, I saw Hannah and Jonas lying down cuddling near a patch of flowers, blissfully unaware of the world around them. Peter and Ruth would return from their holiday to find their daughter besotted. Another foreign traveller had entered their home and won the heart of their child.

The next day, the staffing agency contacted me about another administrative assignment with a different ministry. A large records management project, the tasks looked even more monotonous than those of the last assignment. But knowing Veronique could take care of the animals, and with the greater goal in mind and for the sake of moderate income, I once again expressed my interest. After a short meeting in which the hiring manager expressed her hope that I wouldn't get too bored, I was confirmed to start later that week. Harry agreed to drop me off at the bus stop on the way to school. Jake would be sleeping over the evening before my first day and would also ride with us.

"Is Jake ready? It's getting tight," I said on the first morning, glancing at the clock with concern.

"Jake, we need to go soon," called Harry obligingly.

Jake emerged from the bathroom and sleepily ambled towards the kitchen before reaching in the cupboard for a box of cereal.

"I don't think you'll have time to have breakfast here," I said as I buttoned up my coat.

"No worries, I'll just eat it in the car," he replied, not noticing my sense of urgency.

"Harry, do you want to start the car?" I asked with a hinting tone.

He returned quickly from outside with a look of irritation. "Jake, did you forget to charge the car last night?"

Jake made a guilty face. "Oh, shoot."

I felt a wave of worry. "Are you serious? I can't be late for my first day!"

"We'll just have to take my mom's car."

"Okay, well, can we get moving? We should have left by now." I pulled on my boots and stormed out of the door.

In the silence of the car, I chewed a nail and wondered if it would be this stressful every morning. As we merged onto the highway, I spotted my bus approaching from behind. With a flash of panic, I urged Harry to hurry. He screeched to a halt in front of the stop, and I jumped out of the car without saying goodbye, only to see Julie standing in front of me.

"Sara, what a nice surprise!" She came forward to hug me. "Where are you heading to?"

I followed Julie onto the bus and told her about my new assignment. When she asked what type of work I was looking for, I mentioned my interest in human resources. At her offer to connect me with a contact for an informational interview, I gratefully accepted.

"How's it going living with Harry's family?" she asked as she handed me her business card.

I scratched my brow and sniggered. "It's an adjustment. I know I should be grateful that they're letting me live with them, and I am, but I sometimes find it hard not having as much independence as I'm used to."

"I bet."

I looked down at my hands. "I struggle with Ruth sometimes."

Julie smiled. "I can understand."

"I'm moving closer to Victoria next month, though, so that'll be nice."

"I think that's a wise thing to do. And maybe down the line, Harry will join you."

I hesitated. "Well, actually, I'm not sure what's going to happen between us." At her puzzled gaze, I cleared my throat. "He wants to move east for grad school next September, and he wants to be single when he goes."

Julie scoffed and shook her head in disappointment. "How nice of him to tell you so soon."

"It was hard to hear, but I think I took it more personally than necessary. I've realized his motives for going alone are because he wants to develop himself, and not because of any issues with me."

"Oh, absolutely."

"I could be wrong, of course. He seems to change his mind a lot about what he wants."

Julie tittered. "He's a kid; he doesn't know what he wants."

I looked out of the window as we passed Elk Lake. Early morning rowers glided along its surface. *Maybe that's the problem; he's just a kid.*

As I stood in front of the bathroom mirror the next morning, I noticed a redness on my right eyelid. Realizing it was a stye, I decided against applying mascara. When I looked in the office's washroom mirror an hour later, I was pleasantly surprised by what I saw. While I had never been one to wear much makeup, I had always felt like a ghost without mascara on my eyelashes. But today, I took in my exposed fair features with newfound confidence, and on the next morning, I left the tube of mascara untouched in the makeup bag.

My bus journeys were spent chatting with Julie. I appreciated how easy she was to talk to and how helpful she was. After the HR acquaintance responded to Julie's introductory email, we arranged to meet after work at a swanky hotel later that week.

Wearing my grey dress pants and a smart shirt, I arrived at the hotel reception and looked around uncertainly before taking a seat in the lounge. Minutes later, a woman with dark hair appeared. Sandra had told me in our email exchange that she'd be carrying a red purse, which my language translated to a handbag. I had subsequently felt obligated to dig out my black one that I rarely used.

Sandra was an HR director in a large Crown corporation. I followed her to a table where she scanned the wine menu and swiftly ordered a glass of Merlot. Wary of seeming young and uncultured, I requested the same and silently pleaded that the waitress wouldn't ask to see my ID.

With her easy-going manner, I soon realized that Sandra wasn't as intimidating as I assumed from her title. She asked about my experience and made a few suggestions to my resume to adapt it to the Canadian market. I swigged from my glass to catch up as she responded to my questions, hoping the wine wouldn't stain my lips. We then talked about Victoria in general before she asked for the bill and told the waitress she'd cover it.

I left the hotel feeling like I had passed a social test. My reflection in a bus window showed an adult woman that I didn't seem to recognize. It still seemed like I should be looking back at a skinny twelve-year-old girl wearing wellies and a scruffy sweater handed down from her older brothers.

Shortly after I arrived home, Peter entered the barn. His brother had some cheap tickets to see a famous band in Vancouver that weekend and wondered if we wanted to go.

"I'm definitely going," said Jake, looking excitedly at his cousin.

"I've seen them before," said Harry with a drab tone. "I went with Lauren."

"There's nothing wrong with seeing them again," said Peter.

"Come on, Harry!" said Jake encouragingly.

"I have a lot of work on right now. You could still go, though."

"But wouldn't this be a cool thing to go to together?" asked Jake with imploring eyes. "We've been listening to them since we were kids."

Harry sat back in his chair with a sigh of reluctance. "It's just a lot of time that's taken up to go to Vancouver and come back."

In the end, he was persuaded to go, and I said I would join too. I needed a change of scene from the island.

TWELVE

The ferry left Swartz Bay at three o'clock on Saturday afternoon. I looked out the window in hopes of spotting an orca whale while Harry read a math textbook. His analysis teacher had chosen him to be his summer research assistant, and he was putting pressure on himself to be thoroughly prepared.

As Harry looked through the window in thought, someone caught his eye and made him snigger. "Is that Cody Brooks?"

I followed his eyes to see a man around his age stood on the deck in a uniform, carrying a radio.

Harry shook his head with disappointment. "He was in my graduating year, and now he's working here? That's so sad."

My stomach twisted with discomfort at the memory of all the safety stewards I had come to know through my last job.

"It's a big organization and a good employer," I said.

"Yes, but working on a ferry?" he sneered. "Have some ambition."

He returned his attention to his book, and I looked back out of the window with a sour taste in my mouth.

A thundering roar of traffic greeted us as we emerged from the subway in downtown Vancouver. I looked up at the surrounding glass skyscrapers and was reminded of how different the city was from small Victoria.

The downside of the cheap tickets was that our seats were spread out. I insisted that Harry and Jake take the two adjacent seats and noted a meeting point for later on. I found my seat and sat observing the stadium, ignoring the questioning looks of the couple next to me. As the lights dimmed and the music began, I was quickly swept up in the energy of those around me and soon forgot I was alone. At the opening of a popular song, the man next to me stripped off his shirt and waved it around madly. It almost slapped me in the face, but I laughed and carried on dancing by myself. I hadn't expected to have so much fun alone in a crowd.

When I sat back down, the hype started to fade, and the music began to drown out as I found myself consumed with the question of whether I was having enough fun with Harry. He often seemed too busy to do things together, and when he was available, he seemed to prefer to take the option that was quickest or closer to home. He'd win me over with the promise of "next time we'll go there and do that." I was still waiting for the next time.

An hour later, I stood outside scanning a lively crowd for the boys. With an inward groan, I caught the hazy expression of Jake, his wandering eyes a mysterious pink colour.

"I'm going to stay in a hotel downtown with Derek, and I'll meet you at nine tomorrow morning," said Peter after finding us. "Sara, you're in charge of getting these two to the ferry terminal."

The three of us walked slowly down Granville Street as Jake pondered out loud whether he needed food or not. The street was bustling with drunk night-clubbers while homeless beggars loitered unnoticed among them. Jake and I stepped inside a crepe shop, and he stared dopily at the menu. From behind me, I heard a man with a raspy voice ask someone on the street if they could buy him some food.

Suddenly, my name was called. I turned to see Harry looking at me.

"Hey, I'll pay you back if you buy this guy some food."

My mouth impulsively opened in protest, but Harry continued to look at me expectantly. I glanced behind him to find the eyes of the man on me. He wore a dirty green jacket and scruffy jeans, two sizes too big. My breath caught in my throat at the pressure of being put on the spot.

"Okay." I cleared my throat and addressed the man. "What kind of crepe would you like?"

"Oh, thank you, miss. The only thing is, I'm a celiac." He shrugged his shoulders with a smile that revealed few teeth. "I know a store this way, though."

He pointed in the direction of a side street, and I felt the hair on my arms stand up in suspicion. After a hesitant glance around the area, I stepped forward, and we followed him as he began to walk ahead with a crooked posture.

"How far away is this store exactly?" I asked, looking down the dark street uncertainly.

"Not far at all, just down here," the man said, signalling limply with his arm.

I squinted doubtfully through the dark. "Are you sure it's even open? It's around midnight."

"Oh, yes, it'll be open."

I cautiously followed the man's figure and glanced behind to make sure Jake was keeping up. A moment later, the man turned a corner. A small grocery store came into view, dimly lit with nobody inside.

"It looks like it's closed, sorry." I shrugged my shoulders and stepped backwards in preparation to leave.

"Ah, well, there's an ATM just over there."

The man spoke innocently while pointing his finger and then looked me squarely in the eye. I mirrored his gaze, wondering how many times he had played this game.

I was on the spot again, but this time I felt more powerful. As much as I didn't want to make assumptions, my instinct was telling me to walk away.

"I can give you some change." Keeping my distance, I fished quickly in my wallet. "Here, I have two dollars."

The man groaned and sunk his shoulders. "Come on, miss. I have to go all the way to Stanley Park tonight. My wife is there too."

I looked at Harry and Jake for help, but they stood silently, like cowardly sheep.

"I'm sorry. Please, take this toonie."

I dropped the coin in his open hand and turned around. Blood pulsed through my veins as I quickly walked away, the boys following quietly behind. As soon as we reached the main street, I turned sharply on my heel.

"Don't ever speak on my behalf like that again."

Harry met my glare sheepishly. "I'm sorry, I didn't realize he'd want us to walk that far."

"Why didn't you just say no to him instead of lumping me with the responsibility?"

Harry shrugged. "I wanted to help him."

"Putting that on me was out of order," I said furiously. "He was obviously conning us with the celiac bullshit."

"You don't know that," said Harry defensively. "You've talked before about believing in the goodness of strangers."

"He could have had a knife! He could have forced me to take all my money out! Why else do you think he dragged us all that way to a closed store, only to just *happen* to come across an ATM on an empty street?"

Harry rolled his eyes and laughed. "Come on, Sara."

Rage surged up through my throat. "You're so fucking naïve, Harry! I could have been mugged. How could you be so stupid?"

His eyes flashed with hurt as passersby glanced in our direction. I was too angry to care.

We boarded the bus in frosty silence. Jake's glazed eyes glanced sadly between Harry and me. I could still feel myself shaking inside as I replayed the event in my mind.

And then the memory changed to one from Tacoma, Washington, 2014. A girl no older than nineteen holding a gas can outside a car at some traffic lights, me behind the wheel quietly protesting as Harry told me to wind down the window, her open hand as she approached, a dingy gas station with needles on the ground, a dark bridge, women in fur coats teetering in stilettos, the rush of relief when Harry appeared again, the girl once more by her car, staring at a phone, full gas can neglected at her feet.

He's never lived in a big city before, a voice reminded me as I gazed through the glass into the dark. *He's not street smart.*

The frustration I felt began to give way to disappointment.

He's just a kid.

Our ferry docked in Swartz Bay at ten-thirty the next morning. After dumping my bag in the barn, I muttered a few words to Harry before leaving for the yoga studio.

A bead of sweat started to tickle my forehead halfway through the class. I ignored it and focused on my breathing. At the teacher's command, we turned over and assumed the cobra position. I watched in the mirror as my upper body rose. I looked strong. But the superman pose was coming up next, and that one was harder. I squeezed my core and glutes and raised my arms by my side, urging my torso and legs upwards. I inhaled deeper to distract from the strain, willing myself to maintain the position and hold my strength. The countdown seemed to get slower every time.

We finally rolled back over into the corpse position. The bead of sweat returned, taunting my temple.

"Resist that urge to wipe your face or scratch your skin," said the teacher calmly. "Just breathe and let the feeling pass."

I exhaled and opened my eyes. There was a window in the ceiling above me. I looked up at the blue sky and watched puffy clouds slowly pass by. Time moved on, but clouds always seemed to drift by in the same slow manner. Their course never changed; they were always moving aimlessly in one direction. A lump formed in my throat.

Will it always be like this? Is this how Canadian life will always be?

"You might find your mind starting to wander, to think about things that happened yesterday, things you need to do today. Bring yourself back to focus."

I swallowed and closed my eyes.

"Now is the time for you to release the tension you've been holding onto before this session," the teacher continued soothingly. "Just let it go."

Something wet started trickling down my cheek. It wasn't sweat.

THIRTEEN

On April 24th, my luck miraculously changed. A few days before my assignment at the Ministry was due to end, I received an email from the president of the staffing agency. One of the consultants was leaving to go travelling, and based on my recruiting experience, Eva wondered if I'd be interested in meeting with her to discuss the role.

I stared at the screen in astonishment, wondering if it was a mistake. The opportunity seemed too good to be true, yet it was my name on the addressee line. My fingers trembled with shocked delight as I replied to confirm my availability to meet at five o'clock that coming Monday. It would be a few hours after I met another woman in the HR community for an informational meeting.

I approached the weekend feeling optimistic. I was one good impression away from getting a full-time job, and it was my final weekend of living in the barn before having my own space. Peter and Ruth had gone up island for a few days, and I walked around the property in a happy, relaxed mood. The evenings had grown warm enough that coats were no longer necessary, and with the longer days and budding leaves came the inspiring belief that things were about to get better.

On Saturday evening, we threw a spontaneous party in the barn. We bought beer, and Veronique made brownies with some Belgian chocolate she had approved from the grocery store.

"These really are the best brownies I've ever had," I said appreciatively as I reached for another.

"How many have you had?" asked Harry. "Just one is enough for me."

At Jake's suggestion that we play a drinking game, I agreed with revived enthusiasm. I lost the first round and slowly downed my beer before shuddering at the taste.

After one game, Harry rose from the table, noise-cancelling headphones in his hand. "I need to study. I have more exams next week."

By now, I could feel the alcohol seeping into my senses. Veronique turned on a '90s pop playlist, and the rush of nostalgia sent me spiralling around the room giddily. I felt full of energy, like a young child liberated from her room after being grounded. I called up to Harry, and he stood watching me for a few minutes with an amused smile.

An hour later, my energy suddenly crashed. I stumbled upstairs and collapsed on the bed, only to feel a rush of nausea seconds later. Harry followed me down to the bathroom and held my hair back patiently. I woke groggily in the morning.

"Sorry if I was annoying last night," I said sheepishly, running my finger down Harry's chest.

He tilted his head to the side, straight-faced. "It was a little annoying."

I moved my hand away. "I was just happy and wanted to celebrate. I rarely get drunk."

"I know. It's just, with finals coming up, I was hoping for a quiet night, and it was a little distracting."

I sat up with my arms folded. "Do you know how many times I've been trying to concentrate on something or in bed trying to sleep while you and Jake have been playing music?"

"I'm not trying to argue with you, Sara," he said calmly.

"Don't worry, soon I'll no longer be around here distracting you."

I swiftly left the bed and pulled on some clothes before walking to the main house. Hannah was in the kitchen playing guitar. I took a seat at the table and listened until she finished.

"Was that about Jonas?" I asked teasingly.

Bashful dimples formed in her cheeks, then her eyes widened with excitement. "I have news. Mom called. She's buying a cottage up island. Jonas and I are going to start an Airbnb there over the summer."

"She's buying another house?" I said in disbelief.

"Apparently, it's beautiful. North of Campbell River. Quiet, close to the water, surrounded by mountains."

I looked down at the table, processing. "And has Jonas agreed to all of this? I thought he planned to go back to Austria?"

"He will, in the fall." Her eyes suddenly seemed to glitter with happiness. "And I'll go with him."

My throat clogged with surprise. "That's...are you sure? That's a very big commitment."

She shrugged. "I'm ready. I love him."

I played with my ear, unsure how to phrase myself. "And he's definitely on board with this plan?"

"Oh, yeah, we've talked about it." She twisted her hair between her fingers, staring into the distance in a smitten daze.

"Okay. Well, that's great." I hesitated. "I don't want to sound pessimistic and patronizing but, just be careful. Things can get complicated in this type of relationship. I don't want you to get hurt."

"I know, but I trust him. He's the most mature guy I've met."

I nodded. "I get it. I felt the same way about Harry."

"I just want the type of boyfriend who looks at me the loving way Harry looks at you, like last night, when he was watching you dance," she said with a dreamy smile. "It was so adorable."

I suddenly remembered my squabble with Harry and smiled uncomfortably. At my suggestion of another song for her to play, we took it in turns to attempt the low notes and laughed at the result. Hannah then looked at me quizzically.

"What do you think about doing a duet with me at the Sidney festival? It's on May 13th. We could do this song."

I remembered watching her play the year before to a crowd of around one hundred people.

"Oh, I don't know about that."

"Why not? You can sing. It would be fun."

She beamed at me enthusiastically, and after a moment's pause, I found myself returning the smile. "Okay, let's do it."

On Monday morning, I put on some of my smartest clothes and boarded the bus. It was my final day of the assignment, and I had scheduled my first meeting over my lunch break. Set to finish an exam before, Harry had offered to drive me to and from the first meeting.

I arrived with sweaty palms at the front door of what appeared to be another staffing agency. A trainee receptionist greeted me and directed me to a stiff wooden chair on the Persian carpet. A woman in a mid-length dress and knee-high boots came down to meet me. She had short, greying hair and a sharp face with a smile that seemed insincere. I followed her upstairs, and we sat in silence while she scrutinized the resume I had provided, updated with Sandra's suggestions.

"What exactly is a steward?" asked Denise with a frown.

I cleared my throat. "It's someone that helps patrons at an event. They give directions, answer questions, maintain a safe and secure venue. It's very similar to an air steward, although I suppose people say 'flight attendant' over here…" My voice trailed off with embarrassment.

Denise pursed her lips with what seemed like a faint look of scorn.

"I was responsible for recruiting, training, and coordinating the deployments of up to 500 stewards," I added, feeling inclined to fill the silence.

"And you're looking for a job in human resources?"

"Ideally, yes, with a focus on recruitment." I licked my dry lips. "What would you say the job market is like right now?"

Denise shrugged and uttered a pessimistic sigh. "It's a small job market."

"I see." I rubbed my trousers.

"And it says here that you are on a work permit?" Denise looked up at me with piercing eyes.

"Yes, a two-year work permit." I laughed nervously. "I think that's putting some employers off hiring me."

She raised her eyebrows and nodded. "Well, two years go by faster than you think."

My face fell with disappointment.

"I'm open to temporary work, too," I said, trying to sound enthusiastic.

"That's a shame. We just hired a girl to cover reception," said Denise without a hint of emotion. She scanned the rest of my resume with a look of indifference before tossing it to the side. "Now, did you have any other questions for me?"

"I wanted to ask what you think the most challenging thing is about working in HR." As I spoke, I blushed at what suddenly seemed like a silly, cliché question.

"Oh, people." Denise looked away aloofly as she spoke. "They're the best and worst of it."

Sensing she didn't care to elaborate, I cleared my throat. "Well, I'd welcome any opportunities you might have for me to gain more Canadian experience."

"Mmhmm. And are you confident in your ability to use computers, Sara?" she asked with a sudden sweet tone.

Unsure if there was more to the query, I shifted awkwardly in my seat. "Uh—yes, I think I'm pretty good with computers."

"Well, I'm sure we can find something for you." Denise stood up with her unnerving smile and held out her hand. "Very nice to meet you, Sara."

I walked down the street with my shoulders sagged in despair. I had essentially been told to my face that I was unlikely to find a permanent job because of my work permit. I wanted to cry. Was there even any point meeting with Eva later? For all I knew, she had forgotten I was on a work permit, and upon being reminded, would lean back from me in disappointment before smiling sweetly and sugar-coating her words to suggest the job perhaps wasn't "the best fit."

I spotted Harry's car on the corner and slumped into the passenger seat. "It's hopeless. Nobody will hire me. I'm not sure I should even go to this other meeting."

Harry squeezed my leg. "Be positive. You never know."

I got off the bus a few hours later and took a deep breath before walking through the agency's doors. A woman with long, dark-brown hair walked down the stairs with a warm smile.

"Hi Sara, I'm Eva. It's nice to put a face to the name."

Dressed in a white blouse and wide-legged, tan pants, Eva extended her hand to shake mine with what seemed like genuine affability. She offered me water, and I followed her up to a corner office that looked out onto the street.

"So, where in England are you from?" she asked after taking a seat.

"North Yorkshire. Do you know it?"

"I haven't been, but my husband is from Birmingham."

"Oh, right." I took in her expression, and we shared a knowing smile.

"We moved to Victoria several years ago," she said. "I worked in the States before then."

"Did you find it difficult to find work when you moved here?" I asked.

"Absolutely. That's why I ended up starting this agency."

My nerves vanished. Eva asked me about my job in London, and I described my duties, wondering as I spoke why I sounded so much more confident than in my earlier meeting.

"Well, you've basically described what you would be doing in this role," said Eva with a satisfied shrug. "Now, what are your plans? How long do you think you'll be staying in Canada?"

Here it comes.

"My work permit expires in December 2018, but I would definitely like to stay longer than that," I said assuredly. "I plan to apply for permanent residency."

"Great. Well, I have a job description here if you'd like to take it home and read through."

Eva proceeded to tell me more about the office and the team. I listened attentively, ignoring the voice in my head that wondered why she wasn't concerned about my work permit. The office culture sounded relaxed and open, like it had been in my old job.

"It all sounds great. Thanks so much for contacting me." I remained composed, but my insides were bubbling up in excited anticipation.

"I should be thanking you," said Eva with a smile. "We've received glowing feedback from the Ministries about your work."

I walked carefully back down the stairs, wary of tripping and falling at the last hurdle.

At the door, I held up the job description in my hand and looked at Eva queryingly. "So, I'll take a look at this tonight and get back to you tomorrow?"

"Sounds great. I look forward to hearing from you." Eva smiled at me brightly as she shook my hand.

I walked down the street feeling like I was floating on a cloud. A huge weight seemed to have been lifted from my shoulders. I boarded the bus in a daze, as if I had just woken up from a bad dream that had finally ended. And then came the subtle prick of tears. Tears to celebrate the fruits of my persistence, the worth of my toils.

Warm sunshine surrounded me as I stepped off the bus in Sidney. Recent quarrels and living challenges no longer seemed to matter. All that mattered was that I had found a full-time job, in my field, in Canada. I could breathe.

My start date as a consultant at the agency was confirmed for May 15th, meaning I would have two weeks free to relax and explore my new neighbourhood.

On my move date, I finished packing my bags eagerly, like a kid excited to leave for the airport. As I closed the zip on my suitcase, I felt Harry's hands on my shoulders.

"I'll miss waking up next to you each morning," he said glumly. "There's something so comforting about coming home to you."

I placed a hand on his. "You're welcome to stay over whenever, especially since you'll be at UVic most days working on your project."

I walked downstairs with my suitcase and spotted my water bottle on the table, surrounded by pens and guitar picks. On a notepad, there was a short scribble of lyrics in Harry's writing. Lyrics about me.

After loading my bags into the car, it was time to find Veronique. I entered the kitchen with an ache in my stomach. A sudden timidness surrounded us in the strange way it can when saying goodbye to someone that has become so valued within such a short space of time.

I climbed into the passenger seat while Harry went to find his sunglasses. A glint of something caught my eye as I reached for my seatbelt, and in the storage box between the seats, I saw a SIM card. The sight of it made me titter. How long ago that seemed. *The next chapter is going to be so much brighter.*

PART TWO

FOURTEEN

A small bug landed on my skin before buzzing off again at the flicker of my hand. I turned the page of my new book and adjusted my sunglasses. It was my second full day in my new temporary home, and the forecast predicted upwards of twenty degrees all week. Lucy was in Bali on a group trip for two weeks, and I was grateful for the timing. I finally had the space and freedom to do exactly what I wanted, even if it involved doing very little.

I had spent the previous morning running around the neighbourhood of Cadboro Bay. My route had taken me past secret coves and large bushes that concealed mansions with small families of deer sneaking across the sprawling and immaculately maintained lawns. In the evening, I had walked down to the beach and sat admiring the pastel colours of the sky over the calm bay, before returning home to the comfort of a full tub of ice cream in my freezer and my choice of movie.

As I walked down to the beach hours later, a sign directing to a park I hadn't heard of caught my attention. I decided to follow it. A poster on the gate entrance warned of a recent cougar sighting. I took my phone from my pocket to send Harry a light-hearted text.

> Going on a walk through some woods. If you don't hear from me after two hours, I've probably been mauled by a cougar.

I opened the gate and followed the path into the woodland. Rays of sunlight burst through gaps in the branches overhead, and birdsong echoed from the trees. As the path declined downward, a trickling sound of water grew louder. I looked up to feel the warm sunbeams on my face and briefly closed my eyes. I'd found myself in a tranquil oasis.

Suddenly, a twig snapped under my feet, sending a small bird nearby fleeing the ground in fright. I jerked my head around instinctively and scanned the area. Nothing. I was alone.

I returned home and collapsed comfortably on the couch before opening my laptop to finish a blog post. I had found the motivation to start writing again. It was when I hit the publish button two hours later that I realized Harry hadn't responded to my text.

He came round the next evening for dinner and spoke excitedly about his research project. I listened attentively but struggled to keep up, as if I were listening to a foreign language.

"Are you going to stay over?" I asked hopefully. "We could go down to the beach."

"Nah, Jake and I are going to jam tonight. He wants me to play with him at the concert next weekend."

"That'll be fun. Hannah asked if I would—" I hesitated and looked down at my plate. "She asked if I would come watch."

"You should. She's always one of the crowd favourites."

"You could stay tomorrow if you like?"

"Thanks, but I have a piano lesson at six, so I'll probably just go home after work."

"A piano lesson?" I repeated in surprise.

"I've decided to learn," he said brightly. "Mom paid for twenty lessons as an early birthday present, and I'm going to practise on the piano in the barn. Uncle Derek knows someone who can tune it."

"That's great. I didn't realize you wanted to play."

"I have a lot of goals for this summer." He pushed back his empty plate with a satisfied smile and stretched his arms up behind him.

"Like what?" I asked with a mixture of curiousness and wariness.

Harry leaned forward and rested his interlinked hands on the table. "I want to make an album and design a website. I want to read at least three books, and I plan to bike to campus every day."

"Gee, that's a lot." I raised my glass to my mouth. As it touched my lips, a sense of realization hit. I placed the glass down and ran my fingers around its rim uncertainly, mustering a small laugh. "Hopefully, you'll still give yourself time to visit me now and then."

"Well, I was thinking that it would make sense for you to come up on weekends," he said. "You could borrow one of the bikes, and we could go on rides."

My stomach sank with disappointment as I met his encouraging gaze.

"Sure, we can alternate weekends."

Lucy returned from her trip late the next week. I expected her to be tired after her journey, but before even unpacking, she was on the phone with friends making plans to go out that evening. Club music played from her room as she walked into the living room in a short, glittery dress.

I looked up from reading my book. "I saw your photos from Bali. I'm glad you had a good time."

"It was so fun! The drinks there are insanely cheap, oh my gosh." She laughed to herself in the mirror on the wall as she applied lip gloss.

"Did you do much exploring?" I asked.

"We went to a couple of different beaches. To be honest, I think I was hungover on most days!"

I forced myself to match the expression on her face.

"I'm actually going to Europe in mid-July with my family for three weeks," she continued as she brushed her hair. "We'll be in London for a few days. You'll have to give me some tips, all the famous places and nice bars."

Something told me we had different preferences for how we filled our time in a foreign country.

"Sure, I can do that," I said. "It sounds like you've got an exciting summer planned."

Lucy nodded at me in the mirror, her pencilled eyes gleaming. "I'm pretty happy with myself because, by the end of the summer, I'll have done two continents."

A voice in my head groaned in protest.

Lucy turned to look at me keenly. "Would you like to come out with me and my friends tonight? Thursdays are really fun."

I shifted my position on the couch, noticing in the process that I had an ice cream stain on the thigh of my cropped sweatpants. "I think I'm just going to have a quiet night in, but thanks."

After another check of my decision, Lucy clacked out of the door in her heels, leaving behind an invisible trail of perfume. I rested my head on the arm of the sofa and thought back to the time I was twenty-one and had the energy to go out four times a week. It was only four years ago, but it seemed a lot longer.

Lucy emerged from her room the next morning with puffy eyes. After hearing about her eventful night out, I guiltily declined her invitation to sunbathe at the beach. I had plans to call a friend in Europe before going to Sidney.

Living in privacy made calls with friends and family a more relaxing and authentic experience, and being able to share that I had a job offer made me more enthusiastic ahead of a call. But when I confessed Harry's future plans to my friend, the news was met with disapproval once again. When she asked why I decided to stay with him, I found myself trying to highlight his good qualities. It was hard to explain my reasons to people that had never met him. My justifications were met with a skeptical face and an unconvincing comment of "you know what's best."

The journey to Sidney required me to walk ten minutes to the university campus and take two buses. Comments from friends ran through my mind as I looked out of the window at cyclists riding along the Lochside Trail under the afternoon sun.

"So, Mom rescued a dog," said Harry as I stepped into his car.

"You mean, you have four now?"

"Yep. And this one doesn't seem to like males."

He showed me his forearm and I saw a small pink gash with bruising around it.

"Whoa! And your mum is going to keep him?"

"She wants to take him up to the new cottage to guard it while Hannah and Jonas are there." Harry shook his head disapprovingly. "I don't know what she's thinking."

I stepped out of the car to the sound of threatening barks from the porch of the main house. As we approached the bike shed, I saw a flash of brown through the fence before the dog jumped up with his front paws and flashed his teeth with menacing growls. Harry and I stood back hesitantly.

Suddenly, the front door opened, and out stepped Ruth. "Max, come! Lay down."

The dog jumped back from the fence and sat obediently at her feet.

"We think he doesn't like long hair." Ruth nodded at me with a hint of impatience. "You need to tie your hair up."

Harry regarded her with disbelief. "Mom, do you really think it's a wise idea to have him around Airbnb guests? What if he attacks someone?"

Ruth dismissed his concern with a wave of her hand. "He'll be fine. He just needs to get used to his new home, and we need to earn his trust."

Harry mounted his bike with a frustrated expression lingering on his face. I regarded him with sympathy as he cycled ahead of me towards Joey's house. But the feeling weakened when I watched him let himself in the front door and stride straight through to the dining room to take a seat at the family piano. As he began to play, I stood by the window and watched golden sunlight ooze over the ocean at Patricia Bay.

"You're almost better than me now," Joey remarked to Harry.

Harry looked around the room. "Don't you have any music sheets?"

"I haven't read music in years. I just play by memory."

A look of boredom momentarily crossed Harry's face before his eyes brightened. "Are you coming to watch me play at the festival tomorrow?"

"No," scoffed Joey.

"Why not?" asked Harry with disappointment.

"Because I don't want to," laughed Joey. "It's what all the local grannies go to."

"You're telling me you're not going to support your best friend as he plays in his first music show?" asked Harry with a disapproving tone.

Joey rolled his eyes. "Oh, come on. It's hardly a big event."

"That doesn't matter. Mom will probably have a spare ticket. It's only ten bucks."

"Ten bucks to see a bunch of shitty wannabe musicians," Joey sneered.

"Joey, come on."

"You don't need my support. Sara and your family will be there!"

"I want you to be there as well, though. It's important to me," said Harry with a hint of sulkiness. "Brendan would come if he was here."

"Good for him."

My patience tested, I interrupted the conversation. "What did you get up to today, Joey?"

"Well, I helped fix a dock," he said with feigned enthusiasm. He had just started a summer job at a marina doing maintenance. "But I guess the pay is pretty good, and it's nice being outside."

"Definitely!" I said encouragingly.

"You should apply to do a research project next year," said Harry. "It's so much fun."

Joey looked down with a self-deprecating snigger. "I don't think I have the grades to be offered anything like that."

A rising sense of discomfort made me turn away from them to look out of the window again.

"I'll see you at the concert, then," said Harry as he buckled his chin strap an hour later.

Joey rolled his eyes as he closed the front door. "Whatever."

In the bedroom of the barn, I brushed my hair quietly, deep in thought. Harry sat at his computer, stroking a finger over his top lip. I took a breath.

"I don't like the way you talk to Joey sometimes."

Harry looked at me with surprise. "How do you mean?"

"Not everyone wants to do research, and you know he isn't the most naturally academic person."

"I think it would benefit him greatly if he did something like that," said Harry.

"But what if he doesn't want to?"

"Well, he obviously isn't happy doing the job he currently has."

"For all you know, he only mocks it because he thinks you're going to judge it," I said. "Just like you judged that guy you went to school with for working on the ferry."

Harry furrowed his brows, as if struggling to remember the reference. Then he shook his head with a smile. "Joey has always made fun of himself. You haven't known him as long as I have. I don't think you understand the dynamics of our friendship."

"Actually, I think I do. You try to be the dominant one and expect him to do what you want."

"I disagree," replied Harry. "We just have a playful relationship."

"I don't find it playful; I find it unfair. It almost feels a little manipulative at times."

"Manipulative?" he repeated with a puzzled frown.

I sighed in exasperation. "You know what I mean, Harry."

"Actually, I don't. How am I manipulating Joey, exactly?" He pushed his glasses up his nose and looked at me expectantly, like a teacher waiting for a response from a student.

"The way you just walk around his house like you own the place, touching his things, playing his piano, the way you guilt him into coming to your show."

Harry continued to watch me with a composed gaze. "I still don't understand how that indicates that I'm manipulating him."

Words began to muddle through my head in the presence of his calm confidence. "Just the way you talk to him… it's hard to explain."

Harry's lips parted slightly as he stared at me blankly. "I don't understand."

The words came out slowly and quietly, his brow furrowed in a way that made me feel like an indecipherable fool. I dropped the hairbrush with a huff.

"I'm going to bed."

I faced the wall and lay with a restless mind.

The call of the rooster woke me in the morning. I instinctively went to roll over, only to remember where things had been left with Harry. But he heard me too soon and began to stir. I remained silent, reluctant to be the one to give in. After a moment, his hand rested on my waist. I let him wait and then slowly rolled over. He greeted me with a sheepish smile.

"I'm sorry you felt I was being rude to Joey last night," he said softly.

I shifted down and rested my head on his chest.

"Was there something else upsetting you last night?" he asked.

I swallowed nervously, wondering if it was the right time to say what was on my mind. Unsure how to start, I drew small circles on his skin in thought. His heart beat steadily under the surface.

"I feel like it's hard for my friends to understand why I'm with you when I tell them about our relationship," I said uncomfortably.

Harry breathed out evenly. "Well, most of them haven't met me, so that makes sense."

"It's difficult."

"I can understand that."

We lay in silence. Harry's stomach slowly rose and fell as I filled with apprehension. I cleared my throat awkwardly, still tracing circles on his skin with my index finger. *Just say it.*

"I sometimes wonder if it would be better to break up sooner rather than waiting until next year."

Through my cheek, I felt Harry's heart beat immediately quicken.

"What makes you feel that way?" His voice remained controlled but his heart pounded uneasily.

I swallowed, unsure how to express myself. "Carrying on like this while knowing there's an impending end date…I wonder if it would make more sense to just be friends."

Unable to bring myself to look at him, I watched Harry's stomach rise and fall faster. His arm fastened tighter around me. I heard him open his mouth to speak before stopping. There was something oddly reassuring about the way he seemed so tense.

"I would really like to continue as we are," he said.

"You would?" I asked in surprise.

"I really like being with you, and I believe you like being with me. We make each other happy."

I hesitated. "But do you not think it would be smarter to end things now?"

His confidence slowly rebuilding, Harry shifted into a sitting position, so I was forced to rise and face him.

"Sure, it might make sense. But is it actually what you would want?"

He looked deeply in my eyes, and suddenly in his face I saw all the previous goodbyes we'd shared over the years. Clutches of desperation at the ferry terminal and the airport, a reluctant release, eyes wide with despair, a longing look and a limp wave before I forced myself to turn completely around and not look back.

Trapped in the memory, I shook my head.

It was clear that Hannah's idea of a duet at the concert had faded away, and I accepted the update with both relief and disappointment. Harry and Jake spent the day rehearsing, bickering about song choices and arrangements. They displayed their nerves differently: Jake enthusiastic and over-compensating, Harry quiet and stoic.

In the evening, I found him sitting on the bed, staring into space while absent-mindedly biting his nails. At the sight of me, his face grew panicked. "I'm really nervous. I don't think I can do this."

I sat down behind him and stroked his back. "That's natural, but you can do it. You sounded great earlier."

Harry looked at me with a fearful expression. "But I haven't performed in front of strangers before, and there's a hundred of them watching. I don't feel prepared."

"They're just people," I said. "It'll be fun! You'll only regret it if you don't do it."

Harry shook his head. "I don't know."

"It's going to be fine; you'll have a great time." I paused in thought, then smiled. "Hey, this is your mantra. Repeat it: 'Everything will be fine; I'm going to have a great time.'"

Harry lay down on the bed with his eyes closed and slowly started to repeat the words while I silently massaged his scalp.

Thirty minutes later, we loaded up to leave.

"Ahh, you look so cute!" Hannah cooed from the backseat as I climbed into the car. I looked up in surprise at the unrecognizable voice to see her smiling at me, her arm wrapped around Jonas.

Harry sat quietly during the short journey. I held his hand reassuringly. As I took a seat in the venue, my anxiety for him slowly began to increase. The two of us shared a fairly introverted nature, and I knew he was out of his comfort zone. The venue doors opened a few seconds after the first act had begun. I gazed over through the dark light and saw Joey discreetly climb the stairs to find an available seat.

Hannah was second to play, charming the older guests with her country covers. I looked to my side to see Ruth dabbing her eyes and wondered if she would have reacted the same way had I been on stage with her daughter.

When he and his cousin took to the stage, Harry conveyed quiet confidence, whether intended or not. With a laid-back stance, he focused down on his guitar before daring to look around him more towards the end of the performance. His stage presence was quiet but alluring, and seeing him conquer his nerves filled me with pride.

After the concert ended, attendees gathered in the foyer to congratulate friends and relatives. I spotted Ted and Julie and instinctively headed in their direction. I knew Julie would be excited to hear about my job offer. But a belief that the focus should be on Harry stopped me in my tracks.

From across the hall, I watched him walk out of the backstage room with renewed self-assurance. His confident voice drifted through the air as he responded to his aunt and uncle's praise.

"I was really nervous before," he said self-deprecatingly.

"We couldn't tell at all!"

Harry casually ran a hand through his hair with a smile. "I just kept repeating a mantra to myself, and that really helped."

Something stopped me from approaching. From a few steps away, outside of the frame, I watched invisibly as he basked in his fame.

The next day, it was my turn to feel nervous. I sat on the bus to Victoria with a twisting in my stomach at the thought of starting my new job in less than twenty-four hours. I had felt nervous starting new jobs before, but nothing like this. This opportunity seemed to carry more pressure than the rest. With all the obstacles I'd gone through to get this far, I believed I couldn't afford to put a foot wrong.

No matter what I did to reassure and distract myself, the stream of butterflies refused to change course. I had the suite to myself, but being there alone only made me feel restless. I pulled on a cardigan and went for a walk around the neighbourhood in hopes it would help my nerves subside. Not even the candy cotton skies overlooking the bay could calm me. I returned home in defeat.

I consulted my wardrobe carefully, trying to decide on a first-day outfit that was smart but not too formal. As another rush of nerves hit me, I grabbed my phone in an appeal for comfort and messaged Harry with how I was feeling.

He responded late in the evening as I lay in bed trying and failing to sleep.

> Everything will be fine; you're going to have a great time.

I put the phone down with disappointment. The mantra I had created no longer seemed inspiring. Now it just seemed like a lazy, quick-fix solution.

FIFTEEN

My alarm sounded at seven o'clock. I inhaled slowly in front of the mirror as I gave myself a silent pep talk. *It's normal to be nervous. You're going to do great.* I dabbed concealer under my eyes and swept blush over my cheeks before my hand hovered hesitantly over my tube of mascara. It had been a month since I'd stopped wearing it for work, and I had found the experience strangely freeing. I took my hand away and vowed to save it for special social occasions only.

There was nobody else at the bus stop. I stood swapping my weight from one foot to another as I waited. As the bus appeared around the corner, I felt another swoop of butterflies. A smiley driver with a moustache greeted me as I dropped my coins into the slot with shaking fingers.

The bus wound through a quiet neighbourhood of grand houses and oak trees. The bus driver reported the weather forecast with the cheery tone of someone who had previously worked as a pilot. Passengers would call out thanks to him as they exited the bus. Two more stops, one more stop. My thank you came out faintly. I crossed the street with jelly in my legs and took a deep breath before opening the door of the office.

Eva looked over the stairs with a welcoming smile before reintroducing me to Jenna, the bubbly office administrator. After saying hi to Paige, I walked up the stairs to my office. On the desk, a card was propped against a small vase of flowers. *Welcome to the team!* it read in big curly letters.

"Now, we're not expecting much output from you this week," said Eva warmly as she gave me a tour of the office. "Just take the time to learn about the office and what we do."

I sat down with Paige to learn about the staff database and hear about a typical day. Then I turned on my computer and read through some email templates, making notes for myself and jotting down Canadian terms I was unfamiliar with for further research. The others would call out to each other, sometimes asking work-related questions and sometimes making comments about the news. I sat quietly as they came together on the mezzanine to talk about their weekends. In time I would join them, when I felt more familiar with the team dynamics.

I wanted to get stuck in and make a good impression, so I offered to check some references. Data protection laws regarding sharing employee information seemed to differ slightly from those in the UK. I started dialling a number, only to feel self-conscious as Eva walked past. I had a template of questions to go off, but they sounded unnatural to my speaking style, and I worried I'd fluff up my words. A call went straight to voicemail, and my mind went blank before I mumbled a message in which I almost forgot to provide the number to call back.

A few minutes later, Jenna called upstairs. "Sara, line one is for you, returning your call."

I cleared my throat and picked up the phone.

"I'm sorry, who did you say this reference is for?" asked the man on the other end sharply after I introduced myself with a squeaky voice.

"Betty Kirk."

"Who?"

"Betty Kirk."

"I don't know anyone of that name," said the man with a dismissive tone.

I swallowed. "Oh, really? It says on her resume that she worked for you as an administrative assistant two years ago."

"Oh! Betty Kirk!" he said suddenly. "I'm sorry, your accent confused me."

"Sorry about that," I instinctively replied, feeling my cheeks blush.

Despite the hiccups, I felt more relaxed as the day went on. Everyone in the office seemed relatively laid-back, and the work wasn't new to me. I left the office that afternoon feeling optimistic. My phone showed a message from Harry sent earlier, asking how the day was going. I replied with a smile.

I think I'm going to like working here.

The next morning, I sat in on one of Paige's interviews. There was something surreal about going from being sat in the candidate's position a few months ago to an interviewer position today. Before noon, everyone dressed in workout clothes, and we walked a couple of blocks over to the gym that Eva had recently started a corporate membership with. A converted warehouse, it had an open space with exposed brick and mirrors that ran along the walls. We approached the front desk behind which a man and woman stood chatting.

"This is Sara," said Eva, gesturing towards me. "Could we please add her to our membership?"

"Welcome," said the man with a smile.

He was handsome, with a sharp jaw and broad shoulders. I smiled my thanks and lowered my eyes shyly.

The heavily made-up woman next to him fixed her hair before leaving the desk and calling the group together. We began with a warm-up, and I found myself jogging comfortably ahead of the others. When we started sprints, I surged ahead of the group with an ease that seemed to take the woman by surprise. A satisfied smile played on my lips as I bent to pick up my water bottle.

People had underestimated my abilities in the past, and as a young blonde woman with a soft-spoken voice and foreign accent, I had accepted that assumptions would be made as I navigated Canadian life. Once demoralized by this reality, the experience of it now inspired me to prove people wrong.

Harry's car was parked outside the house when I arrived home later. The warm, sunny weather had inspired me to walk instead of taking the bus, and the ninety minutes allowed me to unwind and discover unfamiliar roads.

Harry listened and smiled as I told him about my first couple of days, but he seemed distracted and restless.

"I feel like I don't have much integrity right now," he said as we lay in my bed later.

"How do you mean?"

"I feel like I'm not making progress on my goals."

I propped myself up on my elbows. "I wouldn't say that reflects your integrity. Integrity is about having moral principles, being honest with yourself and following your values."

"Yes, and I'm not following the values I've set for myself this summer."

I laid a hand on his arm. "I don't think you have low integrity; I think you're just being hard on yourself. It's normal for people to set goals and not accomplish them as quickly as they'd hoped."

Harry frowned. "I don't want to be the norm."

I looked at him blankly, unsure what he wanted to hear.

Harry stared up at the ceiling sulkily. "You're lucky to live away from home."

"There's no reason you couldn't either."

"Well, actually there is," he said with a serious expression. "All the music and recording equipment is in the barn, and I can make as much noise as I need to."

"I suppose."

"With my family around, it's really distracting. Hannah wants to hang out, and Jake wants to do things."

"Well, they are your family," I said pointedly.

"I know, but I think they could be more considerate." Harry shook his head with a disappointed sigh. "It's the same with every friend—there are all these distractions."

My skin prickled at his words.

"I wish I could just escape the island for a month and be on my own so I could actually get things done," he continued, staring grudgingly at the ceiling.

I folded my arms. "You do realize that saying that makes me feel like a burden?"

He turned to me in surprise. "That's not what I meant."

"Then maybe you should think more before you speak."

I got out of bed and pulled on my clothes.

"I'm sorry," he said behind me. "You're right. I could have explained my feelings better."

I turned around. "Promise me you won't be mopey like this when we go sailing with Ted and Julie this weekend. Promise me you'll have fun."

"I will," he said earnestly. "But after that, I really do need to hunker down."

I watched with suspicion from the window as he walked away. I knew exactly what he meant by "hunker down." It meant reduced visits and less time doing things together.

I turned on my laptop and opened social media. An ad referred to my upcoming birthday and suggested creating an event to celebrate with friends. I sniffed sardonically. *What friends?*

As soon as the question passed through my mind, I felt a flicker of sadness, and then it was followed by an intense feeling of dissatisfaction. I, too, was not making progress on my goal.

The next day, I found myself itching to do more at work and be more involved in staffing placements. A new request from a client on the Friday inspired me to take action. After scanning the database for candidates with relevant experience, I made a list, rose from my desk, and gently called for everyone's attention before reading out the names for consideration. Eva met my input with enthusiasm, and within the next hour, I had connected with a few candidates and presented their resumes to the hiring manager.

I boarded the bus to Sidney feeling more content with my contributions. Ted and Julie picked me up with their two young kids in the back. Tom and Milly smiled at me timidly and mumbled shy responses to my questions. Harry was waiting at the marina. I passed food items to Julie on the boat while Ted and Harry untied the ropes.

Clouds were grey, and there was a slight chill in the air as we set sail towards Salt Spring Island. Julie passed me a blanket and poured me a glass of wine as Harry told Ted about his math project.

"Have you ever gone through a period of feeling really unsatisfied with your progress in life?" asked Harry as we ate dinner.

I looked out at the water with a sinking feeling.

Julie sipped her wine in thought. "For a couple of years, I had a job that didn't bring me much satisfaction, but otherwise, I don't think so."

"Why do you ask?" Ted asked curiously.

"I just feel a need to be more productive in achieving my goals," Harry replied. "I'm behind where I'd like to be."

Ted took a swig from his beer and sniggered. "Relax, it's a long weekend."

Harry glanced at me quickly before looking down shamefacedly. "I'm probably going to head back tomorrow evening."

My mouth dropped open in protest. "I thought you were going to join for the whole weekend?"

"I know, I'm sorry. I just really didn't get enough work done these past few days."

I looked away crossly.

"Well, there's no reason you can't stay with us the whole weekend, Sara," said Julie.

Unwilling to let Harry cut short my fun, I turned to her with a smile. "That would be great."

We docked in Fulford Harbour just as the clouds dispersed to reveal a setting sun. Harry and I slept in the compartment at the bow of the boat. Ted's gentle snores from the main cabin carried through the darkness. With a playful grin and a finger to his lips, Harry ran his hand up my thigh. Physical intimacy was an area that he seemed unwilling to compromise on while pursuing academics and personal projects. It had always been a central part of our relationship. Even if he'd recently done something that irritated me, Harry had a charm I found hard to resist. In these moments, I felt his desire for me, and I held onto them as a representation of his devotion.

We woke to glorious sunshine and blue skies, and I quickly regretted not packing shorts. Ted and Julie made bacon and waffles while I drew pictures with the kids.

The Saturday market was in full swing as we walked up from the harbour. Vendors sold handmade soaps and crafted jewellery, vivid paintings of wildlife and oceans, fine scarfs of rich colours, baked goods and homegrown vegetables. In the park, long-haired hippies in ragged tie-dyed clothes danced to marimba drums in a lyrical trance.

"You fit right in, Harry," Ted quipped, nodding at his nephew's bun.

After lunch, we crossed the main square and browsed a local bookshop that was thronged with tourists. I climbed the wooden staircase to the travel writing section while Harry stayed downstairs searching for the mathematics aisle. Milly followed me, and I instinctively took her hand.

"Where's Daddy?" she asked, staring around uncertainly at the sea of legs.

"Daddy's this way." I pointed toward the DIY corner where Ted stood with Julie discussing their shed. As I did so, an elderly lady passed by. She looked down at Milly and beamed at me with a commending expression that made me blush.

I wasn't sure if I wanted to have children or not, but that was perhaps because it was difficult to imagine having them with Harry. I had pictured wedding scenes in the distant future, but the image of him cradling a baby didn't seem to develop. The idea of parenthood seemed to be low on both our priority lists.

Harry boarded the bus to the ferry terminal at four o'clock. I pecked him on the lips with a measure of sullenness before returning to the boat for drinks and snacks. Julie sat playing a game with her kids as they drank their orange juice.

"How do you know Harry?" she asked.

"He's our cousin," said Tom assuredly.

"And Hannah?"

"Cousin!" chipped in Milly.

"What about Sara? How do you know her?" asked Julie.

Both kids fell silent and looked at me with blank faces. I smiled and looked into the distance nonchalantly.

"Sara is Harry's girlfriend. And if they were to get married, she would be his wife," Julie explained. She let the kids absorb the information for a few seconds before leaning towards them intently. "And if Harry and Sara were no longer a couple, she would still be our friend."

I continued to look into the distance as a lump formed in my throat. When I looked back in her direction, Julie's eyes were closed. Continuing as normal, she let the evening sun kiss her face, blissfully unaware of the impact of her words.

SIXTEEN

I returned to the barn on Monday afternoon with cheeks pinked from time spent on the boat deck without sunscreen. Two new WWOOFers had arrived at the property that morning, and they knocked on the door that afternoon to introduce themselves. They were from England and had recently graduated from the same university. Their denim shorts showed their tanned legs, and I felt inclined to make a self-deprecating remark about my sunburn as I introduced myself. After they left, Jake's comment to Harry on the brunette girl's attractiveness caused a sense of unease to creep up inside me.

"Do you think Jake will try something with Kate?" I asked Harry as we sat in my kitchen that evening.

"It wouldn't surprise me; he's fooled around with girls that have stayed with our family before." Harry smiled at me playfully. "We both have."

I played with the salad on my plate and swallowed uncomfortably at a memory different from the one he was referring to. Coming home to his missed calls, the anxiety on his face when he said, "we need to talk," the mechanical delivery of his story, the way it felt like a cruel form of payback.

I looked up with a sigh. "I know it might sound silly, but there's a part of me that can't help but feel a little worried after what happened last summer."

"Last summer?" asked Harry with a puzzled expression.

I let my fork drop onto the plate. "You know what I'm talking about. The two WWOOFers from Oregon."

Harry frowned in thought. "You mean, the massages?"

My jaw clenched as I heard the word.

Harry smiled and shook his head. "I really don't think—"

"You don't think it was inappropriate to be in your bed exchanging massages with other girls?"

Harry looked up in surprise before clearing his throat. "I'm a little confused about where this is coming from. We talked about it at the time. You were upset at first, but then you said you were okay with it and didn't consider it to be cheating."

"Well, I've changed my view on it since then."

Harry sat back calmly in his seat. "This all feels very sudden. I feel like you've suddenly just decided to attack me out of nowhere."

"I'm trying to explain why I'm feeling worried about the two new girls, because of what happened in the past. I'm trying to be open with you about my feelings."

Harry sighed. "I really don't think going back to that time is helpful in any way. There's no point dwelling on the past. I haven't."

His eyes rose to look squarely in mine. I looked away sullenly.

"At the moment, it sounds like you don't trust me," he continued. "And if that's the case, it's quite concerning."

My arms impulsively folded in defence. "It's not like I want to feel this way."

"Then don't let yourself feel that way." Harry leaned forward with a pleading look. "And please stop with the passive-aggressiveness. You know how much I value direct communication."

I unfolded my arms and looked down.

"Anyway, what did you want to do for your birthday?" asked Harry cheerily. "Did you want to do anything that weekend?"

"Eva let me have the Friday off in advance, so I thought it might be nice to go up island for the three days." I glanced up at him. "But I don't know how busy you'll be with the project."

"It's okay. I'll work extra hard these next two weeks so I can be fully available on that weekend."

I sat up with optimism. "Maybe we could go see the new cottage?"

Harry nodded. "That sounds good. Mom was actually suggesting we all do a trip up there one weekend."

I scratched my head in hesitation. "Sure, one weekend, that would be nice. For my birthday, though, I was sort of hoping it would just be you and me. It might be more…relaxing that way."

"I'm fine with whatever you want to do," said Harry.

As I ran the plates under the kitchen tap, the prospect of a birthday adventure boosted my mood. Now I just had to make more friends.

A few days later, I walked down Government Street with a jelly-like feeling in my legs. The lady that responded to my email had told me to meet at the running store at five-thirty. I had made some great friends in my running club at university, but the idea of walking into a room without knowing anyone was still daunting.

I entered the store quietly and saw a group of men and women huddled by the counter. Many of them stood with serious faces, hands on hips with fancy watches glued to their wrists, shiny shoes on their feet. Upon spotting me, the leader checked I had come for the run group. I felt the eyes of the other attendees on me, quick glances up and down in an attempt to estimate my ability.

The leader directed me to the backroom, where I could put my bag. I looked inside and spotted a girl bent down by some lockers, retrieving something from a knapsack.

"Hi," I said tentatively. "Do you know if these lockers can be used by anyone?"

The girl turned in surprise. "Yep, you can use them."

I found an open locker and took a breath. "Are you here for the run group?"

"Yeah, it's just my second time coming."

"Oh, it's my first."

With a petite build, the girl stood up and introduced herself as Carrie. We walked back to the front room and stood slightly outside of the group.

"Do you run often?" she asked me.

"Not as much as I used to, about once or twice a week now."

"Okay, well, I'm very slow, just so you know," she said with a smile.

Carrie's friendly nature made me inclined to stay with her during the run, regardless of her pace. The leader explained the route we'd be taking, and then everyone filed out to the sound of beeping watches. Carrie and I followed, and the group quickly sped farther into the distance.

A physiotherapist, Carrie had moved to Victoria from Vancouver in 2015. We jogged side by side while chatting about our jobs, our families, travel. Tourist season had begun and sightseers thronged the wharf, stopping unexpectedly in front of us to admire the grand legislative building and to take pictures of the harbour.

"Would it be okay if we walked for a bit?" asked Carrie after another kilometre. As she bent over with her hands on her knees, I looked ahead and realized the rest of the group was out of sight.

Carrie rose up to wipe her brow. "I'm sorry, you're not tired at all. If you want to go ahead, please do."

"It's okay. I really don't mind." I licked my lips and looked at the ground, suddenly bitten by shyness. "It's hard to meet people in Victoria."

Carrie raised her eyebrows in agreement. "Isn't it? I'm glad I'm not the only one who thinks that."

"Have you made many friends since moving here?" I asked curiously.

"I have physio friends, but outside of work, not really. I've always lived with my boyfriend since moving here, so I never had roommates." She placed her hands on her lower back. "There seem to be a lot of students here."

"There are."

Across the road, I noticed a group of tourists turn up a path into a large patch of woodland.

"What's that?" I asked impulsively, nodding in its direction.

"Beacon Hill Park." Carrie looked at me in surprise. "Have you not been?"

I smiled sheepishly. "I haven't explored Victoria all that much."

Most runners had already left by the time we returned to the store. As we collected our bags, Carrie asked if I'd like to go for a drink at a café down the street. Feeling like a teenager who'd just been asked on a date, I agreed without hesitation. We took a seat at a table with red-checked tablecloths.

"Does your boyfriend like to travel as much as you?" asked Carrie as she sipped her smoothie.

"Harry isn't really into travelling. At least, he isn't now while he's in school." I cleared my throat. "I don't mind, to be honest. I almost prefer going places alone."

"I find that so brave. I don't think I could do it," said Carrie admiringly. She propped her chin on her elbow thoughtfully before rolling her eyes. "Mind you, the idea of planning something just for myself definitely sounds nice. I tend to do all the planning when Eric and I go away."

There was something so effortless and refreshing about talking with Carrie. She asked questions with genuine interest instead of just going through a checklist of courtesies. She spoke with maturity but had a sense of humour and was down to earth. I felt like I could continue chatting with her for hours.

As we left the restaurant, Carrie suggested we swap numbers and see each other again when she had returned from an upcoming trip to Vancouver. I walked to the bus stop with a dancing feeling in my chest. I already knew in my gut that this date was going to call me again.

My personal achievement seemed to instill a higher level of comfortability in interacting with the team at work. When they gathered on the mezzanine the next morning to talk about something in the news, I stood up to join them.

On Friday afternoon, Eva asked me to conduct my first solo interview. I welcomed the new responsibility with excitement, only to feel my throat tightening with nerves as I walked downstairs to meet the candidate. A man in his fifties in a smart suit gave me a firm handshake. With a squeaky voice, I offered him some water before directing him to my office.

When I asked how he'd heard about the vacancy, the man straightened his tie and told me with a blasé tone that he met the hiring manager at a networking event.

"And how do you feel your experience relates to the position?" I asked.

The man scoffed. "Well, you can clearly see from my resume that I have twenty years of experience within the sales industry."

I felt my face redden at his intensity. "Yes, but what would you say are your particular qualities that apply to this position since it isn't a sales role?"

The man regarded me with a look of impatience. "It's a basic customer service role, and I know how to speak to customers and provide a professional service."

"Have you worked on a help desk before?" I asked.

"No, but I don't see that being an issue," he said haughtily. "I've talked with the hiring manager. She knows my skillset."

I shook the man's hand goodbye fifteen minutes later with a mixture of relief and regret. My mind pictured Eva sitting in her office with a disappointed expression as she heard snippets of conversation. I had interviewed egotistical men before, men whose pride was bruised at being out of work, who felt insulted at the notion of being interviewed by a younger female. Over time I had handled such personalities confidently and held my own. I told myself I would soon get back to that level again.

I walked home feeling guiltily content in the knowledge I had a free house for the weekend. With a bag of cookies by my side, I put on some music while I finished an email to my mum.

As I wrote, I heard the ringing notification of an incoming video call, and Brendan's name appeared on the screen. I groaned in protest. *Maybe it won't be so bad with Harry not around.* I pushed the cookies out of sight and answered.

"Hello there, stranger!" gasped Brendan with feigned surprise. "How's it going?"

When he told me that he'd been accepted to join the University of Waterloo as a tenure-track professor, I tried to conceal my realization of the potential wider consequences. I gave him my congratulations and forced a smile as he proceeded to tell me more details.

"And what's going on with you?" he asked later on. "I hear you started your new job."

"I did. It seems to be going okay so far."

"And how are you finding living away from Harry? Have you seen much of each other?"

"It's fine, and yeah, we'll hang out a few times a week," I replied casually, ignoring the fact I hadn't seen him since the weekend.

"Must be nice having an enclosed bedroom to use," said Brendan with a wink.

I smiled uncomfortably. "It's nice having more privacy, yes."

"Does he stay over often? He's always home when I call him."

"Not often, no. He's been biking to and from UVic. It's part of his new fitness plan."

"So I heard. I hope he won't get too skinny from all that cycling." He followed his disapproving expression with a cheeky smile.

"I suppose you've also heard he's learning piano. He's getting quite into it."

"Tell me about it! He hasn't called me in two days. I'm feeling neglected!" He touched his chest in mock offence and laughed.

I smiled while silently pondering the likelihood that Harry spoke to Brendan more than me.

"I hope you're getting enough time together," he continued.

I shrugged and scratched my neck. "It would be nice to see more of him, but it's fine."

Brendan's face grew serious. "And how are you feeling about the relationship, given what will happen next summer?"

I crossed my arms. "It is what it is, I guess."

"It must be difficult, I'm sure."

"I'm not really thinking about it."

"Mm. I can imagine it's hard."

"It's okay."

Brendan rested his chin on his hand, his eyes narrowing in scrutiny. "Do you feel like it's changed your attraction towards him at all?"

I rubbed my forehead with increasing weariness. "I wouldn't say so."

Brendan studied me silently, then he looked to his side with a deep sigh, as if he'd just completed a demanding task and wasn't quite satisfied with the outcome.

"Well, he really needs to cut his hair," he said. "The man bun isn't a good look for him. I miss sexy Harry."

Feeling myself stiffen, I silenced the voice that agreed with him. "I suppose it's ultimately up to him, isn't it?"

Brendan smirked. "A little pressure won't hurt."

Time up.

"Well, anyway, I should probably make dinner," I said, stretching my arms out behind me.

"We should talk more," he said. "I miss you."

I waved goodbye with a smile and then regarded the black screen coldly. *You don't miss me; you just want to know about Harry.*

SEVENTEEN

Shortly before my twenty-fifth birthday, I spent the evening with a couple I had known since I was eleven years old. Jim and Maureen had run my local modern pentathlon club, and they had arrived in Victoria as part of a vacation tour package. Seeing them waiting for me near the harbour stirred an instant feeling of comfort. Home suddenly seemed closer. As I translated Jim's broad Yorkshire accent for the waitress, it felt surreal to be in Canada sitting in a pub opposite a couple I had known since before puberty. They had gone from seeing my shy self play silly games with others during training breaks as a kid, to getting moody about my performance during competitions in my mid-teens, to living in a foreign country with a professional job as an adult. When I was a teenager, nobody would likely have imagined I'd go on to live on the other side of the world.

I walked Jim and Maureen back to their hotel with legs heavy from the knowledge my closest connection to home was about to end. As we embraced, I asked Maureen to give my mum a hug from me. Then, after a final wave, I was once again a big girl on my own, about to enter my quarter-century.

I arrived at the office on the last day of May to find balloons around my desk. Eva treated us to lunch at a local restaurant, and upon noticing everyone was having a drink, I ordered a lager that left me more light-headed than I wished to admit. The team surprised me with a cake in the afternoon, and I smiled with bashful gratitude as they sang the birthday song.

The evening was spent in my suite with the friends I felt fortunate to have met through Harry. We stayed up chatting and playing cards until the early morning when I fell asleep alongside Harry with the heartening warmth that stems from feeling appreciated and celebrated.

I caught the bus to Sidney the next evening, ready for my weekend away with Harry in Sooke. Peter and Ruth ate dinner quietly with tired faces. A tension seemed to hang in the air that made me unsettled. After filling the dishwasher and scrubbing the pots, I left quietly for the barn.

"Are your parents okay?" I asked Harry as we joined the highway the next day. "They were very quiet last night."

"Dad's tired from working a lot and Mom…" Harry hesitated. "She had a bit of a misunderstanding over something the other day."

I looked at him in concern. "What happened?"

He stroked his chin, considering his words. "Well, she had suggested we go up island with her and Dad this weekend to help them get some stuff set up for the Airbnb. I explained that you'd told me you'd rather go there in private and not with the family."

"You did?" I said in panic.

"Yes, and Mom got quite upset."

"How upset? What did she say?"

"She stormed off to Dad and told him you didn't want to go with them because you didn't want to help—"

"Did you tell her that wasn't the reason?" I asked frantically.

Harry made a calming gesture with his hand. "I explained to her that you had just wanted a weekend alone together for your birthday. However, she went on to bring up the time you'd lived on the property and how she felt you hadn't helped much. And she felt that helping at the cottage wasn't a big ask because of that."

I rubbed my forehead with worry.

"So, I pointed out that there was really only a month or so when you were living there simultaneously because of the times we were house-sitting, and she was on vacation," continued Harry. "I mentioned that during the times you weren't working, you had helped with the animals and so on. I told her how we had typically shared showers to avoid using more water. I said that you always aimed to make dinner for yourself and that I would often have to insist that you eat inside with everyone. And I reminded her that when you did, you would always do the dishes after. And then I highlighted how awkward you would have felt for being the only one not eating with everyone."

I exhaled with mild relief. "And how did she take that?"

"Well, in reference to the dinner issue, she suggested you could have always cooked for everyone so that she didn't have to."

My face scrunched up in protest. "You mean, cook for more than six people with varied preferences while she criticized every little thing I did?"

Harry sighed. "I'm just telling you what she said. I'm not saying I agree with the idea."

"I know, I'm sorry. It's just stressful to hear she's annoyed with me."

"I don't think she is anymore. She came to the barn this morning specifically to apologize. She said she was just tired and felt like she needed more help in general. She pretty much begged that I say nothing to you because she didn't want it to damage her relationship with you."

I chewed my nail in thought. Pricks of guilt were followed by flashes of resistance. Then I felt another pinch of panic.

"What did your dad think about it all?"

"He wasn't bothered."

Feeling another boost of relief, I turned my attention back through the window. I tried to imagine my mum's approach if Harry was staying at my family home. I knew it would be completely different from Ruth's.

"Do you think your mum wants me to give her some money?" I asked.

Harry shook his head. "No, I don't think so. You know my mom; she just sees people as labour."

I sighed. "I sometimes feel like she still sees me as a WWOOFer."

Harry shrugged. "Probably."

I looked down at my lap and wondered if this would always be the case.

We arrived at the campground an hour later and unlocked the door of our rustic cabin to find a cozy room with a large bed and a small kitchen area. From his knapsack, Harry pulled out a bottle of cream liqueur and a small tin of hot chocolate. Out of the bag peeped the white top of a math textbook. My stomach sank with disappointment.

We spent the next day at Sooke Potholes, clambering over the rocks in the river to get upstream. An overcast sky didn't stop two men from stripping to their shorts and jumping off the cliff into the clear pools of water. Later on, they would stop us on the road to ask for a ride, having noticed a black bear in the bushes. I peered through the window in hope, but it had disappeared.

For lunch, we stopped at a family-owned diner. The dulcet tones of a country singer spread through a room with black-and-white floor tiles and turquoise leather booths.

"What can I get you, honey?" a curly-haired waitress asked me with a big smile. She looked no older than twenty-one.

I ordered a burger and then requested a slab of chocolate cream pie that had caught my eye from the dessert counter. The waitress brought it over with an enthusiastic wiggle in her hips.

"Enjoy, sugar!"

Harry took one bite of the pie before laying down his fork. "How can you finish that?" he asked in amazement as I continued eating.

"How can you not?"

"I'm full from my burger, and there's so much of it."

"Well, you know I have a second stomach for desserts," I said with a smile.

Harry wrinkled his face in distaste. "I don't understand how you're not uncomfortable eating it. It's so rich."

"It's delicious. Are you sure you don't want more? I'll finish it otherwise."

He shook his head. "I went off desserts a while ago. We once had a birthday cake at Nana's, and it hit just hit me that I was putting a load of bad stuff into my body."

I looked down at the half-eaten pie, suddenly feeling judged. Then I looked up with a shrug. "Oh well, more for me. It's my birthday treat."

We spent the rest of the day exploring the beaches along the coast. China Beach was deserted except for a couple of surfers riding the waves. In the wind-protected shelter of a fallen tree, Harry played his guitar while I scanned the ground for pebbles with interesting patterns. After the surfers returned to shore and left the beach, Harry motioned to the trees behind us with a hinting smile.

"Isn't that close to a trail?" I asked uncertainly.

"Nobody will see, but we'll keep a lookout."

Moments later, we emerged from the hidden enclave to find the beach still empty. As we walked back, Harry laughed at the thought of what Brendan would say about the story. I looked down quietly at old footprints left in the sand and wondered if there was anything in our relationship that wasn't shared with Brendan.

The next morning, warm sunlight beamed down through the trees as we followed a quiet trail in East Sooke Regional Park down to a small cove where dogs splashed in the water to fetch their sticks. We crossed the beach to climb up a rock plateau and gazed across the dazzling ocean towards the outline of Washington State. I stretched out on a patch of rock and gazed at the clear blue sky above me. Faint echoes of barking dogs came and went; otherwise, the only sound was water lapping against the rocks.

Harry had walked down to the edge and sat looking into the deep blue water thoughtfully, the tips of his ponytail blowing gently in the breeze. I watched his moment of musing through my camera lens and took the photo. It was clear he had things on his mind—projects and goals. I took a deep inhale of the salty air in acceptance that the weekend was over and called his name.

When I got home, a quick read of the news revealed that there had been a terrorist attack in England—the second in two weeks. It had taken place in London on a popular bridge I had walked over many times. I pictured myself a few hours earlier, lying in tranquillity under the sun by the ocean. My present life on Vancouver Island seemed so different from the one I had lived in London. I already knew that I didn't want to go back.

EIGHTEEN

As I settled more into the office environment, my work continued to be stimulating and enjoyable. Lunchtime boot camps at the gym helped me recharge when the workload seemed heavy. And when work ended, I walked home to the comfort of having full control over how I spent my evening.

While it was clear we didn't share many of the same hobbies, Lucy was friendly and straightforward to live with. I always aimed to let her know in advance when Harry was coming over, though his visits tended to be at short notice rather than planned, and they never seemed to last too long. Contrary to my hopes, I almost always found myself boarding the bus to Sidney every Friday evening and waiting at the bus stop for Harry to arrive.

"I really need to pee," I said bluntly as I opened his car door on Friday.

I jumped out of the car before Harry had even finished parking and dashed across to the barn. Jake sat at the table, and I flashed him a wave as I hurried past. I sat down and closed my eyes with relief. My hand reached for the toilet paper, only for my fingers to slip on cardboard. I opened my eyes to find the empty roll hanging on the holder. *Not again.*

"Is it really that hard to replace the toilet paper for the next person?" I asked grumpily as I walked up the stairs to Harry's room. Silence answered me.

Moments later, the barn door opened and Hannah and Jonas appeared.

"Hey, cutie!" said Hannah as she opened her arms for a hug. I felt my face begin to wrinkle in protest at the term of address and quickly stopped myself.

The cousins picked up instruments and began to experiment with different melodies. Harry played the piano surprisingly well after a few weeks of lessons. I sat on the sofa with Jonas to watch. He and I had shared a few chats, and I liked him. He reminded me of my brother, Finn, who worked as a farrier in Australia. They had the same strong build and dexterous hands. They were plain-speaking types but had a good heart and protective nature.

As the cousins played, I broke into German for the sake of practising with Jonas. I was rusty and found it harder to hold a conversation these days. My question to Jonas was followed by a response that left me staring at him incomprehensively. I burst into laughter and he squeezed my knee teasingly.

At the sound of the barn door opening, I turned to see Kate and Holly enter the room. Days spent outside working in the vineyard had made them even more tanned than since I last saw them. I turned back to watch the cousins and noticed Harry watching me curiously. Upon meeting mine, his eyes lowered their focus back to the piano keys.

For the sake of appeasing Ruth, I had offered to help in the vineyard on Saturday. I woke early and turned to lay my arm over Harry's chest. His skin was moist with sweat, and he stared up at the ceiling with a look of unease on his face. I asked what was wrong.

"I had a bad dream last night," he said sadly.

"What happened?"

He continued to look at the ceiling and swallowed. "You cheated on me with Jonas."

I regarded him with surprise. "Oh, Harry, I wouldn't do that. Plus, he's dating your little sister."

"I know. You just found him more attractive, I guess."

I cocked my head to the side. "I can see why people would find him attractive, but I'm not attracted to him in that way."

Harry looked down towards the end of the bed, his bottom lip puffing out slightly. "I just saw you talking together last night and, I don't know..."

"I'm allowed to talk to other guys, Harry."

"I know, it's not that." He raised a hand and rubbed his other arm, as if comforting himself.

I studied him quietly. As I did so, it hit me that the only males he had seen me speak with were his friends. He had never seen men flirt with me.

At the sight of his sullen face, I couldn't help myself. I broke into a smile and hit his arm playfully. "Now you know how I feel when you talk about other girls."

Seeing his face remain unchanged, I began to grow impatient. "Please don't punish me for something I haven't done. It was just a dream."

Harry finally turned to look at me. "I know, it was just a little scary." He frowned in thought. "I don't necessarily think it's that I believed it would happen. I guess it was more the idea of not being enough to maintain your attraction."

I looked down at the pillow. "You mean physical attraction?"

"Yeah, I guess that's sort of what I mean."

I scratched my neck as I decided on my words. "Well, you do look quite different now from how you used to." I swallowed. "And to be honest, I do think you look better with shorter hair."

A slight smile formed at the corner of Harry's lips. "I know, everyone thinks that. But I like it."

I bit my lip at the realization he hadn't understood what I meant. He couldn't read the shallow part of my mind that wished he looked the way he used to.

Outside, Ruth had already rounded up Kate and Holly. Upon approaching them, I instantly resumed my WWOOFer status. We each took a bike from the shed and cycled over to the old house located ten minutes away. Memories of warm evenings and buzzing mosquitoes began flooding back as soon as we turned onto its road.

We worked in the vineyard for a few hours, pulling stray weeds from the vines. I had been nervous when I first helped years ago, worried I might do something wrong. I had worked alone for two days with the hot sun on my back. On one afternoon, I had stood feeling bored and tired when I heard the sound of footsteps followed by the sight of Harry's smile. "Come on. We're going to the beach." His search had saved me, and his invitation had ignited something.

Two days later, we had snuck out of the house together to walk to the local beach. We'd held our arms around the other tightly in the unexpectedly cold air, guided by moonlight. On the beach, we had stood near the water to admire the green phosphorescence, and then we had sat on a log and talked. Soon after, we had our first kiss under the glow of the beaming moon. From that day on, what we had called Midnight Walk Beach had held a special memory in my mind.

After we finished our assigned rows, I invited the girls to see the beach. I led them across the road and down the narrow path that weaved through a patch of trees before reaching some old wooden steps. In the midday heat, we instinctively went to splash our feet in the cool water. A glance over my shoulder showed the log still in the same place, six years later.

Kate was about to turn twenty-two, but she seemed older. In the next few weeks, she and Holly intended to leave Vancouver Island and travel around BC before visiting the Rockies. Ideally, they hoped to find jobs that matched their geography degree, but otherwise, they were happy with any job that allowed them to explore the country and be outdoors. They planned to work in summer camps and do a ski season. They were not tied to one permanent job but free to take on seasonal gigs before moving on to their next destination to spend the money they had earned. We were using our working holiday visas in very different ways, and for a moment, I found myself wondering if I would rather be doing things their way.

Jake came over that evening and organized a game of ping pong. After a few games, we drove to a quiet beach. Jake and Kate brought longboards and asked Harry to pull over at the top of a hill.

I watched Kate mount the board in her sandals with a mixture of envy and admiration. *I used to be like that when I was twenty-two—brave, willing to try new things and take risks.* I looked down and wondered where that daring person had gone. Nowadays, there seemed to be a voice of caution that accompanied each bold idea, one that questioned the pros and cons. What if a candidate I interviewed saw me? What if I got in trouble and it affected my job or eligibility to stay in Canada? What if I hurt myself?

We gathered on a quiet outcrop that overlooked the ocean. The sun was starting to sink and spill over the ocean surface. I felt a strange sense of déjà vu and looked around me in confusion before realizing I had been to this spot before with Harry.

The others pulled drinks and vapes from their bags and shared jokes. I silently resented the noise that came from their chatter and clanking bottles, the way it spoiled the peace of the surroundings. I politely refused all offers of a drink or a vape. I just wanted to watch the sunset, undisturbed.

"Sure you don't want a drink?" asked Kate.

I shook my head. "I'm good, thanks."

Jake looked over and sneered. "Dude, don't be boring. Get drunk."

"I'll do what I want. Thanks, Jake."

He turned back to his drink with the cocky snigger of a nineteen-year-old trying to impress a girl. As he began to play his guitar, laughter filled the evening air. I clasped my arms around my knees and pulled them towards my chest, feeling increasingly out of place.

When we returned home, I withdrew to bed quickly, drained from a day of working in the sun and being around younger people. Music and chatter kept me awake, but at ten-thirty on a Saturday night, I had no grounds on which to complain.

I woke the next morning with the motivation to write. My pen was scribbling fervently over paper as Harry woke.

"What are you writing?" he asked with a yawn as he approached.

"A poem."

Harry glanced over my shoulder. "*Once I was Nineteen*?" After reading the first few lines, he rubbed my shoulder sympathetically. "I had a feeling you felt a little uncomfortable last night."

"I suddenly felt old, even though I know I'm not. I just can't seem to relate to that type of company anymore." I let my cheek fall on my palm. "Maybe I'm just boring. I don't know."

"I don't think so," said Harry gently.

He pulled me down on his lap and handed me one of his earphones. One of our favourite musicians had just released a new album, and the news of it spurred us to recollect memories of going to Vancouver one Halloween to see his gig. The new album was more acoustic, and there was something melancholy about its theme.

I took the melancholy feeling with me as I boarded the bus to Victoria that afternoon. I thought about Holly and Kate and their plans to adventure around Canada for the next two years. A stranger wouldn't be able to tell we were three years apart in age, yet our goals and priorities were so different. Developing a career wasn't on their agenda for now. The idea of having responsibilities and a stable salary to pay monthly bills was alien to them as they commenced their temporary adventure overseas.

I didn't see Canada as temporary. Despite the challenges I'd had so far, I was hungry to keep building on my progress. I was beginning to feel settled, and the prospect of returning to my former life in England made me glum. To return would almost seem like a regression.

But what about Harry? asked a voice of caution. *Would you want to stay here even if you weren't together?*

I inhaled deeply and looked out of the window. The bus rolled past Elk Lake, where bathers had flocked to dip in its waters. The outdoor culture of this country carried so much appeal. *I fell in love with Canada before I fell in love with Harry.*

The distinctive sound of an Irish accent interrupted my thoughts. I turned from the window to see the middle-aged couple in front of me chattering with confusion while staring at a map. I impulsively cleared my throat and asked if they would like some help.

The couple turned around in surprise. "Yes, our Airbnb is on Pemberton Street, and we're unsure how we get there. Do you know that area?" asked the woman.

I leaned forward, recognizing the name from my walks back from work. "That's off Fort Street. You can get off downtown, and then with your day pass, you can take either the number 11 or 14 from here." I pointed at the map. "And your bus stop will be here."

The couple smiled at me gratefully. "Thank you for your help."

I sat back in my seat with a flicker of inspiration.

The remainder of the day became devoted to researching the process of applying for permanent residence. It seemed to involve many hoops. Candidates had to meet certain criteria and would then be selected to apply based on the number of points they had for their age, education, experience, and assessed language skills. There were a few possible programs of entry, and the one I seemed most suited for required one year of Canadian experience in a skilled field. Knowing I was only a few weeks into my job, I felt a tingle of worry. A language exam on July 8th had spaces left, and I paid the three-figure booking fee with hopes my money and efforts wouldn't go to waste.

The workweek was fruitful. I started Monday morning by finding another receptionist to replace the one that withdrew from a placement an hour before the start time. Then I learned that my four candidates had been hired by a Crown corporation for contract positions throughout BC. The successes and subsequent recognition I received felt good, but I didn't let myself get complacent. I knew all too well that the world of recruiting and staffing involved highs and lows. Until I had the confirmation that I had passed my probation period, I would remind myself that this job could end at any moment and leave my prospects of becoming a permanent resident further out of reach.

Despite the stirrings of self-imposed pressure, summer would be over before I knew it, and I wanted to make the most of it. Oak

Bay Village hosted a night market every second Wednesday of the summer months, and I arranged to go with Joey and Liz the next day. Knowing he was busy practising for a piano recital scheduled that Sunday, I decided not to invite Harry. Not only would he probably decline, but I enjoyed developing this trio independently of him. I didn't need him to escort me as I explored the offerings of the place that was beginning to feel like home.

NINETEEN

Grey skies cast a drowsy mood inside the car as Harry drove us back to Cadboro Bay. He was quiet, busy running his recital through his mind for faults. I stared out of the window and wished he would just accept the praise I had given him.

In my bedroom, I lay awake quietly while Harry napped. When he stirred, the disappointment in his eyes had been replaced with motivation, and he pulled me closer. It lasted shorter than I would have liked, and I sat up after with unexpected discontent. When he left, I watched from the window with mild resentment as he walked away.

I turned back to the empty room and put on a movie. Thinking it was one Harry would enjoy, I texted him with the recommendation and repeated how well he had played earlier. By the time I went to bed, I hadn't heard back from him. I set my alarm with a pulsing sense of aggravation as I counted another ignored message.

I tossed and turned, unable to get comfortable. The clock said it was past midnight, and I sighed with impatience. Then there came the sound of the front door opening, followed by muffled giggles from Lucy. I rolled over. Glasses clinked in the kitchen, and inaudible chat continued. Short sentences followed by more giggles. I groaned and changed position. The uneven tiptoes of footsteps sounded outside my door as Lucy led her date to her bedroom. After a few moments of silence, bumps and moans filtered through the walls. I pushed my ear farther into my pillow and closed my eyes tightly, waiting for it to end.

Groggy eyes greeted me in the mirror as I reluctantly stepped out of bed at the order of my alarm. The retired pilot-turned-bus driver greeted me with his usual chirpiness, and I smiled back sleepily. After a busy morning of phone calls and emails, I walked to the gym to release some frustration. The burning feeling in my legs as I squatted and lunged brought a strange sensation of satisfaction. Determined to keep going, I felt a bit stronger with each rep. As we finished another round, I pulled out my hair tie and shook my damp hair to the ground before piling it up once more, ready for the next set. An absent-minded glance in the mirror showed the handsome trainer looking at me intriguingly. I held my gaze for a second before looking away with a brief tingle in my chest.

I had the suite to myself that evening. Unmotivated to make dinner, I slumped on the couch with a cheesecake I'd bought impulsively on the way home. The sweetness brought me comfort, and I continued eating without thinking. An hour later, I lay feeling sick and uncomfortable, and I discarded the box in shame.

With no word from Harry, I opened a pad of paper and began to formulate my feelings into a poem. The sugar had left my head fuzzy, and after a few lines, the poem became a ramble of adjectives I felt too tired to connect together in prose.

At the buzzing of my phone, I picked it up expectantly. It was a new email from my mum. My stomach flipped with guilt when she told me Dad had arrived safely in New Zealand. He was visiting my sister, and I had completely forgotten to wish him a good trip. I put the phone down and listened to the disappointed moans that sounded from my belly.

"How is it so difficult to respond to a text message?" I asked Joey the next evening as we sat in the market square downtown.

Joey shrugged. "I can't say I'm great at replying to messages either."

"He should try harder. It's not impossible."

"Maybe you should ask Harry to check his messages before he goes to bed each night?"

I shook my head. "I don't understand why it has to be that structured. You should want to respond to a partner's messages, not feel like it's a chore."

Joey stretched out his legs and looked down at his shoes. "Harry is being quite selfish with everyone at the moment."

I looked at him quizzically. "I don't know how you're so patient with him."

"I've known him a long time," he said with a smile. He checked his phone and stood up. "So, my sister invited me to play in her softball game tonight. Do you want to come along? It starts at seven."

"But I've never played softball."

"They're really not a great team; it won't matter."

I looked up at the blue sky and shrugged. "Okay, sure."

"I invited Harry as well. He said he'd come along."

"How nice that he responded to your message," I said dryly.

We walked back to his truck and left downtown. Joey wasn't sure of the location, and we ended up driving in circles. It was approaching seven-twenty when we pulled into the parking lot of a school in Royal Oak. I looked across a playing field and heard the tink of a ball being hit, and then I spotted Harry's car. We jogged across the field and found him standing next to a few other players. Upon seeing us, he walked over with folded arms.

"So much for insisting I had to be here no later than seven," he said irritably.

"We got lost, sorry," I said.

Joey's sister introduced us to a team comprising people of various ages and sizes.

"I've never played before, just so you know," I warned Leah as she handed me a bat.

"Don't worry, we'll help you," she said.

At my turn, I walked up to the home plate and glanced back awkwardly at the team. Leah shouted out how to hold the bat. The pitcher threw. I swung and missed and laughed at myself.

"You got this!" someone called encouragingly.

I swung and missed again. More claps of encouragement. I gripped the bat and licked my lips, concentrating on the pitcher's hand. This time I clipped the ball, only for it to fly behind me right into the hands of the catcher.

"Bad luck," said Leah as I left the field blushing.

I took a seat on the grass near Harry. We sat apart, focused on the game.

"How do you know Leah?" a girl to my right asked.

"Her brother is good friends with Harry." I motioned at Harry next to me. He didn't seem to hear me, and I looked down uncomfortably as the girl nodded silently.

The game ended twenty minutes later, with the team losing by a large margin. We walked back across the field, a slight chill now in the air.

"Hey, could you give me a ride home?" I asked Harry, gently touching his arm.

His shoulders sagged with reluctance. "Can't Joey?"

"Why should he?"

Harry sighed. "It's just, I drove all this way when I could have been at home working on my project, only to find you weren't here when I arrived, and now this."

"Jesus, Harry!" said Joey with a snort. "Drive your girlfriend home."

I got into the car in frosty silence and waited until we had left the parking lot to speak.

"What is up with you? You take forever to respond to my texts, and then you complain about giving me—your girlfriend—a ride home. You said you wanted to continue our relationship, yet you don't seem to want to put in the effort. It's rude and unfair, and I'm fed up." I slumped down in the seat and crossed my arms.

"I'm sorry," said Harry meekly. "I've just been in a really nihilistic, lethargic mood recently."

"Fine, but don't take it out on me."

Harry rested a hand on my thigh. "It's nothing personal. It's not that I'm unhappy with you or our relationship; I'm just unhappy in general with my progress this summer. I'm going through what I've called a summer of discontent."

I remained silent, my eyes focused sullenly ahead.

"You're a fantastic girlfriend, Sara," said Harry gently.

"You've said that before. That doesn't make this okay."

"It doesn't, I know."

I looked across at him. "Have you ever thought of just not trying so hard? Nobody will care if you don't make an album by the end of summer."

Harry looked at me with a puzzled expression. "It doesn't matter what other people will think. I'll care. I've set these goals for myself."

"Well, maybe they're unrealistic."

"They're not unrealistic," he replied patiently. "I just need to be more productive with my time."

"You can still be productive and respond to a text. Can you see why I'm upset?"

"Yes, I can."

"So, will you please make an effort to reply sooner?"

Harry nodded. "I will."

Outside of my house, he pulled me towards him for a hug. "You're coming up this weekend, right? Ted and Julie are having a party on Saturday."

I told him I'd catch the bus after work on Friday. Then I walked away from the car without looking back. Music sounded from Lucy's bedroom. Still disgruntled, I took a packet of brownies from my kitchen cupboard and closed my bedroom door behind me.

Piercing punches of menstrual cramps started in the early hours of Friday morning, accompanied by a tickle in my throat. I ran a hand soothingly over my belly, bloated with heavy food that refused to leave my body. The tickle in my throat continued to taunt me as I lay in discomfort. By the morning, it had developed into a cough, and I had a runny nose.

Eva stopped by my door in her gym gear and looked at me in concern. "Allergies?"

"Just a random summer cold," I said as I threw my tissue in the bin. "No workout for me today."

After the others left, I messaged Harry to tell him I wouldn't be able to come that evening. He didn't respond until seven o'clock when I lay on the couch caressing my abdomen. He encouraged me to come up the next morning and offered to learn a song on piano that I could sing at the party. His offer made me soften, but it was quickly clouded by self-doubt. Everything seemed to ache, my pelvis, my stomach, and my sinuses. I couldn't remember when I last felt so uncomfortable.

I woke late the next morning with a husky voice from so much coughing in the night. My stomach felt heavy with a weight that refused to leave. I slowly dressed in shorts and a sleeveless shirt and grabbed my sunglasses. The walk up the hill to the bus stop felt more challenging than normal. Hot sun burned down on my head, and I quickly began to regret not bringing water. I reached the bus stop and gratefully took a seat on the bench. My stomach squirmed in protest, and I breathed out deeply, thankful nobody else was around.

I boarded the bus with a strong feeling of needing to relieve myself. The thought of the long journey ahead made me anxious, and I crossed my legs and tried to calm my breathing, wondering if the other passengers felt as hot as I did. At the second bus shelter, the discomfort grew, and I began to feel flushed with panic. I looked around helplessly, wondering where the closest facility was. I gingerly climbed onto the bus to find it cramped with passengers, with those forced to stand huddled tightly together. With another flicker of trepidation, I licked my dry lips and squeezed through and took hold of a rail.

The air was sticky and hot. I closed my eyes in hopes it would make the journey feel faster, but when I opened them, I only felt more aware of how far I was from comfort. I tried to focus my attention on a sign on the window, but doing so made me feel dizzy. Then black spots began to appear before a dark fog seemed to cloud over my eyes. Unable to see, my limbs began to relax, and I felt a moment of calm.

Suddenly, I felt a hand on my shoulder and heard a man's voice. I opened my eyes blearily to see two blurry faces looking down at me. A woman with grey hair and a warm smile leaned over to touch my forehead.

"Hi, dear," she said. "I'm Edith. Can you hear me? What's your name?"

"Sara." Confused, I looked around and realized I was lying on a seat. "Where are we?"

"We're on the bus. We've pulled over on the highway," she said calmly. "You just fainted."

I tried to sit up, but Edith gently pushed my shoulders back. "It's okay, dear. Just relax. You're very pale. We're going to raise your legs, okay?"

I lowered back down uncertainly while the man next to her lifted my feet into the air.

"Do you have any medical conditions, Sara?" asked Edith, placing two fingers on my wrist.

"No, none," I said weakly. I suddenly felt a shooting pain in my temple and winced.

"Do you have a headache?" asked Edith.

"Yes, it hurts." I opened my eyes to look at her.

"And do you have any pain anywhere else?"

"My stomach." I swallowed, and my mouth was dry.

"Are you on your period?" Edith asked quietly.

I nodded.

"Just sit tight. We've called an ambulance, and some paramedics are on their way."

"I'm sorry," I said feebly, closing my eyes with shame.

"There's no need to be sorry, dear." Edith patted my arm comfortingly. "Now, where are your parents? What's their number?"

"They don't live here," I murmured.

"Where do they live? We'll call them."

"No, they don't live here."

"Well, what's their number?"

"They're in England; they can't do anything." The reality of my words hit me, and suddenly, I wanted to cry.

Edith continued to hold my arm. "Okay, dear. Who else can we contact?"

"My boyfriend," I said faintly. "You can call him. I'm on my way to see him."

I told Edith the number and watched as she called. After a moment, she shook her head and began to leave a voice message. I cursed under my breath and gave her the house number. Someone answered, and minutes later, her phone rang.

"Harry is on his way, and the paramedics should be here shortly," she said reassuringly.

I looked up at the ceiling. "I feel awful. I'm holding up everyone's journey."

'Don't worry about that, dear."

The man holding my ankles began to chat with another passenger. When asked where he was headed, he mentioned the airport.

I impulsively went to sit up, only to feel another sharp pain in my head. "You're going to the airport?" I gasped. "Won't you miss your flight?"

The man smiled down at me. "No, no. I'm just going to see an old war plane they have on display."

I laid my head back down on the seat in relief. Soon I heard an authoritative male voice and the sound of feet stepping on the bus. Two men came either side of me and asked if I wanted a stretcher.

"No, I can walk." I turned slowly to Edith and the man. "Thank you. I'm so sorry."

The paramedics carefully lifted me by the shoulders and escorted me off the bus. My legs felt like jelly. I sheepishly smiled at the faces of the passengers watching me, some sympathetic, some expressionless.

I sat in the ambulance while the paramedics took my blood pressure. "Have you fainted before?" one of them asked.

"Yes, twice before, when I had bad period pains." The cuff squeezed my arm tightly.

"Your blood pressure is pretty low, but that should pick up soon. You seem pretty dehydrated as well. I don't think we need to take you to hospital, though, unless you'd like us to?"

"No, that's okay," I said hastily. Healthcare in Canada required enrollment in a provincial medical services plan, for which monthly premiums had to be paid. As a temporary resident, I hadn't enrolled, and I wanted to avoid using my travel insurance if I could.

The paramedics dropped me outside a nearby care home and remained parked nearby while I sat waiting under the shade of a tree, wishing Harry would hurry up. I would later learn that using ambulances was billable in British Columbia. Perhaps they had assumed I was visiting and taken pity on me. When Harry arrived, I waved them off with bashful thanks and sank down in the passenger seat in relief.

Harry squeezed my arm with a smile. "What happened? A lady said you fainted."

"I feel so bad," I sighed. "I guess I had a vasovagal episode. I was in pain and really hot."

"I brought you water." He handed me a bottle, and I opened it eagerly. "Are you feeling better?"

"A little. I just want to lie down." I took a gulp of water and let a drop fall down my chin. "I might not be able to go to the party tonight."

"Maybe see how you feel closer to the time," suggested Harry.

I crawled onto the bed and lay silently while he worked on his computer. My headache slowly ebbed away, but I still felt tired. My stomach continued to rumble and squeak until a sudden downward pressure forced me to run downstairs to the bathroom.

I remained in bed as Harry was dressing for the party. "You could always bike over later on if you're feeling better," he said. "Or I could come back to get you."

"I'd really like to go," I said wistfully, picturing the pretty wooden cottage that overlooked a bay. "I just don't feel up to being around a lot of people right now."

I listened as he put on his shoes. Then the barn door closed, and all was silent. I looked up at the ceiling with regret. The events of the bus journey ran through my mind and made me cringe. My phone buzzed with a response from Edith to my follow-up thank you text. She told me not to feel bad for needing help, but to simply pay it forward to help someone else. I read the message a few times before lying back with a deep sigh of discontent.

A banging on the barn door distracted me from my thoughts. I walked sluggishly down the stairs and opened the door to find a man I didn't recognize stood outside.

"Sorry to bother you," he said. "I live down the road, and I think one of your horses has got loose. Big fella, brown with a black mane and tail. Nobody was in at the main house, so I thought I'd try here."

My shoulders sank with weariness. "Thanks for letting me know. That'll be Jacob."

I pulled on some boots and went to the barn to fill a bucket with food. The afternoon air was still hot and dry as I walked slowly down the driveway and peered across the field to see Jacob on the verge by the road. Upon noticing my approach, he moved off with a defiant swish of his tail.

I returned to the barn twenty minutes later with a resurgent throbbing in my head. My phone flashed with a missed call from Harry.

"How are you feeling?" he asked after I called back. Faint chatter sounded in the background.

"Pretty shitty. I just spent almost half an hour catching one of the horses that got loose."

"Oh, shoot." His voice brightened. "Do you feel up to coming over, though? Jake and I have been playing music for everyone all evening."

"No, Harry. I'm tired, and I have a banging headache."

"I'm sorry. I'll let Julie know, then. She says hi!"

I tossed the phone on the bed with annoyance before sitting down and letting my face flop wearily into my hands. The barn door creaked open thirty minutes later, and Hannah's voice called my name. I coughed and wiped my wet cheeks. "Up here."

Hannah walked up the stairs in a white cotton dress, followed by Jonas. They sat on the rug in front of me and watched me quietly.

"How's the party?" I asked, forcing a smile.

"It's fun," said Hannah. "We wanted to see how you were doing, though."

I sniffed. "That's sweet. You didn't have to do that."

"How are you feeling?" asked Jonas. "I heard what happened."

I rolled my eyes and wiped my runny nose. "Oh, I'm fine. I wasn't feeling well. I should have stayed home instead of travelling in the heat."

Hannah and Jonas exchanged concerned glances.

"I'm just feeling a little sorry for myself, that's all." I uttered a pathetic laugh.

"Harry should be here looking after you," said Jonas firmly.

I looked down with a dry smile. "Harry only looks out for himself."

Hannah shifted uncomfortably.

"I'm sorry, I don't mean that," I said guiltily. "I've just been finding him a little selfish recently."

Hannah smiled faintly, a sadness in her eyes. "It's okay; I know what you mean."

"Have you told him how you feel?" asked Jonas.

"Yes, a few times. It gets better for a little while, and then I go through phases of feeling ignored again." I rested my chin on my hand glumly.

"You should look out for yourself more," said Jonas.

Hannah played quietly with the hem on her dress, as if questioning her beliefs about a relationship she'd always looked to for inspiration.

TWENTY

Hannah's graduation ceremony took place the following Wednesday. I boarded the bus after work and hoped nobody would recognize me as the fainting girl from the 70 bus to Sidney.

Harry was sat in a lounge outside the auditorium, reading a textbook. As I approached, he took me in appreciatively.

"Why aren't you inside?" I asked.

"I didn't want to pay thirty dollars to sit through a boring ceremony," he said. "Hannah didn't mind."

I sat down next to him and told him about the woman I had interviewed that afternoon. With her heavy makeup and various piercings and tattoos, her presence had seemed quite intimidating at first glance. But she was extremely friendly and articulate, and there was something admirable about the way she was comfortable being different from cookie-cutter candidates and something uplifting about the way she challenged societal stereotypes.

"It's so unfortunate that society still has this idea that someone has to look a certain way to be considered smart," said Harry with a disappointed expression.

"Tell me about it. To this day, people look at me and assume I'm a bimbo."

"Sure, although I'd say your looks have often worked in your favour," said Harry.

I shot him a puzzled look. "How do you mean?"

Harry smiled. "Well, when you got your job in London, for example. The interviewer in his sixties? You even joked at the time that you wondered if he was attracted to you."

My arms impulsively folded in defence. "I did make that joke, yes, but I also know that I earned the position on merit. I was prepared, and I interviewed well."

"Oh, I know." Harry squeezed my shoulder. "But I'm sure your attractiveness played some role in the decision, even if it was subconscious."

I looked down at my shoes in defeat while Harry turned back to his book. When I saw him push his glasses up his nose, I licked my lips in preparation for my counter-attack.

Suddenly, the auditorium doors opened, and a colourful mess of kitschy dresses swarmed out. I stood up and waved when I spotted Hannah. She smiled back bashfully, seeming uncomfortable in the crowd. Her shoulders hunched forward slightly as she walked tentatively in her heels.

"You look beautiful," I said admiringly as I hugged her.

We walked outside into the courtyard, where boys in their suits stood awkwardly while girls gathered for photos, placing hands on hips and blowing kisses. Some girls grabbed the arms of their dates and dragged them unwillingly into the photo with them.

"Let's get a family photo," suggested Ruth, her eyes pink with recent tears.

"I can take it," I offered.

"No, Sara, you get in it," insisted Peter.

Ruth passed her phone to someone nearby, and I joined on the end. As the family discussed options for the remainder of the evening, I found myself standing back quietly.

"Sara, are you going to join us for dinner?" asked Peter.

"There won't be enough room in the car, Pete," said Ruth sharply. "There's already five of us."

I waved my hand nonchalantly to conceal my embarrassment. "It's fine. I'll see you on Friday night for the long weekend."

They walked off loudly towards the parking lot, and I walked off in the opposite direction. The sound of chatter and laughter behind me gradually fell to silence.

On Friday evening, Peter told us over dinner that Sidney was hosting a firework display to mark the 150th Canada Day. He looked hopefully at his daughter after suggesting we go watch. His idea was met with a reluctant face and an excuse of fatigue as Hannah rested her head against Jonas's shoulder.

"I'd be interested," I said upon seeing Peter's disappointed face. I looked probingly at Harry.

"Maybe," he said. "I need to do some work first."

The light on my bike flashed limply as Peter and I cycled towards town an hour later. The main avenue was packed with cars as people tried to find parking. Booming music could be heard in the distance. I came to a squeaky halt near a crowd by the harbour, and we walked our bikes through the throng of people until we found a spot close to the water.

Peter glanced at his watch with a satisfied nod. "Ten minutes to spare."

I looked up at the dark sky and spotted the tiny dot of a light flashing from a plane. June 30th. Six months ago, I had arrived in Canada on a plane, and now here I was, celebrating its special anniversary.

The fireworks began with a burst of red and white colour, and the crowd began to cheer. I watched the display transfixed until a tap on my shoulder distracted me. I turned to see Harry unbuckling his bike helmet.

"You came!" I said in pleasant surprise.

He took my hand, and we gazed into the sky sprinkled by showers of red and gold, silver and violet. Once more, any recent frustrations started to ebb away with the warmth of his hand.

In the morning, I woke to find I had a new email from Amy in Australia. Emails had always been our preferred form of communication when in different countries. They served as a journal of our experiences overseas and were something to look forward to every couple of weeks. Receiving one felt like receiving a parcel; there always seemed to be something valuable inside. I sat reading while Harry worked at his desk.

When Joey called minutes later to propose a swim at Durrance Lake, I welcomed the idea with enthusiasm and looked encouragingly at Harry's conflicted face.

Cars lined the road towards the lake as we approached an hour later. People in board shorts and bikinis walked along the verge carrying floaties and towels. After we managed to sneak into a space in the lot, Joey led the way towards the trail. Signs at the entrance noted that smoking was prohibited.

"Forest fires are getting bad in California," he said. "If the weather stays this dry, we'll probably have a bad season here too."

We found a small patch of uninhabited sand and jumped down the trail bank. Dragonflies skimmed off the calm surface of the lake. I dipped my toes tentatively in the water before stripping off to my bikini and stepping in slowly until the pricking water reached my thighs. Then I dived down for a few seconds, letting myself become immersed. I emerged and lay floating quietly on my back with my eyes closed. The sun spread its warmth over my exposed wet skin, and the water began to feel warmer. I let my ears sink under the surface, so any other noise drowned out. In my privacy, I thought about Amy's email and her comment that everything in my relationship with Harry seemed to be on his terms.

The feeling of something tickling my back sent me springing up with a squeal and kicking away behind me. I turned to see Harry grinning cheekily at me.

"You meanie," I said, splashing water at him.

"Sorry, couldn't resist."

As I treaded water, I took in our surroundings contemplatively. "We're so lucky to live here."

"To be honest, I'm looking forward to getting away for a while," replied Harry. "This has been all I've known my whole life."

"Fair enough, but going away might make you appreciate it more. When I moved to London, I realized I'd taken where I grew up for granted." I let my words sink in before looking at him with a smile. "It's nice to come back here. We haven't been since you lived at your old house."

"I forgot to tell you," said Harry with a hint of reluctance. "We're going for dinner there tonight. The new owner invited us."

The new owner was a Chinese-Canadian who worked in investment banking in Vancouver. She had bought the house as a holiday home with plans to eventually retire in it.

What a waste of the space, I thought as I walked around the house that evening and peeked in the empty rooms. I gave a little smile at the corner room that used to belong to Harry and returned back downstairs, where Judy was roasting chicken and pork.

"This is a lovely red," said Ruth as she examined the wine bottle on the dining table.

"I'm glad there are lots of you here. I made a lot of food, good Chinese food." Judy stirred something on the stove with a smile before taking some plates out of the cupboard.

"In a few days, Hannah and Jonas will be going to our new property up island," said Ruth proudly. "They're going to run an Airbnb for me."

"Very good! You make a lot of money doing that in Vancouver," said Judy, nodding at the young couple enthusiastically.

"Oh, yeah?" Ruth's eyes glistened with scheming intrigue.

"My son—he works in finance too. On top of his job, he makes over three grand a month from having his other house on Airbnb."

Ruth's eyes widened with amazement. "Are you serious? How long's he had the second house?"

Judy placed some dishes of food on the table. "Two years. Bought it to live with a girl, but they're no longer together." She made a dirty face. "Good riddance."

Peter chuckled. "That bad?"

Judy nodded as she took a seat. "Very selfish girl."

"What happened?" asked Ruth nosily as she poured another glass. Harry shifted in his seat next to me.

"She was a Korean girl. Spoiled thing. Daughter of some Samsung exec. Lee met her while she was in Vancouver on holiday, and they kept in touch. You know how it is with all these video calling apps."

I chewed tentatively on a piece of chicken.

"She said she wanted to move to Canada to be with him," Judy continued. "So, he said he'd help her, foolish boy. He was just young at the time, twenty-four or so."

With a hand gripped around her glass, Ruth listened intently.

"So, she applied for a work visa and did one of those partner applications, you know, where a citizen helps sponsor it. Got the visa, moved to Vancouver, got a job in some tacky cosmetics company, and within a few months, she dumped him!"

"No!" Ruth's mouth dropped open in disgust.

Judy raised her eyebrows and shook her head. "Awful girl. Just used my boy to get into Canada. Left him heartbroken."

My eyes instinctively rose to gaze at Ruth. Her face taut, she returned my look with piercing eyes of distrust.

On the drive home, I sat silently, wishing I hadn't already agreed to stay the whole weekend. Peter had arranged a boat trip for the next evening. I rarely said no to such an invitation.

I sat on the top deck, a blanket draped over my legs as I watched sun rays dance and sparkle on the water. As Harry played his guitar, Hannah sat in Jonas's arms, the evening sunlight shining in her eyes as she quietly imagined her summer with her new love.

The cabin window next to me slid open, and Peter pushed out a thick booklet open on a page covered with scribbles.

"Have a look at this," he said with a smile. "September 5th, 2011."

I took the booklet in my hands and ran my eyes down the page until I identified my italic writing, logging the boat trip on my last evening in Canada. I remembered the tugging feeling in my stomach, constantly reminding me that it was all about to come to an end in less than twenty-four hours. I remembered how everyone on the boat seemed to share in the sombre mood, knowing the connection Harry and I had made was about to be cut short.

My handwriting had changed since that time; now, it was smaller and more mature. I took the pen Peter handed me and started a new message on the most recent page. *Six years later and so happy to be living here. Thanks for all the memories.*

On Monday's statutory holiday, I suggested to Harry that we go for breakfast in Sidney. I observed as he sat with his chin on his hand, fiddling with the menu and puffing out his cheeks.

"What's wrong?" I asked. "You're restless."

"I just can't wait to live away from home. It's too much being here sometimes."

I sipped my water, wondering how to respond.

"There's a math conference in Ottawa in a few weeks," he continued. "I'm thinking of going. It'll be nice to get away for a few days and see what it's like out there."

I looked up in surprise. "Flights will be quite expensive at this notice, surely?"

Harry shrugged. "I figured it could be an early birthday present from Nana."

The waitress came to take our order. Harry looked over the menu again indifferently and ordered an omelette.

"Well, that sounds exciting," I said, feeling a pang of envy. "I'd love to go to Ottawa."

"You could always come along, though I'd be spending most of my time at the conference with other math people."

"I couldn't get the time off anyway. My probation doesn't end until mid-August."

"Oh, right."

I casually curled a strand of hair behind my ear. "Do you think you'll do any campus visits?"

Harry shook his head adamantly. "No, that's too scary to think about right now."

"Do you still think you'll apply to an Ontario school, though?"

"Yes, definitely," he said assuredly.

A drip of water began to slide down my glass. I caught it with my finger.

Harry glanced glumly at the other diners. "All the people here just look so miserable."

I followed his gaze and saw an overweight middle-aged couple eating in silence. When I turned back to Harry, his head was resting against his hand, and his eyes were staring into the distance.

"My mom and dad seem really unhappy," he said sadly.

"What makes you think that?"

"They just don't talk about anything. Mom only talks about herself. And Dad doesn't open up. They just sit and talk about nothing and drink too much." He slumped back in his seat with a sigh.

"They don't drink *that* much. By medical standards, I'm pretty sure one glass of red wine a night is fine."

"I disagree," said Harry resolutely. "I think they would benefit from having a week free of alcohol and talking about their feelings. What they need is some counselling."

"And you're going to tell them that?" I asked skeptically.

Harry looked at me seriously. "Yes, I am."

"I'm not sure they'd take that very well."

"I think they need to hear it from their children, to realize how important the matter is."

Our food arrived, and I picked up my cutlery with relief. Harry looked at his food sullenly before stroking his chin and looking out of the window in thought.

"I think I'm going to bike over to Ted and Julie's and hang out with them for a bit today," he said. "I want to ask them about their decisions when it comes to relationships, how they decided to stay with each other, and so on."

I instinctively broke into a sardonic smile. "That sounds worrying. Should I prepare for you to come away from it and break up with me?"

Harry looked at me expressionlessly. "Well, I am going to break up with you. I just don't know when."

The abruptness of his words cut through me like a knife.

"That was a little unnecessary, Harry," I mumbled.

We ate in silence like the middle-aged couple, the food tasting bland in my mouth. Harry's words repeated in my head as we drove home, and yet I still found myself lying next to him an hour later, letting his physical touch compensate for his words.

I boarded the bus to Victoria in the middle of the afternoon and took a seat near the window. Through the glass, I saw Harry's white car drive away, becoming smaller and smaller. His words ran through my mind again and left a wounding feeling.

When I looked away from the window, my mind instinctively flashed back to sitting on a bus in Ontario six years ago, completely independent, not knowing anyone around me. The memory filled me with shame.

In my room, I tore a piece of paper from my notepad and underlined the words *What I Want.*

With my sublet due to end on the last day of August and the awareness I'd be competing with students, I decided to start my search for another house for September. I looked online and arranged a viewing for Thursday evening with a girl who lived in a suite in Oak Bay.

High temperatures were expected all week, and the heat brought with it a slow burn of events. As I introduced myself to an interviewee, I was met with a look of surprise and a comment of "You're so young!" When I spoke, the woman would furrow her brow and jut her chin out in a way that suggested I was incomprehensible. As much as I spoke louder and slower, still, she regarded me with a look that made me stammer my words. I shook her hand with a forced smile and returned to my office to a text from Helena, noting she had to reschedule our plans to meet the next day. On Thursday morning, the girl with the suite emailed to inform me she had decided to stay in Victoria after all, and the room was no longer available. I logged out of my personal email only to see a new email in my work inbox from a client, noting that my candidate hadn't shown up to their scheduled interview.

I walked home feeling like I was being punched repeatedly in multiple parts of my body. Various elements of my life suddenly seemed unstable. I couldn't seem to ensure commitment, and I couldn't seem to be heard.

The grass in the backyard had started to turn yellow from the sun. I sat on my bed with my head against the wall. A cloud of exhaustion appeared out of nowhere and fogged my brain. After a while, the silence seemed deafening, so I turned on my soul music playlist. A small bug slowly crawled across the window while I listened to one of my favourite singers. I had listened to the song many times, but today the words seemed to have more meaning than usual. Unrequited love. Everything suddenly seemed clearer.

What are you more scared of? a voice asked. *Losing Harry as a boyfriend, or losing the comfort of being in a long-term relationship in a foreign country?*

With another round of the chorus came an awareness that I couldn't ignore any longer.

TWENTY-ONE

The retired pilot's cheerful smile faded when I boarded the bus the next morning. I kept my puffy eyes on the ground as I found a seat. Defeated thoughts randomly entered my head at the office, causing sporadic outpourings of tears. Unable to control their arrival, I dabbed at my eyes just as Paige entered my doorway. Upon seeing me, she came to an abrupt halt. I sniffed and looked up with a straight face.

"Uh, I was just going to ask if you saw that email from the law firm wanting to set up interviews," she said awkwardly. "I can contact both candidates if you want?"

"Okay, sounds good." I looked down and quickly wiped my nose.

Paige lingered tentatively in the doorway. "Everything okay?"

I smiled down at my desk. "Yeah, thanks."

"Sure?" she asked probingly.

At my nod, she turned away hesitantly. I chewed my lip with regret. Paige and I had only recently begun to connect over conversations unrelated to work. I didn't want to stall the progress in our relationship, but I hadn't shared anything so personal with her before.

After a moment's thought, I started a new email and briefly summarized the cause of my emotions. Paige replied within a few minutes.

> I'm sorry to hear that. If you decide you need someone to talk or vent to, I'm a pretty good ear.

A soft blanket of comfort fell over me as I read the email. Plans to hide away for the evening and wallow in my own self-pity suddenly seemed foolish. I picked up my phone and replied to Helena's reschedule proposal with a promise I'd meet her at the beach in Cadboro Bay at seven o'clock.

The evening sun was warm on my bare legs as Helena and I sat amongst the driftwood talking about Harry's recent behaviour. At the arrival of Nathan, I forced a smile and tried to push thoughts of Harry away. As we sat talking under the lilac sky, the distraction came easier than I expected.

By dark, we were the only people left on the beach. Nathan pushed his bike next to me as we walked up the hill towards my house.

"Thanks for walking me home, Nathan," I said.

"Of course."

I cleared my throat. "Just so you know, I'm seeing Harry tomorrow evening and, well, I'm not sure how it's going to end."

"I'm sorry to hear that, Sara," said Nathan gently.

"It hasn't been great for a while now."

Nathan extended a long arm over my shoulders. "Just know that you have friends here who care about you."

A lump formed in my throat. "Thank you." I paused and let out a dry laugh. "I definitely need to make more of them, though."

"Since you enjoy running, maybe you should try the run meet-ups at Tracks," he said. "They're every Wednesday at six. Two of my friends work there—Will and my roommate, Tyler."

"I went to one at a different store a few weeks ago. Everyone seemed a little serious, so I didn't go back, but maybe this one will be better."

"I'd go myself if I didn't have classes until then," said Nathan encouragingly.

I smiled up at his face, concealed by the dark. "Okay, I'll look into it."

My English exam was scheduled to start at nine o'clock on Saturday morning. I took the bus downtown and queued up outside the building next to a group of people who stood biting their nails and fidgeting with pencils and water bottles. The reading exam was surprisingly challenging in places, even for a native English speaker. I finished the written portion with a slight headache and a sore hand. When the oral examiner asked me to talk about a person in history that I found interesting, my mind suddenly felt empty. I had studied a history degree, and yet I couldn't think of one particular person to talk about. It was difficult to focus on anything else when I knew what the evening was going to involve. I found myself speaking about a politician I didn't even admire, noting that the most interesting people in history were often also the most infamous.

I had arranged a room viewing for after the exam, but it wasn't what I expected, and I couldn't see myself living there. I walked home resignedly, no longer able to put off what was coming.

A knock on the door came at seven o'clock. I opened it to see a man with a cropped haircut looking at me nervously. It was Harry.

I stared at him in astonishment. "You cut your hair."

He ran his hands through the top of his hair sheepishly. "I brought dinner, too."

As he pulled take-out boxes from his bag, I regarded him silently, waiting for the ponytail to appear again. It was like seeing the old Harry again. He turned to see me looking at him and smiled, anxiety still painted on his face.

"You look so different. I almost forgot..." My voice trailed off and was replaced by confused and conflicted thoughts. *Why now?*

We sat down next to each other, and he looked at me apprehensively, waiting. I looked down and rubbed my thigh in preparation before taking a deep breath.

"I feel like I've been on this really long hike, and there have been a lot of challenges along the trail, but there have also been a lot of great views and rewarding moments too. And then, farther into the hike, things have got more challenging. I've wondered if it's worth carrying on, but I've pushed myself on out of this desire to make it to the end, knowing how far I've already come along the trail. But now I'm just really tired. I'm tired of the rain; I'm tired of the hills and the tumbles and the insect bites. And as much as I don't want to give up, I've come to accept that I can't continue the hike. It's just not worth struggling to the end anymore."

I looked up to see Harry regarding me solemnly.

"I still love you, and I probably will for a while." My lips wavered. "I'm just not sure I like you anymore."

Harry's face suddenly crumpled.

"I hadn't realized how much I hurt you, Sara. I feel awful."

"How could you not realize?" I asked shakily. "All the things you've done and said these past few months; how could you not realize it would hurt me?"

"I was just trying to be honest because I believe that's the best thing to be in a relationship."

"Wanting to be honest doesn't justify being rude or insensitive."

"I know that. I just didn't realize it was making you feel this way." Harry looked at me pleadingly. "Please tell me sooner if I'm hurting you."

"I did! I did tell you!" I flung up my hands in exasperation. "I told you so many times that I was feeling like an inconvenience. How do you not remember this?"

As Harry's brow furrowed in confusion, my shoulders began to quiver with oncoming sobs. "Do you have any idea what it feels like to be with someone who doesn't really want to be with you?"

Harry's eyes widened in alarm. "That's not what this is. I do want to be with you. It's simply a case of 'right person, wrong time.'"

I scowled up at him through eyes blurred with tears. "But you're so cold. The way you are with me in public, the way you take forever to respond to my messages. Why be so cold?"

Harry looked down with guilt. "I'll admit, I thought making less effort would make it easier for you to go off being in a relationship with me."

"Don't you see how cruel that is?"

"I do. The idea really wasn't well thought-out. I'm sorry." He pulled me into him and grasped me tightly. I was too limp to resist and let myself cry until the tears briefly ebbed, and then I pulled myself away from him.

"I really love you, Sara," he said feebly.

I sniffed and turned my face away. "I know you do. I believe you do. You just won't show it."

"I don't want to hurt you anymore."

A silence fell between us. My head began to spin with anticipation.

"So, we'll break up then."

As the words sunk in, Harry studied the floor silently. Then he cleared his throat.

"My preference would be that we break up in September when I go back to school." He sat up straighter and began to speak more confidently. "I suggest this because I'd really like to spend this time with you. I'd like to do another trip with you. And I want us to see our friends during the summer without feeling uncomfortable in each other's presence. We could tell more people the news closer to the time."

I chewed my lip with mixed feelings. I resented his lack of self-awareness, but there was something relieving about the security his proposal offered.

After a moment of consideration, I nodded slowly. "Okay. We can do that."

We ate dinner with a strange calmness, appeased by this new treaty we had agreed to.

When Harry left, I closed the door and leaned back against it, drained from the medley of emotions running through my mind. I told the voice of fear and doubt that it was for the best and that I had the rest of the summer to come to terms with it. But the voice continued to tremble and moan, convinced I wouldn't find anyone else like the boy that searched for me among the vines six years ago.

TWENTY-TWO

My eyes gazed uncertainly at my laptop screen as I debated whether I should tell my mum the news in my response to her latest email.

Twenty-four hours had passed since my conversation with Harry. I had spent the day at the Pride Parade with him, Joey and Lucy. Despite my support for the movement, I had been in an irritable mood all day, drained by the hot sun and the colourful crowds of people with an energy I didn't seem to possess. And I had been offended by the sight of Harry seeming so cheerful and enthusiastic in spite of our circumstances.

I looked back at my laptop. The idea of telling my mum the whole context over email seemed exhausting. Instead, I finished the email by noting how nice it would be if she were able to visit. My mum had always had a strange yet fascinating ability to be able to tell when something was going on—a telepathy of sorts. There were times when I would wake up randomly in the middle of the night, only to get up the next day and learn that she had emailed me around the time I woke up. The same thing used to happen with Harry when I lived in London.

"I think you could probably meet someone more suitable, to be honest," said Joey as we walked along Dallas Road a few days later.

I crossed my arms and looked towards the ocean. "It's really not helpful when people say that."

"Sorry," said Joey with a shrug. "But you just both seem to want different things. I know people always say this, but there might be someone else you have more in common with."

I looked down as the face of the fitness trainer entered my mind. We had locked eyes through the window as I'd left the gym that day, his attention diverted towards me as he spoke with a client at the front desk. We had shared a secret smile that had left a tingling in the back of my neck. It wasn't the first time we had exchanged curious glances. But a voice warned me he probably looked at other girls the same way. After all the uncertainty over Harry's commitment, I wanted someone who only had eyes for me.

"I don't really feel like looking for someone else right now," I said.

"I'm not saying you have to right now, but in time, when you're ready, there might be someone better for you."

A spaniel trotted happily towards us. I bent to pet him with a smile, and then I straightened up with a sigh.

"It's hard to imagine being with someone else. It's even hard to imagine not spending time with Harry's family. I'm so used to them." A sudden wave of sadness hit me at the thought of how Hannah would react to the news.

A buzzing sounded from my bag. A girl I'd emailed about a room asked if I was available for a viewing that evening. Joey offered to drive me to the house in Oaklands. The room I had expressed interest in had been taken, but the girl said another room was available. She led the way to a tiny room with a single bed and no window.

"You could probably fit in a double bed if you wanted," the girl said brightly.

I nodded quietly, pondering whether that would even be necessary.

When Harry called me that evening, I gazed at him through the screen with a mixture of longing and irritation. It seemed almost cruel, the way he had sparked a renewal of attraction just before our decision was made.

"My mum's booked a flight to visit," I said. "She'll be arriving on August 3rd for one week."

"That's great," he said with a smile.

"I thought I'd tell her about us when she's here."

"I think that's a good idea."

I cleared my throat and looked down. "Also, when I started my job, I put you as my emergency contact. I was wondering if you'd be okay remaining so after we break up?"

"Of course." Harry shook his head. "Sara, you're tiptoeing too much. I'm not moving to Russia."

"I just wanted to be sure." I brushed a speck of dust off my keyboard, reluctant to look at him.

"I booked some flights too," said Harry chirpily. "I'm going to Ottawa next Wednesday for the math conference I told you about. My friend that's going with me knows a girl who studies at Carleton. We're going to stay at her place."

"That's nice." A flicker of worry entered my stomach out of nowhere.

"So, are you coming up this weekend?" asked Harry.

"I guess, if that's okay with you?"

"Of course."

After we said goodbye, I stared solemnly at the black screen.

The bus journey to Sidney had a different feel to it that weekend. A clock ticked quickly in the back of my mind as I looked out of the window at the white sailboats on the ocean.

At the property, I followed Harry into the barn with resentment, but I pulled him down beside me longingly. We lay together in a satisfied daze until the clock began to tick once more, triggering a feeling of dread.

"It's weird to think that soon we won't do this again," I said quietly.

Suddenly emotional, I rolled over and sat on the edge of the bed with my elbows on my thighs.

"What are you thinking?" asked Harry.

I looked at the whiteboard on the wall. It was covered in math equations, with only a small space in the top right corner devoted to a love note I had written a few months ago.

"I'm thinking that you'll find someone better, someone who makes you happier and ready to commit to a relationship. I'm scared of how that will make me feel, like I've failed in some way. I'm scared that I'll be quickly and easily replaced."

Harry exhaled calmly and sat up beside me. "I could never forget you."

"If you met someone else, you could."

"You could meet someone else too. It's not just me."

I shook my head skeptically. "You're going to be surrounded by girls at school."

"That doesn't mean anything will happen. You need to stop making predictions. You're just willing yourself to feel sad."

"Can you blame me?" I asked defensively.

"You could meet a guy if you wanted, if you put yourself out there."

My cheeks grew hot with discomfort. "I can't see myself doing that."

"Of course you can't if you tell yourself you can't. You shouldn't hold yourself back like that." Harry placed his hand gently on my back. "I'd be happy for you if you found someone, Sara."

I rose to my feet. "Why would you say that? It's just weird."

"It's not weird; it's important. I don't want you to put me on a pedestal."

I turned around sharply. "How can you be so calm about this? It's like you want me to go look for someone else."

Harry shrugged. "I just want you to be happy."

"Or you just don't want to feel as guilty when you start dating other girls."

Harry's face tightened with impatience. "I don't plan on feeling guilty if I end up meeting someone else, even though I've told you many times that I see myself being too busy to be in a committed relationship."

"But not too busy to have polyamorous relationships."

"When have I ever said that's my intention?"

"You don't have to. I can tell it's what you want."

Harry regarded me steadily. "If we're single, neither of us should feel guilty dating others."

I stood silently, staring sullenly at the carpet.

"And if I heard you were seeing someone, yes, I'm sure it would hurt a little at first," continued Harry. "But ultimately, I'd be happy for you."

I chewed my lip, fighting back tears. "I'm sorry, but I can't see myself feeling the same way."

A hopeless silence fell between us. Feeling a need to escape, I pulled my shorts from my bag.

I ran quickly down the driveway, darting through the patch of forest and down towards the bay. My breath came out unevenly as my feet pounded the ground. Upon reaching the beach, I jumped down the bank onto the pebbles and bent with my hands on my knees, gasping deeply. When I straightened up, I felt physically strong, but mentally I felt deflated.

I was used to having control over things. I could control how well I did in school because of the effort I made to study. I could control how well I did in my job because of the effort I made to work. I could control how well I did at running because of the effort I made to train. But I couldn't control Harry's feelings, no matter how much effort I made to win his commitment.

When Peter invited me on a boat trip the next morning, something blocked my usual enthusiasm. It was difficult to be around the family and pretend that everything was normal. At the bus stop, I hugged Harry awkwardly as I wished him a good trip to Ottawa. Regret swirled around my head as soon as I sat down on the bus. *I should be making the most of the time I have left with him.*

Staying in my suite only made me glum, so I walked down to the beach with a book. It told the story of a spirited young woman who seduced a mysterious man that visited her hometown for a work project. But when she found him in the city, pregnant with his child, he rejected her, intent on pursuing his career. An ambitious young man with his future ahead of him, he had no desire to make room in his life for her.

The sound of a shouting child nearby broke my thoughts, and I looked up to see a small girl run over to her mother. At the news that the younger sister had fallen in the playground and cut her toe, the mother stood up in a flap, panicking about the sight of blood.

The words of the woman that helped me on the bus suddenly ran through my mind. *Pay it forward.* I impulsively reached in my bag for a band-aid I always carried with me, and approached the flustered mother. Five minutes later, she and her daughters waved me off with grateful smiles. As I washed my hands in the public washroom, I smiled in amused recollection. But when I looked up at myself in the mirror, the smile began to fade. A band-aid couldn't fix everything.

At home, I decided to email Peter to let him know the news. My fingers moved clumsily over the keys, heavy with the reality of it all. I asked that he didn't tell anyone else. In his reply, he told me my friendship with the family extended farther than my relationship with Harry and that I was always welcome to visit them in future. I closed my laptop with tears in my eyes.

When I arrived at work on Monday, I found myself opening up to Paige and Jenna. At my confession that I was struggling to come to terms with the impending change, Paige suggested I write down a list of goals to focus on for when I became single. I took a sheet from my notepad and began to scribble down some bullet points of things I wanted to do. *Travel somewhere new in Canada. Start practising German again. Run competitively again.*

As I wrote, Nathan's suggestion popped in my head, and I searched online for the Tracks website. The next run meet-up was scheduled for Wednesday evening, and I decided to give it a try.

My mood began to lift. I caught up on reference checks I'd put off on the sluggish Friday afternoon and finished the lunchtime boot camp with an invigorated sense of energy.

In the afternoon, Eva stopped by my office and handed me a leaflet.

"Work BC is hosting a roundtable event for job-seekers next month, answering questions on how to prepare for interviews and so on," she said. "They've asked one of us to be on the panel. I wondered if you'd like to represent us?"

I scanned the leaflet in surprise. The date of the event was Harry's birthday. And past my probation end date.

"I'd love to," I said enthusiastically, only to hesitate. "If you're sure you'd like me to do it?"

"Of course. It'll be a good experience for you," said Eva with a smile. "But if you change your mind, no worries. I know some people don't like public speaking."

"It's okay, I can do it," I said assuredly.

Public speaking was something I found daunting, but I felt driven to impress. I sat a little higher in my chair, flattered by the invitation. This opportunity was exactly what I needed. I walked home with a spring in my step, feeling like the future might be bright after all.

TWENTY-THREE

Wednesday, July 19th started with a text from Harry at six o'clock as he boarded his early flight to Ottawa. Although a part of me was genuinely excited for him to be having the experience, bitterness began to build up during the day as I reflected on the past six months. The sadness I used to feel over his selfish ways began to transition into resentment. The ten days of time apart suddenly seemed like a blessing, a chance to process everything and come to terms with our future status.

As the clock approached four-thirty, I changed into my sports bra and running shorts. The butterflies began to flicker again as I tied my laces. I looked in the mirror and asked myself why it was that I could interview strangers every day, yet found myself nervous about going to a run group.

I walked timidly into Tracks and passed through the clothing area towards the shoe section before looking around in confusion. A man pointed me through a side door towards a courtyard. I swung my ponytail over my shoulder and took a deep breath before walking out to see a group of people stood around chatting quietly.

"Hey, is this the run meet-up?" I asked, giving a shy wave of my hand.

As I finished speaking, my eyes landed on a man whose bright blue eyes caught me by surprise. They seemed to widen at the sight of me, and in turn, I felt a spark of electricity shoot through me.

After a moment, the man swallowed and said, "Yeah, this is us." As I approached the table, he held out a tanned hand. "I'm Will."

"Sara." His hand was warm as our eyes met once more. After removing his hand, he ruffled his light-brown hair that curled slightly on the top. The shortened sides highlighted his chiselled cheekbones.

"There are just a couple of forms to sign," he said. "Here's a pen."

The tips of our fingers touched as I took the biro from him, and my thanks came out barely audible. The form asked me to list an emergency contact. The pen hovered over the sheet hesitantly before writing Harry's name, followed by *Friend.* I put the forms on the table and wondered if Will was the friend Nathan had mentioned.

The group was made up of a mix of ages, with a few more males than females. I approached a blonde woman who looked nice enough, and we began to chat. My eyes occasionally wandered curiously back to Will, taking in the way he seemed to carry himself with a cool, quiet confidence. Another woman with a big smile and fit physique joined and introduced herself as Zoe, the other run leader, before going on to explain the route plan.

I set off running next to the blonde woman. Her pace was slower than mine, and I didn't find her particularly interesting. We ran down the wharf past the harbour filled with tourists enjoying the summer weather before looping around the floating houses at Fisherman's Wharf and coming to a stop near Ogden Point. I stood quietly, barely out of breath.

Will took off his backwards baseball cap and pushed a few curls of hair off his forehead before replacing the cap. I looked away just before he looked back at the group. The option was to continue on a longer route with him along Dallas Road or return to the store with Zoe.

"Would anyone be interested in doing the longer route?" he asked.

Members of the group looked at each other indecisively. I raised my hand casually. "I would."

Will's eyes met mine, seeming even brighter than before, and then he looked away and nodded at another man who raised his hand. We continued along the ocean path with its cooling breeze, and Neil proposed picking up the pace.

"You go ahead, I'm good," said Will.

Neil spurted ahead, leaving Will and I running side by side.

"Feel free to join him. I'll be fine," I said.

"Nah, it's okay. I'm actually a little sore today, anyway." His voice sounded different from anyone else I knew. It had a mild twang, but there was a lightness to the tone.

We turned down a path to the right, into the direction of the sun. I licked my lips.

"So, do you know Nathan?" I asked.

"I do not know Nathan," replied Will with an amused smile.

"Oh." I laughed in self-deprecation. "He's my friend. He recommended I join this group and said his friend Will works at the store."

"There are a lot of Wills at Tracks, in fairness. I just do the weekly run meet-ups." He wiped his brow. "And what about you? Do you live here or just visiting?"

"Yeah, I live here. I moved in late December."

"From...New Zealand?"

I couldn't help but smile. "No, England."

Now Will laughed sheepishly at himself. "You don't sound very English."

"My accent is all over the place. New Zealand would be more exciting. Sorry to disappoint."

"I'll let you off." He pointed to a path on the left, and his arm brushed mine accidentally. "What made you move to Victoria?"

I looked at the ground hesitantly. "A few reasons, really. I travelled here a few years ago and really liked it. I wanted a change from England and, well, my boyfriend is here."

"Oh, right."

"It's a bit of a weird situation. We're actually breaking up at the end of summer."

I wrinkled my nose in embarrassment as I heard myself.

"Ah, I'm sorry to hear that," said Will.

"It's okay. It's part of the reason I came today, actually. I'm taking it as a time to focus on some personal goals."

"Good for you," he said. "And what are some of your goals?"

"I'd like to run competitively again. It's been a couple of years."

"Well, you're in the right place." Will's hands gestured at the path in front of us. "What's your distance?"

Two loose dogs tore up the path, and we side-stepped them clumsily before sharing an amused look.

"Anything under 8k. 3k was the distance I ran in pentathlon."

"Pentathlon?" repeated Will. "You mean, with the hammer throwing and stuff?"

I smiled. "No, modern pentathlon. Running, swimming, shooting, fencing, show jumping."

"What did you shoot?" asked Will with intrigue.

"An air pistol. We had to shoot at targets one-handed."

"Geez. I won't get on the wrong side of you, then."

"I'm actually really good, too."

"It's a good thing you're modest," he joked. "But no, I'm impressed. How long did you do it for?"

"Around six years. It was fun, but my swim stopped me getting anywhere far with it. I wasn't fast enough, and I didn't care enough to train more for it."

"I know what you mean. I used to play soccer pretty seriously, but it required so much commitment, and I got tired of getting injured, so I focused on running instead."

"Striker?"

"Winger."

"Close enough." I brushed a strand of hair out of my eyes. "How long have you led these runs?"

"Just under a year." Will cleared his throat. "Actually, next Wednesday will be my last session. I'm going on a trip for a few months. I guess you could call it a run-cation."

"Oh." I tried to mask the unexpected disappointment I suddenly felt. "That'll be fun. Where are you going?"

"Possibly New Zealand at some point, but just through BC and into the States for now. There are some big running communities down there."

I listened with envy. "I'm jealous. I love the western USA."

"You've been?" asked Will.

"Yeah, a few times. We—I was there a few summers ago." I scratched my brow. "It's nice you can go away for that long."

"I've wanted to do it for a while. I'm looking forward to it." Will ruffled his hair before pointing to his left. "Let's go down here."

I followed him onto a street where Neil could be seen waiting at the end of the road.

"I'm planning to go for drinks after the next session," said Will casually. "You're welcome to join if you'd like."

I rubbed my lips together to suppress a developing smile. "Thanks, that sounds nice."

Upon reaching Neil, Will led the way back to the store. I watched his lean figure as it ran with an easy, smooth gait. The two of them surged off in a final light-hearted race against each other, and I watched with amusement. In the courtyard, Neil held up his hand for a high five. I returned it cheerfully, lifted by endorphins.

Zoe was filling out some forms in the corner. As Neil left, I took my water bottle from my bag and sipped slowly while she chatted with Will behind me. She seemed to be in the middle of a long story. I zipped my bag shut in acceptance and walked towards the gate quietly. Will's face turned towards me.

"That was fun, thanks," I said with sudden shyness.

"See you next week?" he asked.

I met his hopeful eyes with a ripple in my chest. "Yeah, I'll come."

As I walked through the gate, a curious glance back through the railings showed Zoe raising her eyebrows cheekily at Will. He shrugged and looked down with a bashful smile. I looked away and let myself do the same.

Lucy left for her family vacation to Europe the next day, and I welcomed the time alone. It seemed to complement the process of restoring my independence. As the week went on, I felt my pessimism towards the future circumstances with Harry begin to fade in place of growing acceptance. Joey's words ran through my mind, and I wondered if there might be better people for me after all.

I arrived home from a friend's potluck dinner on Friday to find a missed video call from Harry. Aware it was late in Ottawa, I decided against calling back and instead focused on preparing for my permanent residence application. Research had informed me that my educational credentials had to be assessed, and I had to contact my university to request copies of my transcript.

As I prepared to turn off my laptop, Harry called again. Muffled conversations sounded in the background as he greeted me.

"I can definitely see myself living here for a couple of years," he said brightly. "We had such an awesome day. I really want to tell you about it, but we're heading out shortly."

I glanced at the time on my laptop. "It's midnight there. Seems a little late to go out."

"That's just what they do here," he said, taking a swig from a beer bottle.

As I went to speak, a female voice called his name.

"Sounds like the cab is on its way. But anyway, I wanted to tell you about the conference we—" he hesitated and then sighed resignedly. "Ah, maybe I'll just see you next Friday and tell you then."

My mouth began to tighten.

"And, how are you?" he asked hurriedly. "Quickly."

"Don't burden yourself."

I hung up on his surprised face and exhaled with annoyance.

Why stay with him, if he annoys you? asked a voice. *Why not call the shots and end it now?*

I pictured myself showing Harry the door, telling him I didn't want to see him again. Convenience, history, physical intimacy, mutual friends—all seemed to cut the scene in my head.

I picked up my notepad from the coffee table and wrote the words *Dear Harry*. We had always written each other goodbye letters. I would read them on the ferry with an aching inside as I gravely resigned myself to another installment of long-distance.

When I looked down at the blank sheet of paper now, nothing came to me. I didn't know what I wanted to say. I closed my eyes and sat back with a sigh.

"I just want to feel loved by someone," I said to the empty room.

TWENTY-FOUR

The smoke from the wildfires of California and Washington began to spread north, filling the sky with a faint grey haze and turning the evening sun a blood orange colour. Environmental scientists were calling it the driest year on record.

A tension hung in the air between Harry and me, lingering silently like the smoke in the sky. When we next spoke, fiery jabs about communication style were followed by a moody simmer, and the call ended quickly.

With the heat and smoke came a sense of sluggishness. On Wednesday afternoon, I rubbed my eyes wearily and stared grudgingly at the pile of employee files on my desk. I was waiting for certain applicants to provide references and send updated resumes with the edits I'd suggested. I didn't want to follow up again. I didn't want to chase people that weren't willing to dedicate themselves.

Seeing the clock turn four-fifteen, I glanced at my gym bag. The run meet-up was later, but I wasn't sure I had the energy to run in the heat. I considered going to the gym instead, but something convinced me the run would be the better option. I put on a t-shirt to cover the pimples on my shoulders and walked to Tracks. The butterflies began to flutter once more as I approached the store, but they felt different from last time. Less anxiety, more anticipation.

The group seemed slightly larger this week. Something stirred inside me at the way Will said my name when he saw me, the way a faint smile played on his lips as he looked back down at his pile of forms. I wiped my sweaty palms on my shorts and listened as Zoe called for everyone's attention and reminded us that it was Will's last day. My eyes met his briefly as she spoke, and a slight blush formed on his face as the group responded with a collective bemoan.

When the group split at Dallas Road, I ran quietly next to Neil while a woman with curly hair chatted animatedly to Will in front. As we climbed a hill on the oceanside path and took a left down a side street, my bladder began to wince. I interrupted the chatty woman with an apologetic smile and asked if there was a public washroom nearby. Will led the way through a cemetery and pointed to a small building just outside the gates. I emerged a minute later and was surprised to find him standing solely outside, fiddling with his shirt.

"Thanks for waiting," I said.

"The others know where to go."

We proceeded to jog side by side up a mounting road that curved to the left.

"How's your week so far?" asked Will.

"Pretty slow. I thought I was going to fall asleep at work today, especially with this heat."

"I never asked what you do for work," he said curiously.

"I'm a recruitment consultant at an employment agency in town," I said.

"So, you interview people for jobs?"

"I do, and a lot of them seem to think I'm Australian."

"Pfft. You're obviously English."

I turned to see the smile on his face before I glanced around at the unfamiliar road. "I'm glad you know where we're going."

"Just up here." He gestured with his hand and then scratched his temple. "This is Fairfield. I actually live around here."

"Not for long. When do you leave for your trip?"

"I'm planning to leave on Saturday. Got to pack up a few things from my place."

"If only I'd met you sooner," I said playfully. "I'm looking for a place for September 1st."

"Where do you and your boyfriend live now?" he asked nonchalantly.

I brushed a stray curl of hair from my eyes. "Actually, I moved from his family's place in May. I wanted more of my own space, so I got a sublet in Cadboro Bay."

We turned up a side road that led to a large rock. The other runners could be seen at the top, pulling quad stretches. I climbed up and stood at the top, catching my breath. In front of us, the pink sun shone down on the calm ocean, the distant mountains of Washington barely visible through the smoky haze.

Will stood beside me. "This is Moss Rock. Have you been here?"

"I haven't. It's lovely." I dug my shoe into a crevice and smiled embarrassedly. "I still haven't been to a lot of places, to be honest. On the bus to Sidney, I always see a sign for Island View Beach. Is it nice there?"

Will smiled amusingly. "I can tell from the way you called it Cadboro Bay. Most people say 'Caddy.' And yeah, it's a nice beach."

"What will I do when you're gone, and I no longer have my local guide?"

We shared a playful smile. The sun reflected in Will's blue eyes and cast a glow over his skin. I looked away and swallowed, and my mouth felt dry.

Back at the store, Neil offered to find a table at The Anchor while Will finished some paperwork. I followed the group down the street to a pub with wooden tables and high ceilings. Unfamiliar with any of the local beers on the menu, I ordered a cider and showed the bartender my ID. As I glanced through the window on the other side of the room, Will appeared in view, pushing a road bike. A girl walked by his side. My shoulders automatically drooped with disappointment. *Of course, why wouldn't he?*

I returned to the table and listened as members of the group talked about something in the news. My eyes occasionally drifted to the bar where Will and the girl stood looking at the menu, he dressed in a loose white t-shirt and faded blue jeans. The girl was pretty with dyed blonde hair and an athletic build that was slightly shorter than mine. Will took the seat in front of me, and she the one next to him, and I acknowledged her with a bashful smile.

"Cheers," said Will, raising his glass towards me.

Our eyes met as our glasses clinked. I glanced self-consciously at the girl as I drank. She was texting on her phone.

"It's a nice pub," I said, gazing around the room. "I like the pictures."

"I take it you haven't been here either?" asked Will.

"I don't really go out that much," I said sheepishly.

"I don't either, to be honest."

Suddenly, a man approached and tapped the girl on the shoulder before bending to kiss her. I took in their passionate display of affection with relieved surprise before looking away.

"Where in England are you from, anyway?" asked Will, scratching his ear.

"North Yorkshire. Have you heard of it?"

"Yorkshire, yeah. It has a lot of sheep farmers, right?"

"I guess you could say that," I laughed. "In the dale I grew up in, there were more sheep than people."

"The dale?" asked Will with intrigue.

"It's like a valley." I motioned a bowl shape with my hands, and Will nodded with an amused smile. "We technically live in a national park on the moors, and there are all these dales."

"So, you're from a family of shepherds?"

"Not quite. My parents were in the medical field, but we grew up with animals and my mum started breeding sheep ten years ago. We have around forty of them." I smiled fondly. "And they all have names."

"That's impressive. What's your favourite called?"

My face straightened sarcastically. "You can't have favourites, Will."

"Ah, of course. Wouldn't want the others to get jealous." He smiled and looked down at his drink. "Well, it sounds like a nice place to grow up."

My feet accidentally touched his, and I instinctively moved them away.

"What about you?" I asked. "Are you from the island?"

"No, I'm from a small city in Alberta called Grande Prairie. If you haven't been, don't bother going."

As Will finished his sentence, a smiling Zoe approached and placed a drink in front of him.

"I can't stay," she said sadly. "I have a friend's birthday dinner."

Will stood up to give her a hug, and I saw her whisper something in his ear. I looked away as they spoke, and when Will sat back down, there was a faint blush on his cheeks.

"Zoe seems really nice," I said as I watched her walk away.

"She is. She's like a big sister to me," he said warmly.

"Do you have any siblings?"

"Nope. Precious only child here."

"I bet those blue eyes came in handy as a kid." With a smile, I rose my eyes to briefly meet his own. "Did you ever wish you had siblings?"

Will shrugged. "Having a brother or sister would have been nice, but I had friends close by to play with."

"I can't imagine being the only child. I'm the youngest of five."

Will's eyes widened in surprise before he gazed up at my hair. "And are you all really blonde?"

"Yes, but I'm the blondest." I flicked my ponytail cheekily. "We have Dutch heritage from my mum's side."

"That makes sense." He leaned forward and rested an elbow on the table with a relaxed smile. "Do you think any of them would want to move here?"

"I don't think so. Everyone seems pretty happy where they are." I traced my fingers over the wooden table. "I kind of like that Canada is my own place, if you know what I mean. It's something that's my own and not a toy or piece of clothing that used to belong to an older sibling."

"I see what you mean." Will looked at me curiously. "How old are you, anyway?"

"How old do you think I am?" I replied, smiling with scrutinizing eyes.

Will studied my face carefully for a moment. "Twenty-four?"

"Close. I turned twenty-five in May. I was expecting you'd think younger."

"No, you can tell from the way you act." His eyes lingered on mine for a moment before he lowered his gaze. "I'm actually only a year older than you."

I tore my eyes away from his face and looked at my drink. "How come you moved to Victoria?"

"I transferred to UVic a couple years ago. I wanted to get out of Alberta and be near the ocean."

"People seem a lot happier here," I remarked. "I like that it's slower-paced and that people thank the bus driver and speak to other passengers. That rarely happened in London."

"You lived in London?"

"For a few years, yeah. I went to uni there." I twisted my glass in thought. "It was fun for a while, but it wasn't for me long-term. I found the crowds and the pace and the culture draining. People just seemed very..." I paused, pondering my word choice.

"Cold?"

I looked up and caught his eye. "Exactly." I rubbed my lips together before clearing my throat. "What did you study at uni?"

Will scratched his neck. "I haven't actually graduated yet. I wanted to take some time off to travel. But I'm studying political science."

"It's nice that universities let you do that here. Take time off."

Will nodded and tilted his near-empty glass. Then he asked about my travels and watched with a smile as I spoke.

"Have you mostly travelled by yourself?" he asked.

I nodded. "Canada was my first solo trip, actually."

Will looked impressed. "Good for you. I don't know many girls who would want to do that."

I shrugged. "Most countries I've gone to have been pretty safe. But yes, I was a little nervous before Canada, and losing my backpack was quite stressful. But otherwise—"

"You lost your backpack?" asked Will dubiously. "How did that happen?"

I rolled my eyes. "It's a long story."

"I'm all ears."

I rested my elbows on the table, and Will leaned forward, listening attentively as I spoke. As I finished, I found myself laughing at the expression on his face. "It sounded better when I wrote it on my blog."

"What's your blog called?" His eyes twinkled mischievously. "'The Amazing Adventures of Sara from the Shire?'"

I shook my head with a smile and explained the meaning behind its name. Then I waved my hand, suddenly embarrassed. Will nodded, his brow slowly furrowing in thought.

"So, where is North Yorkshire in relation to Liverpool?" he asked.

"You've been to Liverpool?"

"No, but it's my Premier League team."

"You watch the Premier League?" I asked in surprise. "I thought Canadians only cared about baseball and ice hockey."

Will rubbed his lips together with amusement before smiling affectionately. "We just say hockey over here, not ice hockey."

"Whatever." I reached out and punched him gently on the arm.

Will watched my hand move back to the table. "Anyway. Liverpool."

"Oh, right." I moved my glass out of the way, and Will watched closely as I drew a map on the table with my fingers.

"Can you even understand the Liverpool accent?" I asked curiously.

"Remind me what it sounds like, again?"

"Okay, wait." I swallowed and opened my mouth, only to second guess myself and start giggling. "I can't do it when someone is watching."

Will smiled and covered his eyes.

"You don't want to hear. It's not that attractive. At least, to me, it isn't."

"Can you recognize differences within the Canadian accent?" asked Will.

I rested my chin back on my hand. "I think so. Your accent is different. It sounds a bit drawly."

"Drawly? Like hick?"

"What's hick?"

"Hick is someone from the country. Where you grew up in England, for example, you would be considered a hick."

"Why does something tell me that I don't want to be known as a hick?"

"Just see it as a term of endearment."

Our eyes lingered friskily for a few seconds. Feeling my face grow warm, I dropped my gaze and tucked a strand of hair behind my ear.

"Do you think you'll live in Victoria for a while?" I asked. "I mean, whenever it is you come back."

"I think so. I definitely want to do more travelling, though."

"So, you're going away for a while, then?" I asked casually.

"Until December is my plan for now." Will played with a coaster on the table. "What about you? Can you see yourself staying here?"

I rubbed my arm. "I think so. I like it here. In spite of the breakup, I don't want to leave."

"Right." Will scratched his brow. "How are you feeling about that whole situation?"

"It's sad, but it's the right thing to do." I hesitated before letting my elbows sink back onto the table. "It sounds lame, but I suppose there's a part of me that feels like I've failed in some way."

I looked up at Will's face. He nodded slowly.

"I get what you mean. I actually went through a similar breakup last summer. It's hard."

A pause ensued between us as our eyes locked together. Then a loud call of Will's name sent me sitting back in my seat in surprise. My ears suddenly filled with the noise of the room. I looked around in a mild daze, as if I'd been sat in a private bubble that had just burst.

Will turned to greet the man who had called him, and at his invitation, went to join him at the bar. I looked to the group sat on my right, trying to pick up their topic of conversation. A glimpse towards the bar showed Will talking with his friend, hands casually in his pockets. As I observed them, his eyes drifted away from his friend and found me.

The friend held out his hand confidently as they returned, a smile on his face. "Hi, I'm Tyler."

I gazed at him inquiringly before a lightbulb flashed and told me he was Nathan's roommate. A student at UVic, he also worked for Tracks and would be taking over the Wednesday sessions in Will's absence. He had a cheeky but endearing smile, and in the easy-going company of him and Will, I found myself oozing a confidence and sense of humour that seemed to have been locked away for the past few months. A smile would linger between Will and me at the end of a joke, and when our feet accidentally touched again, I let mine stay a moment longer before moving them away.

I looked in the washroom mirror with beaming eyes. A glance at my phone revealed that it was already nearing ten-thirty. My shoulders sank. The party would soon have to come to an end. I returned to the table and reached in my bag for my cardigan while the others continued to speak. Will shifted in his seat as I pulled it over my shoulders.

"I think you might have to finish this for me," I said, pushing my half-finished second glass of cider towards the centre of the table.

"You're heading out?" asked Tyler in disappointment. Next to him, Will ran a hand quietly through his hair.

"I'm up early for work." I rose to my feet and slung my bag over my shoulder. "It was great to meet you, Tyler. I'll see you next week."

"Sara, it was a pleasure," he replied through merry eyes.

Will's eyes met mine with a sudden hint of shyness. I placed a hand on his shoulder and kept it there briefly. "Well, I hope you have a great trip."

"Thanks, see you." He smiled warmly before his eyes fell bashfully to the table.

I walked towards the door with a mild tugging of reluctance. The sky was dark, and the late-night air sent goosebumps up my bare legs. I shoved my hands in my cardigan pockets and wrapped the sweater tightly around me. As I walked up the street, cold air brushed my skin, but I felt warm inside. A bittersweet smile formed on my lips as I reached the street corner. Instinctively I stopped under the glow of a streetlamp and turned to look back behind me curiously. *No, that would be too much.* I turned back around in acceptance and jogged to make the final few seconds of the pedestrian light before quickly making my way to the bus stop.

TWENTY-FIVE

The next day passed slowly, a sleepy haze of waiting for clients to provide feedback on candidates. In the dry heat, I walked home to the jingle of an ice-cream truck in the neighbourhood. The jingle would quieten down only to burst into life again as it turned onto a new street. A similar pattern had ensued in my head all day as flashbacks to my conversation with Will continuously drifted into my head. But December was months away, and I told myself to let go of the daydreams.

Friday remained quiet in the office. After finishing some interview notes, I gazed absent-mindedly out of my window. People in dresses and polo shirts crossed the street on their lunch break. Unattracted by the thought of going outside in the hot weather, I found myself logging into my personal email account. I was waiting to hear back from a girl about a room viewing. My inbox showed a new email from the contact page of my blog. Assuming it was a spam advert, I opened it with apathy.

> Hey Sara, this is Will from the Tracks meet-up. I meant to get your number on Wednesday but foolishly let the opportunity pass, then I tried to chase you down, but you had evidently disappeared into the night. As such, I've been

> forced to (creepily) track you down via the internet. Anyway, it would be great to keep in touch whilst I'm off doing my thing and potentially get together some time when I get back. Here's my number if you want to send a text. Be warned: my sensitive male ego will be extremely damaged if you decide not to.

I sat back slowly in my chair, stunned. The room suddenly felt warmer, the skin under my blouse dampened with shock. I leaned forward to read the email again. A goofy smile of glee began to take over my face as I pictured Will jogging up the street to find me. *No way. He didn't do that.*

A balloon seemed to swell in my chest as I read the message once more. An inflating feeling from having stayed in the mind of someone who could spark a rush of delightful tremors with one quiet glance and make the rest of the room disappear with one secret smile. That moment of realizing they felt the same way.

The jingle pattern resumed once more as I walked home, oblivious to the looks of strangers who witnessed the smile that would intermittently sneak over my face.

A white car was parked outside my house. The sight of it stirred an uncomfortable jolt back to reality. I swallowed as I watched Harry step out of the door in a colourful t-shirt I didn't recognize. He held out his arms for an embrace, and I responded obligingly.

"I can't stay long, but I wanted to see you," he said.

"That's okay. I have some stuff to do anyway."

I pulled away from him and led the way to the house while he chatted animatedly behind me.

"Man, Ottawa was so great. There was a speaker at the conference who—"

"Could you take off your shoes? Keeps the carpet clean."

Harry kicked them off while continuing his story. My ears began to close off as he spoke about the various talks he'd attended. I scrubbed dirty dishes with increasing impatience before the guilt over my disinterest set in. At the door, I told him I'd visit him over the weekend.

But as I boarded the bus to Sidney on Saturday afternoon, I felt lethargic. When Harry slowly began to unbutton my blouse in his room, I stood lazily with my hands by my sides. He swiftly lowered himself on top of me, and I looked into his eyes, trying to feel something. On impact, I winced and looked away from him, hoping it would soon be over.

When we walked into the house to have dinner, Peter gave me an understanding nod.

"It's strange without Hannah here," I said to end the silence. "How are things going with the Airbnb?"

"Great!" said Ruth. "They currently have a couple from Brazil staying. The previous ones left early because they didn't like Max. They obviously weren't dog people."

"You do have something on the website that mentions him, don't you?" asked Harry with raised eyebrows.

"Of course, Harry," said Ruth, rolling her eyes.

"And it mentions he can be aggressive?" he asked.

"He's not aggressive. You just have to be respectful and give him space."

Harry put down his fork with a sigh. "Mom, people are paying to stay in the bed and breakfast. Don't you think their experience should be prioritized over a dog's desire for space?"

"When did you become so patronizing?" asked Ruth disapprovingly.

I sipped my water with a dose of satisfaction.

"I'm just saying that it could harm your business, having Max there," said Harry. "He could hurt someone."

Ruth's face tautened. "I'm not going to give him away, Harry. You don't just give up on an animal. That's not fair." Searching for support, her eyes fell on me. "Aren't I right, Sara?"

My throat tightened under her expecting gaze. I played with my fork, carefully considering my words.

"I think it's the case that not every animal can be saved, no matter how hard you try."

A look of offence crossed Ruth's face. "Are you saying you don't think Max will get better?"

At the intensity of her stare, I swallowed. "I just mean in general. I'm sure Max will get better in time."

Ruth stiffly sipped her wine, as if unsatisfied with my response.

Peter cleared his throat. "I hear your mother is coming to visit, Sara. When does she arrive?"

"This Thursday, for a week."

"Well, we'd love to see her again," he said with a smile.

I returned his smile as Ruth continued to eat in silence.

Harry and I returned to the barn shortly after, and I collapsed on the bed with a sigh.

"I wish your mum wouldn't always bring me into things and try to get my support like that. One minute she wants me to be her ally, and the next she's acting like she dislikes me again."

"She doesn't dislike you," said Harry reassuringly. "You know how she is with everyone. She's stubborn and finds it hard to consider other perspectives."

"I guess." I sat up and looked at him. "I told your dad, by the way. About us."

Harry nodded. "He mentioned it."

"I asked him not to tell your mum, just because…you know."

"That was probably a good idea."

"I would prefer that Hannah hears it from us."

"I agree."

I turned my head away to end the conversation and noticed my phone was flashing with a new message. Will's name showed up when I opened the screen. I put the phone down with a mixture of excitement and guilt.

"I'm just going to do some piano practise, and then we could watch a movie later if you like?" proposed Harry.

"Sure."

As he walked downstairs, I picked up my phone again. Will had asked for my address so he could send me postcards from his trip. There was a dancing in my chest as I read the request. I had never received postcards from a boy before. There was something gratifying about discovering that he wanted to share his experiences with me.

But as Harry began to play a tune, the idea of him seeing my mail and getting the wrong idea made me hesitant. I looked back at the message, and excitement at the novelty of it gave way to skepticism. Was it normal to make this gesture after having only met a person twice? Or was it just that it wasn't normal for me to experience this type of gesture from someone?

After a moment's hesitation, I put the phone away and took a seat on the stairs to watch Harry play.

"I heard this song in a bar in Ottawa," he said as he started a new tune. "It's so good."

I recognized the song instantly.

At my comment, Harry turned in surprise. "You know it?"

"I grew up listening to old soul music, remember?"

Harry continued to play, and I sang a few lines absent-mindedly. He smiled contentedly as his fingers moved across the keys. I watched him quietly, and as I did so, I found myself wondering if he'd flirted with other girls in Ottawa. Part of me wondered whether I even cared.

In the morning, Harry proposed we go for breakfast at a local café down the road. We chose a table outside on the patio in the shade, and after passing the menu back to the waitress, Harry crossed his hands together on top of the table and sat in thought.

"What is it?" I asked expectantly.

Harry cleared his throat. "I haven't been very good to you recently."

I looked him calmly in the eye, waiting for the confession.

"I've been quite cold and distant at times, and for that, I want to apologize," he said.

I looked away with a shrug as another couple walked onto the patio. "What's done is done."

Harry regarded me with mild tentativeness. "You've been really great to me in spite of all this, and I really appreciate it."

I sat back in my chair and took a sip of juice. "I think it's admirable that you're able to identify where you're dissatisfied in life. I just worry that it will damage your other relationships as well."

Harry nodded, his brow furrowing pensively. "After attending the conference, I've realized that I really want to pursue academia and get a PhD."

His face was serious. An ambitious young man with his future ahead of him. His words seemed to bring me a relieving sense of confirmation. I couldn't go on competing with this passion he was so devoted to.

"Well, that's great," I said.

We ate our food with minimal conversation.

"We should invite Joey if we come here again," I said.

"We could see what he's up to this afternoon if you like?"

I popped the last piece of toast into my mouth. "Can't. I've got an apartment viewing this afternoon, remember?"

Harry clicked his fingers. "Right."

I chewed quietly, contemplating. "It'll be nice when we can all hang out as friends."

"It will."

I fiddled with my napkin. "My friend Amy is coming to visit in October. The one in Australia. You could meet her if you'd like."

Harry smiled. "I would like that. I know she's an important friend of yours."

At the bus stop, he switched off the car's motor and sat with the windows down.

"You don't have to stay," I said as I unbuckled my seatbelt. "I'll probably just wait outside. There's shade in the shelter."

"Okay." Harry smiled faintly, then his face straightened with a memory, and he reached behind his seat and handed me a letter. "This came for you on Friday."

"Thanks." I looked down at the writing. "So, I'll see you on Thursday? To collect my mum from the airport?"

Harry nodded.

When the bus arrived, I boarded with a different feeling from before. No tears, no disappointment.

The apartment I viewed happened to be one that I walked past every day on my way home from work. A timid girl with brown hair greeted me at the door, with her twin sister in the background. The twin was going to study in France for a year, and it would be their first time apart ever. The apartment was nicely furnished with wooden floors and a refurbished bathroom. The bedroom had a double bed and a side closet. I peaked through the blinds at the road below and wondered how loud it would be. Then I looked back at the bed and tried to imagine how comfortable Catherine would feel if I brought a date home.

At home, I opened the letter Harry had given me and found my language exam results. The perfectionist in me grumbled at the writing score. I'd been told a few times that my handwriting was hard to read. I tossed the letter on my desk, and it landed next to the notepad on which I had started writing Harry's goodbye letter. I still hadn't got further than writing his name.

I slumped on the couch and thought of the apartment again, trying to picture myself waking up in the room. Will's face suddenly entered my mind, and just as the tingles began, a voice scolded me for getting ahead of myself over someone I had only just met.

With limited other options and a desire to finalize my search before my mum arrived, I texted Catherine to express my interest in the room. She said she'd send me the paperwork in the next few days, and I exhaled with relief. Then I let myself think of Will again, where he might be and what he might be doing.

Skepticism reverted back to excitement, and before I knew it, I was picking up my phone and giving him my address. He replied to say he was on a ferry heading to the mainland. When I told him that I didn't want to get to know him over text, he said he felt the same way.

As I walked into Tracks on Wednesday evening, I felt a pang of disappointment, as if I'd hoped it was all a trick and Will would appear behind the desk with his backward baseball cap. Tyler led the group along the Galloping Goose Trail, sharing jokes and observations. I kept up with his pace, and when I got home, I smiled at his social media connection request and accompanying message that praised my running ability.

Tyler wasn't the only person who had requested to connect. After closing his message, I hovered my mouse over the thumbnail of Will's profile photo. The few photos he shared showed him running or hiking. He seemed to live the kind of outdoor life I wanted to live. Tagged photos from almost two years earlier showed him with his university running team in Strathcona Provincial Park. In one of them, he stood in front of a glacial lake with his arm around a girl I assumed was the ex he had mentioned. I peered closely at the screen, curious to see her face. Her name no longer showed in his friends list, and I wondered what had happened between them.

I clicked back onto my profile and gazed uncertainly at the cover photo. A painting by a German artist, it showed a girl with long blonde hair sitting on a roof, looking up at a violet sky to watch a boy with dark hair balance on the moon. I had found a postcard of the painting in a Christmas market in Switzerland and had instantly seen myself and Harry in the picture.

Now when I looked at the painting, I saw a girl sitting and watching her boyfriend as he ambitiously reached for the moon, she only able to watch from below as he explored new heights on his own.

TWENTY-SIX

My excitement increased throughout Thursday as I counted down to my mum's arrival. I quickly finished a candidate's talent summary before dashing out of the door at four-thirty on the dot. My feet tapped on the floor in anticipation as the bus made its way up the highway.

Harry typed away on his laptop while I bustled around restlessly, finding clothes to put away and guitar picks to collect.

"Her flight lands at six, so I suppose we should probably leave at twenty to?" I asked.

He shook his head. "They always take ages to unload luggage. We'll be fine if we leave five minutes before."

I chewed my nails while watching the clock.

"Okay, let's go," I said agitatedly as the clock approached five to six.

"One second," he said as he squinted at something on his screen.

"Harry, come on! We'll be late."

"It's an airport; we're not going to lose her," he said, closing his laptop with a sigh.

"That's not the point. I want to be there when she walks through the doors."

As soon as we pulled into the parking lot, I got out of the car and jogged over to the arrivals entrance. People were walking through the doors with their luggage, and I looked around expectantly, peeking past people embracing. A glance at the arrivals board showed the plane had landed at 17:58. Another person walked out of the doors, followed by nobody. I squinted through the glass, but no other figures were approaching. I looked around worriedly as Harry joined me.

Suddenly, there was a tap on my shoulder. I turned to see Mum smiling through tired eyes.

"Mum!" I flung my arms around her and buried my nose in her neck, taking in the familiar smell of her favourite moisturizer. "Where were you?"

"Well, I walked through and didn't see you, so I wondered if I was in the wrong place," she said with a shrug.

I shot an irritated glance at Harry. "Sorry we missed you."

Harry stepped forward with a sweet smile for a hug. "Nice to see you again, Janet."

The skies were a soft lilac infused with grey as Harry drove us back to Victoria.

"They're quite bad, aren't they, the fires?" Mum remarked from the backseat. "I'd hoped to catch a view of the Rockies from the window but couldn't see anything through the smoke."

"And how was your flight otherwise?" asked Harry.

"Oh, fine thanks," said Mum with a yawn. "Air Canada seems generous with the booze, which is nice."

Harry stroked his chin in thought. I chewed my lip with apprehension before slumping in my seat as he brought up his parents and initiated a debate about the definition of alcoholism.

"Well, to be an alcoholic means you have to be dependent on it. It means that you struggle to function without the stuff, and struggle to find satisfaction in life without it," said Mum in response. "It's very normal for people to have a glass of wine in the evening to help relax. This doesn't mean they have an addiction."

"I struggle to agree with that," replied Harry. "To feel the need to drink every day in order to relax seems quite concerning to me. How can that be healthy?"

"I imagine Mum's pretty tired to have this kind of conversation right now," I said.

I changed the subject to ask about Dad and our dog, and before I knew it, we were pulling into my cul-de-sac. I turned on the kitchen light and put the kettle on to make Mum a cup of tea.

"I can sleep on the couch so you can sleep over, Harry," offered Mum.

"It's fine. Harry will be going home," I said.

After he left, Mum rested her feet on the coffee table with a contented sigh. "I hope Harry didn't notice my smelly feet."

"Sorry we were late," I said sadly. "I did ask that we set off sooner."

"That's all right, love. I knew I'd find you at some point." She sipped her tea thoughtfully. "He's very serious, isn't he?"

"Yes, he can be."

"Almost aggressively so."

I scratched my elbow. "I know. He didn't used to be like that."

Mum tossed and turned in the bed, struggling with jetlag. I left her a map of the local area the next morning and walked to the bus stop with heavy eyelids.

A vibration sounded from my bag during an interview with a man who spoke very fast. Something told me it was Will. Sure enough, the text asked if he could call me sometime during the week. The message sent a firework fizzing up my chest. I told him my mum was visiting and proposed next week instead. My fingers hovered over the keypad before sending another message.

> I'm telling her about my breakup tonight, so that'll be fun…

Mum was sitting in the backyard reading a book when I returned home.

"Another soppy romance," she said as she removed her reading glasses. "Very unrealistic."

"I hope you weren't too bored."

"Oh, no. I had a relaxed morning. There was a deer sitting out here when I woke up."

"He comes quite often. I call him Stanley," I said over my shoulder as I walked to the bedroom. My phone flashed with a new text.

> I'm sorry about this situation you're going through. Keep your head up. I see you, I hear you, and I'm with you.

The words left me in a state of light-headed surprise, until Mum's voice from the kitchen shook me from my daze.

I took a blanket from the couch, and we walked down to the beach. Mum wore a blouse I didn't recognize—"Just something I found in the charity shop." I was glad to see she was spending more money on herself.

We sat against a piece of driftwood, looking out at the sailboats docked in the bay. When I told her the news, she snorted with a tone I couldn't identify—unimpressed but not overly surprised.

"Well, it sounds like he's been quite selfish, hasn't he?" she said after I told her Harry's plans. "You can't just take all and give nothing in a relationship."

"He seems to now realize how selfish he's been, but yes, you're right."

"You seem pretty calm about it," she remarked. "What do you think you'll do? Do you still want to be here?"

"Definitely. I really like it here."

"Well, that's the main thing, isn't it? That you're happy." Mum looked into the distance reflectively. "I did have a feeling something was up, just from your emails."

"I was quite upset for a while, but I'm getting used to the idea. I think it's for the best."

"Someone else will probably come along before you know it," she said lightly.

I rubbed my lips together secretively as we sat silently observing the hazy pink sky. As I put my arm gently over her shoulder, she took a few strands of my hair in her hand. "Looks like you've been picking at the ends again. Good thing I brought my scissors."

At home, I turned on the TV and found one of Mum's favourite films. My phone buzzed to show Catherine's name as we watched, and I groaned as I read the message.

"The room I was planning to take is no longer available. Apparently, there's been some sort of family emergency, and her sister has decided to stay." I rubbed my forehead, feeling the stress already build.

"Oh, bugger," said Mum disappointedly. "Well, you focus on looking for a new place."

"But I want to spend this time with you," I said sadly.

Mum waved her hand with a smile. "Don't worry about me; I'm quite all right."

I turned on my laptop and began frantically searching online for vacancies while Mum continued watching the movie. Within several minutes, her head had lolled back, and she was asleep in the chair, her cup of tea still in her hands, just the way I remembered.

Ted and Julie invited us to their house for dinner on Saturday evening. As we sat on their deck eating fresh salmon, their kids smiled shyly at my mum. Then they quietly took her hands as we walked down to the beach after dinner. When Julie suggested we sleep in the guest room instead of staying in Harry's barn, I accepted the offer gratefully.

Shortly after waking in the morning came the sound of pattering feet. I sat up to see Tom and Milly approaching with books in their hands and hopeful faces. At Mum's welcoming smile, they climbed onto the bed and made themselves comfortable next to her. I watched with a smile. I had seen my mum engage with many children, and she was a natural with them all. She had an ability to make anyone feel special.

The skies were overcast as Mum and I boarded a whale-watching boat in our large float suits later that morning. The zodiac boat zoomed over the water, captained by a boy I suspected was an old high school friend of Harry's. We saw no whales during the ninety minutes and were invited to come back for a complimentary tour that evening. After removing our suits, we walked up to the fish and chip café I'd been to a few times with Harry. The service was slower than usual, and I found myself growing disappointed with a sense that the day wasn't turning out to be what I'd envisioned.

Twenty minutes later, Harry drove us back to the property to spend the afternoon with his parents.

"We were expecting you last night," said a smiling Ruth upon seeing us. "I put together the sofa bed for you in the barn."

"That's very kind of you, but we thought it might be easier for everyone if we stayed in Ted's guest room," said Mum before I had a chance to speak. She gazed around at the buildings to change the subject. "What a lovely spot."

"Not as lovely as your home," replied Ruth with a shrill laugh.

We sat chatting at the dinner table while Harry played guitar in the living room.

"I just don't know how you can let all your kids move away like they have," remarked Ruth.

"I can," said Peter with a grin.

Mum shrugged. "Well, you can't hold them back from what they want to do, can you?"

Harry came over for his water glass, only to grin at the plate of cookies on the table. "I'm amazed there are any of those left. I've never known anyone to be able to eat desserts like Sara."

"I wish I could eat cookies and stay so skinny," said Ruth with another unnatural-sounding laugh.

"The kids didn't have many sugary treats when they were young," said Mum. "Pop was only for special occasions, and so on."

Ruth turned to look at me with a sweet smile that made me squirm inside. "No wonder you have such beautiful teeth."

I returned her smile bashfully, wishing I could believe her admiration would last.

As the zodiac boat left the harbour that evening, I let my mind switch off, reprieved from its task of maintaining positive normality in circumstances that would be changing in a month. The pink sun filtered its rays through the hazy smoke and danced on the surface of the water as the boat stopped to wait. After a few minutes, a burst of steam blew up from the water two hundred metres away. A humpback whale slowly curved up out of the water before dipping below with a flick of the tail. A few more times, the whale rose majestically, catching those in the boat by surprise. Then she flashed us the white bottom of her tail as a farewell before diving deep below. Mum patted my hand to signify the moment and sat back with a content smile as we followed a golden path back to shore.

We started Monday's statutory holiday with a bus to Fernwood, where I had an apartment viewing. Mum wished me luck as I approached the building entrance. The apartment was nice, but when the engineering student told me she was a night owl, I sensed she would prefer someone on a different schedule from mine.

I found Mum outside sitting on the wall reading her book. We walked down to the harbour and followed the loop round to Fisherman's Wharf before carrying on to Ogden Point. A snooty girl in an over-priced bistro reluctantly allowed Mum to use the washroom as a non-paying guest. I checked the time as I waited.

"We'll need to head back to Douglas Street so we can get the bus to Butchart Gardens," I said as she emerged from the restaurant.

"More walking?" she said with a protesting face. "Crikey, my legs aren't used to the tarmac."

"I'm not sure where the bus goes from here, and because it's a holiday, they aren't running as frequently." A hint of grumpiness entered my voice, but really it was directed at myself for not having thought to check the transit map.

I led the way back, occasionally glancing over my shoulder to check Mum was keeping up. A sense of stress began to build inside me, and I wasn't sure why.

"Just a minute, Sara," called Mum from behind. "My leg's starting to spasm."

I turned with impatience to see her leaning against a railing with discomfort on her face, stretching the leg she'd broken as a teenager. Upon seeing her, a flurry of guilt hit me. Then came the fear at an unwelcome realization.

Mum was getting older, and I couldn't deny it. Naivety and wishful thinking had convinced me that she would always maintain a certain level of health and strength. It had blocked me from accepting that a time would come when she wouldn't be able to walk as fast, read the small fonts, recall every detail. And as she entered this stage of life, I had moved thousands of miles away from her. I turned away to dab at my watering eyes and slowed my pace, so I was walking by her side.

Crowds of tourists thronged the Butchart Gardens, enjoying the warm afternoon weather and vibrant colours of the flowers. They would block pathways as they continuously stopped to take photos of various bushes and floral arrangements. I watched Mum quietly smell a bunch of sweet peas and felt awful. I had dragged her around walking in pain, only to lead her to an expensive tourist trap.

At home, I left Mum dozing on the couch and ran a shower. The water mixed with my tears as I recalled the look on her face earlier that day.

When I arrived home on Wednesday, a chair stood outside the door with Mum's scissors lying on the seat. I quickly washed and conditioned my hair before sitting down. I had been to a hair salon once in my life, on the day of my brother's wedding. Twice a year, I would sit in our kitchen in North Yorkshire while Mum quietly worked away at my ends, occasionally reminding me to sit up straight and stop tilting my head. In these moments, we would talk about various topics. Today we talked about Harry.

"Julie is very fond of you," said Mum. "And disappointed in Harry, too. Told me I wouldn't believe how he's acted towards you at times."

I looked down at my lap pensively, only for Mum to remind me to sit up.

An hour later, we sat with Harry in a Thai restaurant down in the village. His mood was light and playful, and Mum looked between our laughing faces questioningly.

"I just don't understand how a couple can be so normal and happy with each other and then suddenly end things on one date," she said.

Harry's mouth straightened. "We just wanted to enjoy the time together."

Mum studied her beer glass. "I suppose I'm just quite confused as to why you want to break up."

"I have a lot of academic ambitions, and I don't think it's fair for Sara to be my partner while I pursue those ambitions," said Harry calmly.

I shifted in my seat with sudden irritation. "I'm not sure that was really your main concern. It's ultimately about what you want."

Harry looked at me blankly. "Well, yes, but while taking into consideration—"

"I don't think you can realistically say you've given thought to what's fair to me in this decision."

Harry looked at the table in thought and pushed his glasses up his nose.

"You've changed a lot in the past few years, haven't you?" remarked Mum.

Harry sat up straighter. "I have, but I believe in a good way. Had I not met my mentor, I don't know what I'd be doing today."

"Who's your mentor?" asked Mum curiously.

I downed the last of my water and sucked through my teeth.

"Brendan, my math teacher and friend. He's the one that really inspired me to pursue math."

"What do you mean by 'friend?'"

"He's also a great friend. He's taught me a lot about communication and relationships." Harry smiled. "He sadly moved a year ago, but if I get into Waterloo, I might have him as a teacher again."

Upon seeing Mum's expression, I cleared my throat. "They became friends outside the classroom when Brendan taught him in his first year."

Harry glanced between us with a perplexed look as Mum furrowed her brow in concern.

"To have a person of authority involved in your personal life like that, I wouldn't consider it very healthy," she said.

"Define 'healthy.' What does that mean, exactly?" asked Harry.

"Well, there's a person of power and their subordinate," began Mum.

"A subordinate?" repeated Harry. "You seem to be suggesting I was controlled in some way."

Mum's face remained serious. "Well, unfortunately, that can be an issue in this case."

Harry shook his head. "That seems like a generalization. This is an equal friendship."

My grip on my glass tightened. Just as Mum opened her mouth to respond, the waitress came by to take our plates. I sat back in relief and gathered together my cutlery.

We walked back up the road quietly, with occasional bits of small talk here and there. "Thanks for dinner," "That was nice service," "Your curry looked good."

Harry said goodbye with the agreement he'd pick us up at noon the next day to take us to the airport. The reality of Mum's impending departure began to hit in waves of sadness. In bed, I snuggled into her tightly, smelling the familiar shampoo in her hair, trying to absorb as much of her as I could.

At the airport, Harry and Mum exchanged a hug before I led her away for a private goodbye.

"I promise I really am happy, in spite of everything," I said as I linked my arm in hers.

"I hope so," she said.

We turned to face each other. As I saw Mum's watering eyes, my mind flashed back to standing outside Gatwick Airport in 2011, ready for my first flight to Canada. Turning around with the expectation of seeing a calm and encouraging smile, the surprise and devastation of seeing her sobbing, forcing myself to turn back around and continue walking. Now I was older, but the goodbye remained just as difficult.

"You'd better leave before I start crying too much," she said as we hugged.

I pulled away with tears streaming down my cheeks and watched as she walked towards the security doors before turning with a final wave. When she was out of sight, Harry put his arm over my shoulders and led me back to the car.

I returned home to find my bed sheets neatly folded, with a note left on my pillow. As I lay down and inhaled Mum's comforting scent, I wished the time with her hadn't gone so quickly.

TWENTY-SEVEN

As the clock approached seven, my fingers drummed on the armrest in anticipation. When I had texted Will to propose a call, I'd sent it with the expectation he would have lost interest, but his reply had come quickly.

The phone rang on the dot, and my stomach somersaulted with nervous excitement. Upon hearing his voice, I relaxed slightly.

"How was the time with your mom?" he asked.

"It was really nice. It was hard saying goodbye this morning."

"Are you and her pretty close?"

"We are. We spent a lot of time together when I was growing up. She used to drive me around the country for training and competitions."

"That's nice. I'm not sure my mom would have done that," he said. "And it was just your mom? Not your dad too?"

"No, he stayed home to look after the animals."

"Someone's got to take care of the sheep, I guess," he said playfully.

"Exactly." I smiled and then grew curious. "What are your parents like?"

"Miserable. Unhealthy. You know, classic suburban life."

"That's too bad. I'm sorry."

When he asked about my mum's reaction to the breakup plan, I found myself delving into my relationship with Harry.

"I'm sorry, that became a really long ramble," I said a few minutes later.

"It's okay; it sounds like it's been a tough time."

Keen to change the subject from Harry, I asked Will about his trip. He was currently in a provincial park near the Washington State border. He spoke about mountain runs, wildlife encounters, and observations of strangers he'd come across. I listened intently, picturing the scenes in my mind and enjoying the sound of his voice.

"And then I was in Chilliwack for the past few nights," he finished.

"Chilliwack?" I repeated with interest. "I know that place. I recruited someone for a client there just recently."

Will uttered a gentle laugh, and the sound sent a warm tingle up my spine.

"What is it?"

"It's Chilliwack," he said. "Not Chillee-wack."

"Oh, great. I've been saying that to candidates this whole time."

"They probably find it endearing."

"You've said that before, and I was skeptical then."

We spoke more about the geography of British Columbia, and I was reminded how little of the vast province I had explored.

"What's the weather like where you are right now?" I asked. "You're not near any fires?

"No fires close by, but it's hot. I was thinking I might sleep on the car roof tonight."

"Is that safe?" I asked with concern.

"It'll be fine, plus it's a great view. No light pollution, clear skies—at least, when there isn't smoke around."

I closed my eyes and pictured lying on top of a car under a starry sky in the middle of nowhere.

"I should probably go soon," said Will with a hint of disappointment in his voice. "My phone battery is starting to get low."

I glanced at the clock and was amazed to see two hours had passed. "Well, I enjoyed talking to you."

"Me too," he said. "I mailed you a postcard the other day. Hopefully, the beavers will get it to you soon."

"I'll look out for them," I said with a smile. "Stay safe, and watch out for cougars. I hear the animals are pretty dangerous, too."

Will laughed before saying bye softly. I sat back in my chair with a feeling of content.

I continued my room search saga with a viewing in Oak Bay a few evenings later. The apartment building was at the end of a long street on the corner of a small road close to my current bus route, and it was only a ten-minute walk from the beach. A twenty-six-year-old PhD student from the Maritimes, Connor seemed easy-going and mature as we sat talking in an open living room with wooden floors and large windows. The bedroom was spacious, and I could see myself being there. I emailed him later to confirm my interest and hoped I'd made a good impression.

Once home, I had a text from Will asking if the postcard had arrived. It hadn't. I had been checking the mailbox every day.

I closed the message and sat down on the couch before opening up Amy's latest email.

> Have you and Harry talked about having some space from each other after the breakup?

The question caught me by surprise. I hadn't given any consideration to how things would be between us after that day.

I hadn't even thought of who would help me move house on September 1st. I had simply just assumed I would ask Harry.

I closed my eyes and rubbed my forehead wearily. One more issue to address. I wished I could escape for a few days and return to find that everything had been sorted out for me. I exhaled slowly before opening my eyes. *It's time to have a break from this island.*

I spent the next day's lunch break studying a map of BC, reminding myself of places I'd visited and finding names of places I'd heard of or read about. Ideas of trips occupied my mind as I walked home, distracting me to the point where I almost forgot to check the mailbox. The sight of a postcard filled me with excitement. I read the small but neat writing with a smile, picturing the scenes Will had described from his campsite.

As I placed the card on my bedside desk, my eyes fell on the letter to Harry, still untouched. My stomach flipped with guilt. It had seemed to flip back and forth between different emotions in recent days. The increased reality of the impending breakup stirred flickers of trepidation, but when contacted by Will, thoughts of the breakup promptly left my mind. My communications with him were a welcome distraction, yet something told me there was more to my feelings.

When Will requested a second phone call, I felt like a child that had been presented with a surprise birthday cake. With him, I spoke calmly and confidently. Conversation flowed, and there was an ease between us as we got to know more layers of each other. As the call went on, I found myself wanting to dig in further and have another slice.

Then, after an hour, the line suddenly cut off. I looked at the phone in dismay and called back, but it went straight to voicemail. I sat back in my chair with disappointment, waiting for him to call. After another call went straight to voicemail, I began to regret not asking for his specific location. I didn't even know what type of car he drove or what his parents were called. There was little I could do if something happened to him. He was just an intriguing man that had randomly come into my life and relit a spark. But for now, the candles had gone out, and I had little power to do anything.

The next day signified the end of my probation period at work. The three months had passed in the blink of an eye. I knocked on Eva's door and sat down for my performance review. She said it was clear I knew what I was doing, and she hadn't felt a need to hold my hand over the past few months. I admitted that I tended to be fairly quiet when joining a new team and was pleased when she said she liked my approach to work and communication.

At the end of our conversation, I requested to take a few days off in early September.

"Any plans to go anywhere?" she asked as she made a note in the calendar.

"I'm thinking of going to the Rockies," I said. "It's been a while since I went."

"With Harry?" she asked with a smile.

"No, just me." I cleared my throat and smiled sheepishly. "We're actually breaking up at the end of the month."

Eva's eyes widened in shock. "What happened?"

"We're just not on the same path anymore," I said with a shrug. "He's got his own ambitions, and we're at different life stages."

"I'm so sorry, Sara. Are you okay?"

"I'm fine. It's been on the cards for a while, to be honest."

Eva twirled her pen in her hands in thought. "And so, has this affected your desire to be in Canada at all?"

I shook my head firmly. "No, I definitely want to stay and apply for permanent residence. I really like Victoria and this job."

Eva's face relaxed into a smile. "Well, I'm glad to hear that. We really like having you here." She leaned forward, eyes wide with intention. "And whatever help you need with the application, let me know."

I walked home with a bounce in my step. My phone began to ring just after I stepped through the front door, and I sighed with relief when I saw Will's name.

"You weren't eaten by a bear, then?" I asked upon answering.

"I managed to fight it off with my huge muscles."

"Well, I'm glad. It would have been a faff to head all the way to Grande Prairie for your funeral."

"A faff?"

"Yeah, you know, like a hassle."

"You and your funny words."

"In all seriousness, I'm glad you're okay," I said.

"Sorry about that, my battery died," he said. "How was your day?"

I told him about my performance review and time booked off in early September.

"That's exciting. Where would you go?" he asked.

"Either Kelowna or the Rockies."

"The Rockies?" he repeated with intrigue. "That would be fun."

"It would, though I haven't been to Kelowna before, and I do like the Okanagan Valley."

"Kelowna's nice, though the fires are pretty bad there."

"That's true. I hadn't thought of that."

Will cleared his throat. "Anyway, I'm actually about to head out for a run. I just wanted to call, so you knew I wasn't hanging up on you last night or anything."

"It's okay. I only cried in my pillow for a little bit."

An hour later, I received a text.

> It's totally your call, of course, but personally, I'd advocate for you going to the Rockies for purely selfish reasons of it being a chance to see you.

Will explained that he had a friend's thirtieth birthday party in Edmonton the weekend I would be in Alberta. The prospect of seeing him filled me with sudden excitement, but when I considered my initial purpose for going away, I became hesitant.

> It would be nice to see you, but I kind of wanted to be alone for that time.

He replied quickly.

> No worries at all. I completely understand. You do what you've got to do.

I put the phone down and chewed my lip. As much as I appreciated his understanding of my desire for alone time, I felt myself becoming torn. Flashbacks of our first meets stirred a ripple inside me as I considered the opportunity in front of me.

I opened my laptop to assess flight options. An hour later, I had booked a return flight to Calgary.

The next morning, I sat pondering over word choices as I wrote a summary about a candidate. A stay-at-home mum for the past eight years, she had been struggling to return to the workforce. Demoralized by her lack of success, she had reviewed a job lead I sent her with a mixture of interest and doubt. I had told her it was worth trying, that she ever knew what might happen. Now I had to present her to the hiring manager in the best way I could.

The client responded that afternoon with a request to interview the woman. She received my call with astonishment.

"See, it *was* worth trying," I said encouragingly. "There's nothing to lose in giving it a shot."

My own words of advice echoed in my mind as I left the office and walked to Carrie's condo. I had only told Amy about Will, and I craved to share the secret with someone in person, someone who didn't know Harry.

At the news I had met someone, Carrie's eyes lit up with interest. She listened keenly as I told her about my first meet with Will, the interactions that had followed, and his proposal of meeting in the Rockies.

"Wow, he seems really into you!" said Carrie. "Are you going to meet him?"

"I don't know. It is tempting, but I don't know." I looked at her hesitantly. "Do you think it's a bad idea?"

"Not necessarily. It's quite soon, but it sounds like you've already got to know each other quite a bit." She paused before regarding me squarely. "Do you think you can trust him?"

I nodded assuredly. "I know it sounds cliché, but there's something different about him. He's easy to talk to and seems really caring, and we seem to have a lot in common. It's like we see things the same way."

"What is it about him that you like so much?"

I smiled down at my glass with a shrug. "When you were growing up, did you ever have a vision of the type of person that you saw yourself being with? Will seems to fit the image of the person I saw. Physically and emotionally, he just seems to have the qualities I'm looking for."

"How so?" asked Carrie curiously. "What's he like?"

"He has this smart wit that I really like, and he has a very calm energy and presence—he's not loud or trying to be the centre of attention; he just has a quiet confidence that's always appealed to me. He's thoughtful and mature, and you can tell he really thinks before he speaks, but he doesn't take himself too seriously. There's a depth and perceptiveness to him, but it doesn't feel like he's trying to be someone else." I sat up straighter. "I really like how adventurous and outdoorsy he is. But he's not like one of those adrenaline junkies; he seems to like his downtime too. We even have the same taste in music. And he doesn't seem motivated by materialistic things or wealth. I feel like we value the same things and would want the same lifestyle." I smiled fondly. "I feel like life would be fun with him."

Carrie's face beamed. "Sara, this is so exciting!"

"It's all just happened out of nowhere, but it feels really good. It's kind of revitalizing."

As she sipped her cider and processed the news, a quizzical expression crossed Carrie's face. "Where would you sleep if you met up with him?"

I pursed my lips. "I'm not sure. I haven't thought that far ahead yet. I might not even end up meeting him, and if I do, it will probably only be for a couple of hours."

Carrie sniggered. "No guy I know would drive from Edmonton to Banff just to hang out with a girl for a couple of hours." She looked at me cheekily. "If you ended up staying somewhere together, would you sleep with him?"

I suppressed a giggle. "I don't know. That wouldn't be the purpose of seeing each other."

"Yeah, okay." Carrie rolled her eyes sarcastically.

"It's really not like that," I said with a laugh. "There's more to it. I wouldn't want to just hook up with him, and I think he feels the same way."

"Okay, okay. But if it did come to that situation—hell, why not?"

I shook my head. "I'd only just be single. It wouldn't be right."

Carrie shrugged. "I met Eric pretty much the week after my ex and I broke up. Sometimes it's just timing."

I drank from my glass in thought.

"Don't think about it too much. Just go with the flow, and maybe shave your legs just in case," continued Carrie with a grin.

"I love that I haven't even confirmed I'm meeting with him, yet we're already planning this far ahead," I said in amusement.

"Well, it sounds like you like him, and he likes you, so why not?"

I twirled a strand of hair around my finger. "It seems a little wrong to even be talking about this when I'm still technically with Harry. It almost feels like emotional cheating."

Carrie waved her hand dismissively. "There's nothing wrong with thinking about your future if you know you're about to be single. For all you know, Harry's doing the same."

I pictured Harry messaging a girl he'd met on campus. The image of it didn't seem to hurt.

On Friday morning, I was informed my candidate had been offered the six-month contract.

> Thank you so much for encouraging me. The hiring manager was really nice and I have a feeling this could turn into something long-term.

I read the woman's email with a smile before sitting back in my chair contemplatively. *Nothing to lose.*

With a deep breath, I picked up my phone and messaged Will to ask if he'd like to meet me in Banff for a couple of days.

The question of what would happen if he agreed to meet lingered on my mind as I caught the bus to Sidney that afternoon for Joey's birthday party. Meeting Will had given me a renewed sense of optimism, but past experiences told me to be skeptical. I had put faith in the feelings of others before, only to feel disappointment and self-doubt. Things with Will seemed almost effortless, too good to be true. I was just waiting for the balloon to burst.

Harry's car was waiting in the parking lot as the bus pulled to a stop. I returned his wave with a feeling of guilt and pushed Will out of my mind.

Harry seemed different today, more attentive and generous. His hands stroked my back tenderly as we sat on Joey's deck in the evening sun. When Nathan showed up with Tyler, I shifted awkwardly in my seat as Will's face immediately entered my mind once more. Connections suddenly seemed uncomfortably close.

As everyone began jumping into the pool, I removed my t-shirt slowly, self-conscious about the skin on my back. Harry had never cared about the break-outs I'd dealt with since I was a teenager, never made me feel less attractive for them. There was something daunting about the knowledge that this physical part of me would one day be exposed to a new person.

The next morning, I received a text from Connor inviting me to be his roommate. The initial feeling of relief was followed by a sense of optimism. I could truly start looking forward.

"How typical that we discovered this place just before we break up," I joked as I buttered my toast at the café down the road from Harry's house.

Harry looked up at me with sadness in his eyes and swallowed. "I've been feeling quite emotional about it, to be honest."

A feeling of pity was challenged by a cheering sense of victory in my head.

Harry played with his bottom lip. "I noticed the other day that you deleted your cover photo on your page. The painting—us."

I chewed uncomfortably. "I didn't think you'd notice, to be honest."

Harry's shoulders drooped slightly, and he fixed his eyes sincerely on mine. "I want you to know how much I love you."

It was clear that the reality of the situation had begun to hit him, but there was something irksome about his behaviour. *You made this happen. It didn't have to be this way.*

I cleared my throat and fiddled with my napkin. "I was thinking that we should probably give each other some space after we break up to allow us to move on."

Harry's eyes gazed gloomily into the distance. "It's sad to think of it like that—moving on."

I let out a sigh. "You know what I mean."

Harry looked down at his fork, held limply in his hand. "I'm feeling quite emotional at the thought I'm about to lose one of my closest friends in a certain capacity."

I finished my mouthful in silence, unsure what to say.

"The family is going up to the cottage next weekend," he continued. "I was hoping you'd come. I'd really like you to see it."

I nodded. "Thanks, I'd like that."

With no other plans for my day, I agreed to watch him and Joey play in a softball tournament in Saanichton that afternoon. We arrived at a park where various teams were practising throwing and catching. I set down a picnic rug on the grass and pulled a bottle of sunscreen from my bag. Harry offered to do my back.

"Sounds like your phone is ringing," he said as he rubbed the lotion over my shoulders.

I looked down and quickly closed the screen upon seeing Will's name. "Probably nothing urgent."

I watched Harry and Joey walk towards the diamond before turning back to my phone and opening the new message.

> I'd love to spend a couple of days in Banff with you!
> Could I call you tomorrow?

The fizzing feeling rushed up through my chest. After replying, I looked up with a smile to see that Harry was about to go up to bat. Jerked back to the present, I watched him hit the ball and make it to second base. After making it home, he glanced over in my direction, as if checking for my reaction. I had watched him perform many times, always sitting patiently and devotedly. Sitting and watching him reach for the moon.

It was frustrating to see Harry acting so attentive and attached, the way I had always wanted him to be. For a while, I had hoped he'd have second thoughts about the breakup, but just as he started showing signs of hesitation, I found myself being pulled in another direction.

TWENTY-EIGHT

On the morning of the roundtable event, I woke early and picked up my notes. They sat between the birthday card I'd bought for Harry and the second postcard I'd received from Will. As I visualized speaking in a room full of strangers, I felt an onset of the Imposter Syndrome that had seemed to come and go as I'd grown older. There was a voice that told me I didn't deserve to be in my position, that people would soon discover I didn't know what I was doing.

"The other panel speakers will probably be older and have more years of experience, but don't let that worry you," said Eva as I prepared to leave the office later. "You have a right to be there."

I fixed my favourite blouse in the mirror before walking to the employment centre with a trickle of nerves. The organizers gave me a name badge and showed me the room, with attendees already starting to arrive and sit down. I took a seat and exchanged handshakes with the other speakers—an HR Manager at a reputable hotel, a man who ran a construction staffing company, and an HR Advisor to a non-profit organization.

Most of the fifty attendees appeared to be middle-aged. I remained calm as their eyes focused on me while the host read out my bio. Some eyes seemed curious; others seemed skeptical. The host would read out a question from the audience and let a member of the panel offer to answer first. When someone's query about how to best answer a certain question was met with silence, I found myself speaking up to provide my opinion. My voice rose to the occasion more confidently than expected. When the HR Manager jumped in to say she agreed with me, I felt a surge of self-assurance flow through my arms. My answer was met with grateful nods from the audience, and I sat up higher in my seat, eager to take more questions.

As the roundtable ended, attendees approached to shake hands and request business cards. I received their thanks with a growing sense of fulfillment and left the building on a high. I felt like I had proved myself.

My uplifted mood continued all through the afternoon and remained on the bus journey to Sidney. Moments from the event would pop up in my mind—the time I made the room laugh, the time I offered a new perspective, the time a cynical expression changed to one of respect. As the bus passed the buildings and street signs I had come to know, I recalled the many times I had ridden the bus home from a temporary assignment and glumly wondered when I would be invited for job interviews. Now I had sat on a panel, giving people advice on the interview process. Life in Canada had moved forward hugely since the beginning of the year. It felt surreal, and I let myself feel proud.

Peter and Ruth had already set off up island to the cottage. I walked through the barn door and gently nudged out of the way the cycling shoes I'd bought Harry a few months ago as an early birthday present. An hour later, several of his friends arrived to celebrate his twenty-third birthday. In the kitchen, an old high school friend invited Harry to join him for a hike the next weekend. When he turned to ask if I would be interested in joining, my eyes met Harry's awkwardly.

"Thanks, but I'll actually be in Alberta next weekend."

Some of the guests requested a tour of the property. I looked at the buildings with a sad sense of nostalgia as I pointed out the ducks and chickens and horses. As I reached through the fence to scratch Jacob's withers, my mind flashed back to Hannah telling me his name six years ago. I pulled back my arm quietly.

I kept a distance from Harry throughout the evening, hoping to avoid any uncomfortable conversations. At eleven o'clock, my socializing capacity had reached its limit for the day, and I snuck upstairs discreetly as guests turned up the music. As I looked around the room, my eyes fell on a sweater I'd left behind a few weeks ago. I picked it up and placed it in my bag, knowing that the next time I'd be in this room would be the day before I went to the airport. Then I sat and opened the bedside cabinet drawer. A lump formed in my throat as I took in all the cards and letters I'd sent Harry over the years.

Footsteps sounded on the stairs. I closed the drawer and looked up to see Joey.

"How are you doing?" he asked.

"Fine. Just thinking."

He took a seat next to me. "So, who are you going to Alberta with?"

"Nobody, just myself." I smiled nonchalantly. It wasn't a complete lie.

With another round of footsteps appeared Liz. At the sound of music starting, I rose and walked to the ledge, resting my arms on the railing as I looked down below. Harry played bass next to a girl on the guitar, flashing her smiles as they made up a tune. I shifted my weight onto the other foot and thought about the fact that he and I had never ended up recording anything. There had been no chance to when he was so focused on advancing himself.

"Excited for your trip up island?" asked Liz as she came to stand next to me.

"It'll be a nice way to spend a final weekend with the family. I'm excited to see Hannah." I smiled at the prospect of the reunion, only to swallow uncomfortably when I remembered the impending conversation.

Liz lowered her voice. "When I spoke with Harry a few days ago, he said he felt like you were handling the breakup better than him."

"Really?" I scratched my arm. "I suppose he was a little emotional the last time I saw him."

Liz rolled her eyes and sighed. "One day we'll meet a guy who really knows what he wants."

I nodded and shifted my weight once more.

Harry and I set off in the middle of the next morning for the five-hour drive up island. I fiddled with the radio station, but none of the songs met my taste, and I turned it off with a sigh.

"So hard to find good music these days," I muttered.

"I don't know about that," said Harry. "I'd say there are some pretty good artists out there."

"I mean on the radio."

"Well, that's just one avenue. There are plenty of other streaming sites where you can find great music."

"I know that, I'm just talking about music played on the radio specifically."

"Okay, that wasn't very clear in your initial sentence."

I sucked through my teeth and regretted saying anything.

"I'm so excited to see Hannah," said Harry brightly as we drove up the Malahat. "Not seeing her as often has made me realize just how awesome a human she is."

"She did get a little precocious since she started dating Jonas," I remarked. "But I get why. Being with him made her feel more confident."

Harry pushed his glasses up his nose, his brow furrowed. "How was she precocious?"

"The way she started calling me pet names when she's never done that before."

"Surely that's just her showing affection, not being precocious?" said Harry with a smile.

I shook my head. "It didn't seem natural. It felt like she was trying to act older than she was and be someone else."

"I disagree," said Harry. "I think that was more likely her way of expressing fondness towards you."

"Do you have to disagree with everything I say?"

"What do you mean?" asked Harry in surprise.

"I feel like you always have some counterpoint to make. You can never simply agree with me on anything or just accept something I've said."

Harry smirked. "I'm not going to agree with something if I think it's wrong."

"I'm not saying you should," I said impatiently. "I just feel like your comments are unnecessary sometimes. You can be difficult to communicate with."

"How exactly am I difficult to communicate with?" he asked collectedly.

"Because you're always picking at things people say, questioning them. I feel like I'm constantly being assessed."

"Well, I am a mathematician, Sara."

"So what?"

"So, I'm trained to analyze and critique things."

A shot of repulsion ran through me. "And I'm a history major. I was trained to do the exact same, Harry. That doesn't mean I feel a need to nitpick everything someone says."

"I understand," replied Harry calmly. "But with math, it's slightly different—"

"This isn't about math! It's about you and your communication style. Stop attributing everything to math." I closed my eyes with a disgruntled sigh and rubbed my temple.

Harry paused in thought. "I'm a little confused about how me analyzing things relates to my communication style."

"It's your character. You've changed so much." I felt a pinch of sadness as I said the words.

"I'm still not understanding how—"

"You have a tendency to come off arrogant and dogmatic."

"Dogmatic?" he asked incredulously.

"The way you try to get your point across and question people, it comes off that way sometimes. Even my mum said so."

A look of irritation crossed Harry's face. "Your mom isn't exactly a great communicator herself. She's really rigid in her ideas. That whole thing about Brendan? That was really frustrating for me."

"Can you not see why she'd find it a little concerning that you're close friends with your teacher?" I asked defensively.

"No, I can't," said Harry. "I think it's narrow-minded to assume there's something wrong with a healthy friendship like that."

My face tightened. "You really think your friendship with Brendan is healthy?"

Harry glanced at me earnestly. "Yes, I do."

I flopped my head back against the rest with a snort.

"I don't understand why you have such an issue with Brendan," continued Harry with a tone of sadness. "You don't seem to make any effort with him. He calls, and you always have an excuse to not speak for long, or at all."

"He only wants to speak to you."

"That's not true."

"Then how come whenever I talk with him, he's mostly interested in asking about you?"

"I find that hard to believe."

I rolled my eyes and crossed my arms. "Of course you do."

We stopped at a red light, and Harry cleared his throat. "Look, Sara, I understand you might be a little jealous of Brendan—"

"I'm not jealous of him." The boiling liquid I had kept a lid on for so long began to hiss and spit threateningly.

"Okay, well, you seem a little resentful."

"Can you really blame me?" My palms began to sweat in anticipation.

"I don't know because I don't know why you're resentful of him," said Harry calmly. "He's been a great friend to me. I just wish you'd accept him like you accept Joey. Brendan is no different."

"Of course he is; he's attracted to you."

"Sure, but he's never acted on those feelings or disrespected you and our relationship," said Harry assuredly.

As the light turned green, the hot water began to surge to the surface. A piece of knowledge that I had never been able to let go of entered my mind. A stain I had never been able to remove from the relationship. I felt myself start to shake with anger.

"How can you think that, after what happened?"

Harry frowned with perplexity. "I don't know what you mean."

My skin prickled with discomfort as I spoke. At his recollection of the memory, Harry broke into a smile.

"Come on, Sara. It wasn't a big deal. It's no different to seeing boys in the showers at school."

"It's completely different! He was your teacher. It was totally inappropriate."

"I don't see it that way at all. We had been friends for a while by that point."

I scrunched up my hands with frustration. "Can you not see how manipulative it was?"

"I can see why someone who didn't know Brendan like I do would think that way," said Harry calmly.

There was an aggravated pounding in my chest as I tried to gather my words. It was hopeless; he was completely taken in.

"Please continue," said Harry. "I want to understand why you feel the way you do about this."

"What's the point?" I grumbled. "You'll never listen."

"Can you please stop with this passive-aggressive tone?" asked Harry with a sigh. "I'm trying to have a conversation and understand how you feel."

"Why does it even matter? This time next week, we'll have broken up."

Harry fell quiet at the sharpness of my words. I turned on the radio to drown out the tense silence that filled the car. *Soon you won't have to think about Brendan.*

After passing Parksville, the highway began to quieten. Around four o'clock, we passed a sign indicating that our destination was five kilometres away. We turned off the highway and crossed a bridge over a wide river where men sat on the banks with their fishing rods. Minutes later, a track road led us down to a pretty cottage that sat under the gaze of looming mountains overlooking the river.

I stepped out of the stuffy car and inhaled the clean air as I gazed at the Swedish barns. I hadn't been anywhere so quiet since I was home in Yorkshire.

Suddenly, I heard a loud squeal, and then Hannah was running towards us with flailing arms. She flung them around me before leading us to the house excitedly. Max watched from the bottom of the steps with suspicious eyes as I followed Hannah into a large kitchen with a long wooden table that was covered with boxes of vegetables.

"Did you grow all of these?" I asked in amazement.

Ruth came through the door before Hannah could answer and looked me up and down. "Ah, you're here finally."

"It's a lovely spot," I said politely.

Ruth ignored me and strode towards Harry with her arms out. "Happy Birthday, sweetheart."

"Max seems a lot calmer," I said in an attempt to elicit a smile.

Ruth straightened up stiffly. "Yes, as I knew would happen."

She turned to the oven, from where a sweet smell was coming. I shifted awkwardly out of the way for her to open the door, and Hannah led me to the living room with duck-egg blue walls and white wooden furniture. An open door led to a sprawling lawn, and in the distance, I noticed Jake lying in a hammock hung between two trees, with Jonas sitting close by. I walked down to greet them and looked down the bank to the gently flowing river.

"We have paddleboards if you and Harry want to use one," said Jonas.

I looked questioningly at Harry, and he shrugged indifferently. I dragged the board down the bank into the water and climbed onto it precariously. I had never paddle-boarded before and quickly found myself heading in the direction of some low-hanging branches. When I turned to Harry for advice, his response carried a touch of impatience.

Once back on course, I lay down on the board and studied the clear water. Harry lay on his a few feet away, deep in thought. A sense of apathy seemed to hang between us, as if both were counting the days until we no longer had to care. We were like marathon runners that lacked the energy for the final five miles.

"I need some practice," I joked to Jonas as I dragged the board back up the bank.

Hannah approached me hesitantly. "Hey Sara, could I talk to you for a sec?"

We walked away from the boys and sat down under the shade of a tree.

"What's up?" I asked, casting a quizzical look in Jonas's direction.

Hannah looked down at her hands. "I just wanted to ask what was going on because I heard that you and Harry are breaking up, and I'm a little confused."

She looked up at me sadly, and my shoulders sank. Caught off guard, I scratched my neck as I pondered how to respond. Then I grew suspicious.

"Who told you?" I asked.

"Mom mentioned it this morning."

Something jabbed at me as I heard her, and my eyes began to sting warningly. *Of course.*

"I was planning to tell you myself or with Harry," I said. "That's how I always wanted it to be."

Hannah looked at me in dismay. "What happened?"

I brought my knees up to my chest. "We're just not right for each other anymore. Things got worse over summer, and we agreed back in July that we'd end things at the start of September."

Hannah nodded slowly, her eyes focusing on a daisy she twirled between two fingers. "I remember you being upset with him back in June." She looked up with big questioning eyes. "And you couldn't work through it?"

I rested my chin on my knee in defeat. "Not anymore. Your brother is just a different person from the one I used to know. Our personalities and goals and interests don't really align anymore."

Hannah nodded again. "I understand. I know he's been really focused on himself the past few months." Her mouth began to droop despondently. "You just seemed so great for each other."

I watched her with a pulling in my chest. "We still are in some ways, but it's not enough."

Hannah picked slowly at the daisy petals. I leaned forward and touched her knee.

"This doesn't mean everything has to change. I'll still be a part of your life, Han. I want to be. You mean a lot to me."

A tear began to roll down Hannah's cheek as she smiled bashfully, then she leaned forward quietly into my embrace.

Footsteps approached, and I opened my eyes to see Jonas standing a few feet away.

"Dinner's ready," he said quietly. "When you're ready."

I walked into the dining room to see Ruth and Peter sitting at the table with Peter's brother.

"Did you tell your mum?" I whispered irritably to Harry as we sat down.

"No, why?"

"Hannah just asked me about us. She's really upset."

"Dad must have mentioned it to Mom."

"I wanted us to tell Hannah," I said shakily.

I coughed and took a breath. The adults chatted loudly, discussing the cottage. I ate quietly, my jaw tensing every time I heard Ruth's voice.

Shortly after everyone had finished, Ruth went into the kitchen and brought back a plate with a cake. As she placed it in front of Harry, I joined the birthday song stiffly.

"We don't have any candles, so you'll just have to pretend," said Ruth.

Harry grinned and pretended to blow.

"How many girlfriends?" piped up Derek jokily.

Ruth sneered. "Zero."

The table went silent, puzzled by her scornful tone. I felt myself wince with discomfort. Then came the inner voice of regret, asking me why I had come.

"What time are we leaving for the pub?" asked Peter.

"Eight o'clock." Ruth turned to her brother-in-law proudly. "Hannah sings at the local bar every Saturday night."

"It's really not that big of a deal, Mom," sighed Hannah.

"You boys should bring your guitars," continued Ruth. "The three of you can play together."

An hour later, Ruth's voice could be heard ordering everyone to get into the car. I gave myself a pitying look in the bathroom mirror before walking resignedly down the creaky stairs.

A typical dive bar with old stale carpets, a pool table, and a slot machine, the pub attracted a handful of locals. On the walls hung trophy heads and photos of the logging community from earlier decades. Served by a busty brunette woman, tired old men sat at the bar staring at their beers. Occasionally they would glance up to take in the three men playing slow country tunes on the makeshift stage.

I sat silently with a glass of water, observing as Ruth tried to chat with the locals. Her idea of a chat always seemed to involve some sort of sales pitch, and her voice punctured the quiet atmosphere in the room with a lack of self-awareness.

"We need to get these boring old guys off the stage," she said, grinning back at the table as she sipped her wine.

As Hannah went up to sing her favourite country cover, Ruth watched loyally, dropping scowls on anyone at the bar who was talking. A smug smile was cast around the room at the final applause before she nodded at Harry and Jake to go up. Jake sat at the drums and kicked off a quick beat while Harry started a quirky tune on the guitar. The locals watched with a mixture of surprise and distaste. I took a long gulp of water and slumped in my seat as Ruth's eyes remained glued to the stage.

Ruth's devotion to watching her kids was admirable, but something about it made me feel sad. It was the belief that in Ruth's eyes, her kids would always be shining stars, while I would just be a speck of dust loitering on the surface, ready to discard with the flick of a finger. Winning admiration from her had always been my struggle, and if I was successful, it never seemed to last.

The boys finished to quiet applause, and the old men resumed their seats on the stage. The Indigenous man on the guitar started to play a tune, pulling faces as he tried to remember the chords. The drummer waited for him patiently, and then the guitarist gave an accomplished smile as he figured out the tune. I recognized the distinctive sound of one of my favourite songs instantly.

"Oh, he doesn't know the words," remarked Derek to the table. "Too bad, I love this song."

Within seconds, I was on my feet and being pulled towards the stage by an invisible force. Without further thought, I told the guitarist I would sing the song.

Encouraging cheers rang out as I took a seat and pulled the microphone towards me. I took a breath and smiled timidly at the guitarist. He nodded at me when it was my cue, and my voice came out softly. I knew the lyrics off by heart, and the guitarist grinned at me after joining me on the final note of the chorus. The audience was covered in darkness as I continued to sing under a golden haze. When we finished, there came a round of applause and cheers. Suddenly filled with shyness, I bumped the guitarist's hand and jumped off the stool with a numb feeling in my legs. I walked dizzily past the table to the sounds of praise and claps on the back from everyone at the table. Everyone except Ruth.

"That was awesome," grinned Peter as I walked towards him and Harry at the pool table.

"Thanks, it was surprisingly fun." I shook out my shoulders and laughed.

"I got it on video," said Harry with a smile. "Want to join our game?"

I took the pool cue and potted the first shot.

Ruth sat silently in the passenger seat as we drove back to the cottage. Still feeling a buzz, I looked out of the window at the moon and felt glad I'd visited after all.

The open mic event was still a topic of discussion the next morning as I went on a walk with Harry, Peter, and Derek.

"It honestly made my night hearing you sing that song, Sara," said Derek cheerily as we walked through a field of long grass. "Harry, did you know Sara could sing so beautifully?"

"I did." The proud tone of his voice sent a bittersweet pang through me.

Peter led us to a small beach on the river, from where we could see huge pools of salmon in the clear water. Eagles soared overhead, waiting to catch a meal. I looked across at the opposite bank and almost expected a bear to appear from behind the trees. There was no doubt that Ruth had found a beautiful part of Vancouver Island.

When we returned, a clatter of tins and pans sounded through the kitchen window. I walked inside to find Ruth sieving flour into a bowl.

"Do you know where Peter is?" she asked sharply. "I need him to look at the roof."

"I think he's outside with Derek looking at the car."

Ruth briskly brushed her hands off on her apron and left the room without a word. I looked at the mixture in the bowl and impulsively picked up the wooden spoon in an attempt to be helpful.

When Ruth returned, her face dropped with horror. "What are you doing?" she gasped, dashing towards the table.

I dropped the spoon and swallowed nervously. "Stirring the mixture?"

Ruth's hands rushed to her cheeks, her face etching with despair as she surveyed the bowl. "You're supposed to fold muffin batter, not stir it."

My face burned. "Oh, sorry. I didn't—"

"They'll be ruined now."

"Does it really make that much difference?" I asked limply.

Ruth's eyes regarded me scathingly. "Of course it does."

I stood numb with humiliation, and then I felt Harry's hands on my shoulders.

"Let's go see what Hannah is doing," he said gently.

He guided me out of the kitchen as my legs remained logged down with heaviness.

"I was just trying to help," I said as I battled the urge to cry.

"I know." Harry squeezed my waist comfortingly. "Don't worry. She'll get over it."

Two hours later, we drove to the small harbour where Peter had a boat docked. I climbed on board gingerly, wary of putting another foot wrong. Peter released the anchor out in the bay and picked up his fishing rod. The cousins and Jonas bickered over correct techniques as they took turns trying to catch something. Reluctant to receive Ruth's scrutiny, I politely declined Peter's offer to try.

After a few fish had been caught, we headed east towards a cluster of tiny islands. A colony of sea lions lounged lazily on a large rock. Upon hearing the boat, one raised its head in the air suspiciously, and its frame clashed perfectly with a snowy mountain in the far distance.

We docked at a nearby beach, and the cousins goofed around, clambering over rocks, walking along large, fallen logs, skimming stones, and pulling silly poses for photos. In the midst of the normality, the reality suddenly hit that this would be the last time I would be with the family. There would be no more boat trips, no more birthday dinners, no more vacations. No matter what Peter had said in his email, things would never be quite the same again.

"We should hike up the mountain tomorrow," said Peter as we sat looking at the menu in a local fish café that afternoon. "They have a fell race up to the top every year."

"We're actually heading back tonight," said Harry.

"You are?" asked Ruth with a frown. "Why? You only just got here."

"Sara works tomorrow," said Harry.

Ruth's eyes flashed towards me accusingly, and I felt my cheeks begin to redden. "Can't you just call in sick?" she asked.

"Not really," I mumbled. "We have a deadline for a big campaign this week, so I really need to be there."

Here you go again, ruining the family plans, said an ashamed voice.

"That's a long drive to do on an evening," said Peter with concern.

And now you've annoyed Peter too.

"We don't have to set off right away," I said hastily. "And we'll share the driving."

Ruth continued to look at me unfavourably, her lips sealed tightly. I swallowed and looked out of the window. In the far distance, a movement from the ocean caught my eye. I stared curiously, and a moment later, a pod of dolphins sprung out of the surface and into the air. I instinctively opened my mouth to tell the others, but something held me back from speaking.

"Well, I know what Sara will be getting," said Harry teasingly. "That chocolate milkshake has her name all over it."

When it arrived, Hannah made a protesting face at the waitress. "No straws, please."

The waitress smiled and put a hand on her curvy hips. "How is she going to drink it? It's so thick."

"A spoon," suggested Hannah with a hint of sass.

I removed the straw and picked up my spoon. It was clumsy to eat with, and I felt like a child.

"I don't know how you can drink all that," said Ruth. "I'd feel sick."

An unsettling feeling crept inside me. Suddenly, I felt unwelcome, an inconvenience to everyone around me—the bakers, the hikers, the environmentalists, the family in general.

"So, what exactly is your job again?" asked Ruth as our food began to arrive.

"I work at a staffing agency. We interview people that are looking for work and match them with temporary placements or permanent jobs our clients have."

"Oh, so you place people." Ruth wrinkled her nose in objection. "Don't you feel mean telling people they're not good enough?"

Isn't that what you do all the time?

I cleared my throat. "Well, there's a nice way of giving feedback."

Ruth looked unconvinced.

"It's really great being able to help connect people with their ideal job," I continued.

Ruth pursed her lips with what seemed like disdain before looking away with a bored expression. Another swoop to the gut, only this time, instead of leaving me numb, it left me angry. I wanted to ask what entitled her to be so snooty. What had she done by the time she was twenty-five that gave her the right to put me down?

The reality was that I would never be good enough for Ruth. So long as I didn't know the exact steps for baking muffins and didn't give my full support to her ideas, I would never meet her standards. For too long, I had tried to be empathetic and let go of her hurtful comments and behaviours. Every time I had criticized myself for thinking down on her, I was only kicked and sent rolling into a state of inadequacy. In a few days, I wouldn't have to be in her presence ever again. At the thought of it, I realized the sad truth of how much lighter my life would be without her in it.

Harry and I left the cottage just before eight, with me promising Hannah I would see her next weekend before she and Jonas left for Europe.

"I'm sorry you had to leave early," I said to Harry as we turned out of the driveway.

"It's fine. I have some work I want to do tomorrow anyway."

I resisted the urge to ask why he had pinned the reason for leaving on me. There seemed to be no point in arguing anymore.

"It was really great to see you sing last night," said Harry.

I shifted in my seat. "Thanks."

An hour later, my phone signal returned, and a text came through from Will.

Really stoked to see you soon.

I closed the message with a warm feeling that had been missing all day.

TWENTY-NINE

The final countdown began. After meeting with Connor during the week to sign the tenancy papers, I started to pack up my room. Music played quietly as I folded clothes, debating which ones to put in my holdall for Alberta. Certain items of clothing stirred a particular memory that was associated with Harry. A dress I'd worn the one and only time he visited me in London, shorts I'd worn hiking with him in Utah, a bikini I'd worn in Hawaii. Old memories being creased and placed in a bag.

My phone began to ring with Will's name. I lay on my bed with my head on my pillow.

"How are you doing?" he asked.

"A little sad, to be honest." I uttered a dry laugh. "I'm just packing and listening to this song about a guy who's broken up with a girl, but there's a part of him that still loves her."

"That does sound sad."

I shook away the feelings and smiled. "Where are you right now?'

"I'm at home, actually. I realized that I'm seriously lacking in nice shirts, so I need to go shopping before my friend's birthday party."

"I can't imagine you wearing anything but running clothes, though I suppose I have only seen you in person twice."

"Not for long," he said with an enthusiastic tone.

Fireflies danced through my chest. "Actually, I need to talk to you about that. I was looking for an Airbnb and, well, there aren't really any available in Banff, and if there are, they're really expensive."

"I figured," said Will. "But how much time did you want to spend in Banff, anyway? I just ask because I'm going to borrow my dad's truck, so we could go somewhere else if you wanted."

I sat up with interest. "That would be fun. I suppose Banff will be really busy, given it's the Labour Day long weekend."

"Definitely."

I twirled a strand of hair around my finger, suddenly timid. "So, do you have a tent? Because I don't."

Will cleared his throat. "The truck is pretty big. It has a lot of space in the back."

My palms began to moisten at the indirect response to my question. "Okay, sounds good."

We agreed to meet on Monday afternoon. After the call ended, I lay back down slowly as my mind filled with imagined scenarios.

A knock on my door brought me out of my daydream. Lucy smiled from the doorway, back from her serving shift. Her suggestion that we keep in touch and hang out once I had moved was kind, but something told me it wouldn't happen. She was a nice person, but we lacked much in common.

I looked around the room, deciding what to organize next. My eyes fell on Harry's goodbye letter, sitting neglected on my desk. Still, I felt short of inspiration. *Why make it harder?*

I scrunched up the piece of paper and dropped it in the bin.

Friday came round swiftly. I checked in for my flight and felt a flutter of excitement as the email with my boarding pass arrived in my inbox.

"Be safe out there, hiking alone and all," said Eva as she passed my door on her way out. "Do you have bear spray?"

I looked up from writing a to-do list for when I returned to the office. "No, but I'm sure I'll be okay. I don't think I'll be going anywhere super wild."

Harry arrived at the suite shortly after I got back from work, and we began to load bags and boxes into his car to take to the new apartment in Oak Bay.

"These are yours," I said quietly, passing him a pair of socks he'd left in my room weeks earlier.

I then reached for a rich-blue collared shirt. Harry has given it to me during one of my visits, as a memento to make him seem closer while we were apart. Now I held it out towards him awkwardly.

Harry swallowed as he took in the shirt. "You can keep it."

Hannah was in her room when we returned to the property, staring indecisively at a pile of clothes heaped messily on her bed. She looked at me in relief when I knocked on the doorway.

"I'm trying to decide what to pack," she said. "We'll be gone for at least five months."

I took a seat on the bed and scanned the pile. "People often end up packing more than they need." I picked up a long-sleeved top. "This could be a good underlayer for winter or for sleeping."

Hannah nodded, then sat down next to me and laid her head against my shoulder.

"Are you excited?" I asked as I put my arm around her.

"Yeah. It'll just be weird being away from home for that long."

"You'll be having so much fun you won't have time to think about home," I said reassuringly.

"I hope Jonas's family will like me."

"Why wouldn't they?"

Hannah's shoulders shrugged limply. "I don't know."

"I know what you mean, though. It's natural to care how your partner's parents feel about you." I sucked in my cheeks before my face brightened with an idea. "If you ever end up in England, you're always welcome to stay with my parents. They'd probably love some help in the garden."

Hannah sniffed and smiled. "That'd be nice."

We sat quietly for a moment, arms around each other.

"Remember to hold your money in different places instead of just your wallet," I said.

"Okay."

"And trust your gut, but also remember that strangers can be kind."

Hannah nodded and then sat up and wiped her nose. "I wrote you something." She stood up to take something from her drawer and handed a folded piece of paper to me. "You don't have to read it right away. Maybe read it on the plane."

I took the folded note carefully and then reached inside my pocket with a smile. "I wrote you something too. Definitely don't read it just yet."

We shared a knowing smile, and the room was filled with bittersweet silence.

The next morning, Harry took his time getting ready. I stood with my arms folded by the door, tired of waiting for him. The goodbyes with his family felt rushed, but I wondered if it was better this way. I concealed my relief when I learned Ruth was out running errands. Peter's eyes were sad, Jonas's arms were strong and comforting, and Hannah's mouth wobbled. I gathered up my holdall and gave a final look back at the barn with a lump in my throat.

And so began the familiar journey to the airport. A journey I had taken many times before with similar emotions, only this time it was different. This time it was final. A sense of realization began to set in that left me panicked. I wiped my nostalgic tears from my eyes and took a deep breath, and then I felt calm again.

Harry and I walked quietly towards the security doors before I stopped and turned to face him. I hadn't given much thought to what I wanted to say to him in our parting moments, and my mind suddenly felt blank. Six years, and then blankness.

"Well, thanks for everything," I said with a shrug. "We made a lot of fun memories together."

Harry smiled fondly. "We did. I won't forget them."

I looked down and cleared my throat. "Good luck with your first week back at school."

"Thank you. Final year, it's going to be really hard."

I shook my head with a smile. "Just like you always say."

"I hope you have a good trip."

I nodded, and when our eyes met, he bent down to kiss me. I opened my eyes to see him smiling down at me tenderly.

I stepped back and hitched my bag higher up my shoulder. "Well, see you."

Harry grabbed my hand as I turned, and I looked back with surprise to see him smiling.

"Try not to weigh others against me too much, okay? And try to be more selfish."

With the sight of his encouraging smile came a rush of revulsion. The hammer hit home with a resounding confirmation that leaving him was the best thing I could do for myself. Without saying a word, I turned around and walked away.

Harry's final words were still repeating in my head when a female screening officer called me forward and looked me up and down.

"So, you'll be around eighteen, nineteen, right?" she asked, a quizzical expression on her face.

"I'm twenty-five," I replied.

The woman laughed with embarrassment. "That used to happen to me too. Take it as a compliment."

I walked through the scanner and retrieved my bag, and this time my words repeated in my head. *I'm twenty-five. I'm twenty-five, and I'm free.*

I took a seat in the waiting area, and shortly after, my phone vibrated to show a text from Will. I read it with a fresh feeling of excitement, and thoughts of Harry promptly left my mind.

PART THREE

THIRTY

Huge mushroom clouds of smoke hung motionless in the air as the plane glided over the mountains of Washington State. An eerie reminder of the summer's wildfires. After we crossed the smoky Rocky Mountains, we descended through the haze, and I looked out of my window to see bare, brown, flat land. In the distance loomed the skyscrapers of Calgary, and the sun sparkled off the winding Bow River. I counted the swimming pools that were dotted through the suburbs.

The prairie heat hit me as soon as I stepped out of the airport and walked towards the bus stop. I got off in the middle of the city, grateful for some shade offered by the tall buildings. Taxis beeped, trains hissed, and people bustled about as I walked in search of my hostel. It was strange to think that such a busy city could be located in the middle of nowhere.

After finally locating my hostel, I dumped my bag in the small dorm and changed out of my sweaty t-shirt before walking back through the town. I passed through a park where a large Zumba dance event was being held and crossed a rainbow-coloured crosswalk down a main street where glamorously dressed people sat chatting on bar patios. I had interviewed a few people who had moved to Victoria from Calgary after losing jobs in the oil industry, and all of them had complained about Victoria's lower salaries. I felt like I was walking through a strip in Canadian Las Vegas. In my khaki shorts and thrifted t-shirt, I looked out of place amongst the women with heels and Botox.

Guided by my city map, I located a grocery store and ate my snacks on a bench that overlooked the river. The sun was a striking orange-pink against the smoke. Laughter and chatter sounded from the pebble river bank, where a group sat listening to music and drinking. Sometimes such sights would give me a pang of loneliness during a solo trip, but today I felt grateful to be alone in a new place where I knew no one.

Will called me in the evening to arrange a time and place to meet on Monday. Now officially single, I let myself feel even more excited. Combined with the itchy sheets and heat of the room, the anticipation made it hard to fall asleep. I let my feet slip out of the covers to find cool air just as two girls burst through the door in a fit of giggles. I rolled over and remembered my last trip, when I'd told myself I wouldn't sleep in shared hostel dorms anymore.

After a morning of walking around the city, I arrived at the Greyhound depot early the next afternoon to find the staff asking customers to form a line to have their carry-on bags searched. Operations seemed a lot more formal since the days of 2011 when nobody had checked what I was bringing on board.

I took a seat near the window and watched as the view changed from glass buildings to suburbs to open land. Suddenly overcome with tiredness, I let my head tilt to the side as I listened to the old man behind me speaking to his fellow passenger. A banging of my head against the window woke me with a start, and I opened my eyes to see a display of mountains, grey with ash. A sense of déjà vu suddenly crept in as I recalled seeing this same view from the bus six years ago.

Banff town was packed with tourists enjoying the Labour Day weekend. As I slowly trudged through the crowds, a lady walking on the opposite side of the road with a man caught my eye. I recognized her as a girl that had been in the year above me at school. I looked away with surprise and noticed a fast-food restaurant that hadn't been there when I last visited.

I had booked a room in the same hostel I stayed in in 2011, across the bridge and on a hill. Thankfully, my dorm was just as quiet as it had been six years ago, with only a timid girl for a dorm-mate.

My plan for the afternoon was to hike up Tunnel Mountain. The trail was busy with people in designer brands who didn't give a greeting or say thanks when I was forced to move to the side to make room for them. The summit looked down on the town below, framed by distant mountains with a beam of sunlight streaking through the clouds above them. A group of girls in crop tops asked me to take a photo of them, then sat reviewing the result and debating which filter would look best for the social media post.

I walked back down the trail feeling disappointed. Banff had become so commercialized since my last visit. I supported making travel more accessible, but something seemed to have been lost in the process.

I bought food from the crowded grocery store and ate my salad in the hostel kitchen, where I chatted with a sweet boy from Italy. He had been travelling for a few months, and his eyes watered when he talked about his grandma.

In the dark of the hostel dorm, I thought about the next day, conjuring up scenarios in my mind. My phone buzzed through the night with texts from Will while he was at his friend's party. The fact that I was on his mind gave me a hope that countered the voice in my head, warning that the situation might change. *At least there would be a bed for me here,* I thought as I looked into the darkness. I ran my hands over my legs and wondered if I should have bought a razor from the store for the tiny prickles that had started to bud.

I woke early and pulled on my trainers to go for a run. The air smelled sweet with pine as I jogged along the riverside, casting a smile at the rock I'd sat on years earlier to watch the water go by. The trail led to a waterfall, with only a couple of other tourists around. I welcomed the peace and quiet.

My dorm-mate was awake when I returned to the hostel. Her eyes had been glued to a laptop every time I had seen her. I showered and brushed my teeth and turned in the mirror to examine the skin on my back. To my relief, it looked clear.

After checking out, I read in a public garden until a group of loud and obnoxious American tourists compelled me to move away from the bench I'd been sitting on. I crossed the bridge and took a seat in the park. My hands occasionally reached for my phone, still expecting the text from Will telling me he wouldn't be able to make it after all. That message never came, only one that told me he'd be in Canmore by five o'clock.

I put the phone away and looked contentedly towards the water, thinking about all that had happened in the six years since I had last sat in this park: meeting Harry, university, romantic flings, travel, jobs, moving to Canada, breaking up with Harry.

As I returned to my book, a man approached and sat down a few feet away. I returned his hello and politely answered when he asked me what I was reading, and then where I was from, and what I was doing in Banff. After a lingering look came the question of whether I'd like to go for coffee. I felt myself stiffen awkwardly at the unexpected proposal, not wanting to say yes but not wanting to appear rude.

"Thanks, but I'm happy sitting here with my book," I said with a smile before lowering my eyes.

"Are you sure?"

"Yes." I kept my eyes on the page.

"You don't want a break from reading?"

"No."

The man sniggered. "Do you have a boyfriend or something?"

My jaw clenched with irritation at the assumption that always seemed to explain why a female might not want to be pursued by a man.

"I'm happy staying where I am, alone," I said, feeling my voice grow firm.

I felt the man's eyes continue to look at me as I studied my book. Then with another snort of offence, he stood up and slouched off, leaving me feeling more shame-faced than he should have.

The bus for Canmore arrived late. As I dropped coins into the farebox, I felt sad that I was glad to be leaving Banff, a place I had previously found so exciting in its novelty.

Will and I had agreed to meet in the parking lot outside a grocery store. I leant against a wall and scanned the cars intently while trying to look casual. As a silver truck pulled in, I swallowed in anticipation, only to realize it wasn't him.

When the text came that he was ten minutes away, I shifted my feet with a fresh wave of butterflies. Suddenly, it felt real. More trucks pulled into the parking lot that turned out not to be him. I folded my arms and slouched back further against the wall, conscious of the looks I was receiving in my short denim shorts and baggy white t-shirt with a few small tears in the shoulder.

Another silver truck, then an opening window, then Will's face, and a rush of blood to my skin. I took a breath and approached his car as he pulled into a parking space.

"Is it a law in Alberta that everyone has to own a truck?" I asked teasingly as he stepped out of the door.

"Pretty much." Even more tanned than when I had first met him, he ruffled the top of his freshly cut hair, the front curls lightened by time outside in the sun. "I hope you weren't waiting too long."

"No, it was okay, though I'm pretty sure a few people thought I was a prostitute." I picked at my shirt with a laugh and felt a wobble in my knees when I noticed him gazing down at my legs.

"Is there something you didn't tell me?" he asked with feigned suspicion.

I stepped forward. "Well, good to see you again." We embraced lightly with a hint of shyness.

"You pack light," he remarked, nodding at my holdall with an impressed face.

In the trunk was some bedding and a cooler with food Will had packed for us.

"Thanks for driving all this way," I said as I buckled my seatbelt. "You must be pretty tired."

"It's all good." Will reversed out of the space and pulled onto the road, one hand on the wheel and the other elbow resting on the door ledge. When he pulled up at a gas station, I jumped out to buy a map.

"So, where are we going?" I asked as I opened it up next to him.

At his question of whether I'd been to Waterton Lakes National Park, I studied the map and saw it was situated right next to the border with Montana. As it was a few hours away, Will said we'd have to camp somewhere else for the night.

I traced my finger down a line on the map that indicated a small road. "What about this? It looks like there are some provincial parks down there."

Will leaned close enough that I could hear his calm breathing. "Sure, let's do that."

We set off again and talked about his trip, his friend's party, my time in Banff and the disappointments it had involved. When I told him about the man in the park, he smiled.

"I'm not excusing him, but I will say that approaching girls is scary. Look at me as an example—I resorted to online stalker tactics."

"I suppose." I looked out of the window at the pink sky. "And now I'm in a car with you heading into the middle of nowhere."

We exchanged a quiet smile before turning off onto the smaller road. It soon turned into a gravel track and went on to wind past a reservoir. A full moon was rising as we entered dense forest. Suddenly, a movement along the side of the road caught my eye. Will braked and slowly turned around, and in the glow of the headlights, a moose walked calmly past the car, unfazed by our presence. I admired its huge frame with awe.

We continued slowly along the road before eventually turning into the parking lot of a provincial park. No other cars were in sight. I stepped out of the truck and shivered as crickets chatted from secret places. The sky was dotted with stars, and I could just decipher the dark outline of the surrounding mountains.

Will and I moved around each other comfortably—him moving things into the middle seat, me finding clothes to sleep in, sharing toothpaste. My legs dangled outside of the passenger door as I pulled off my t-shirt and bra. As my hair fell around my shoulders, the driver door behind me opened. My exposed skin tingled with the sense that Will's eyes were on my back. I climbed into the back of the truck and into my sleeping bag. Will wore a loose shirt as he hung a torch from the ceiling. It shone a soft light over us as we spoke.

"My nose sometimes makes whistling noises when I sleep, just so you know," I said.

Will chuckled. "Why?"

"It's bent, from when I broke it. That's why it's all arched and gross."

"I've never noticed." Will turned to study me.

I covered my nose with my hand and turned to face him with a sheepish smile. "You just haven't seen me enough."

Our eyes met, and the sleeping bags rustled as we shifted slightly closer. Will leaned on his side, resting the side of his face against his forearm so he could look at me.

"How did you break your nose?" he asked.

I rolled over to mirror his position. "When I was ten, I fell off a horse and landed on my face."

"Jesus, that's terrible." Will bit his lip to stop smiling.

I reached over and punched him gently on the arm. "Why are you laughing?"

"I'm just trying to picture the scene."

I smiled with recollection. "The worst thing was having to go to school the next day. I had a black eye and this huge swollen nose across my face, and my teacher decided to point me out in front of the entire class and ask what happened."

Will's amused face straightened. "I honestly wouldn't have thought you'd broken it."

"What about you?" I asked playfully. "Any deep insecurities you have that you'd like to share?"

"I have funny ears."

"I like your ears."

"They're big."

"You know what they say about big ears."

"What's that?"

"Big listeners."

We shared a frisky smile as our eyes locked together once more. Another shift closer.

"Have you ever broken anything?" I asked.

"Just a broken heart."

"Oh, Will!" My hand brushed his arm with mock pity.

He smiled. "I'm kidding, sort of. But no, I just had a few soft tissue injuries when I played soccer."

"Do you ever regret stopping?"

Will stretched his arm out in thought, his hand now close to my head. "Sometimes I'll think about it. For a long time, I wanted to be professional. But overall, not really. I've met some great people through running, especially since I moved to Victoria."

Our eyes met, and I realized the bottoms of our sleeping bags were now touching so that I could feel his feet. A pounding began in my chest.

"Well, I'm glad you came to Victoria," I said softly.

Will's eyes studied my face yearningly, and then a ripple ran through me as he leaned forward and kissed me gently.

After a moment, he pulled back, suddenly uncertain.

"Is this okay? You just got out of a relationship."

I took a breath. "It's okay. I've been thinking about you. It's just weird timing."

"Yeah, I know." Will moved back towards his mat humbly.

I swallowed, still buzzing inside from the feeling of his lips. "I obviously like you. I'm just wary of rushing things."

"I understand. It's totally your call."

I glanced across at him hesitantly as we lay back down on our mats in our small space in a secluded park in the middle of the mountains. Will began to speak, and I leaned on my side and watched him closely, studying his long eyelashes, the curls of his hair, the movement of his lips as he smiled. Under the gentle glow of the lamp, I watched him with a deepening sense of trust and a developing sense of desire.

As his eyes met mine once more, I released myself from any restrictions and tenderly pulled him towards me. The skin on his back was warm and smooth as I removed his shirt and pulled him closer. We explored each other slowly and curiously until we paused to look at each other and acknowledged our shared wish.

Afterwards, I lay on my side again with my head resting relaxed on his arm, basking in the increased level of comfortability between us. We talked about our thoughts towards the other when we first met, the signs and statements that had made us think the other was interested, the way Zoe had suggested Will look me up online to make contact.

The truck was warm from the mingling of bodies. Will opened the door for air and stepped towards the bushes. With a smile, I watched his bare body, just visible in the moonlight.

"Uh...Will?" I called, feigning fear in my voice. "There's a bear."

Will stopped in his tracks and slowly turned his head to scan the area. I burst into laughter and then lay back down with a smile that carried me into my sleep.

Morning light shone through the windows as I woke to the sight of Will sleeping peacefully. The brief sense of surrealness was followed by warm contentment. As we dressed, I looked around for my hair tie that had been removed at some point during the slow dance of the night. I had forgotten to bring another with me, and my hair fell messily over my shoulders as I stood eating a breakfast of fruit and bagels and talking about university.

"Sometimes it doesn't seem worth working so hard for a piece of paper that doesn't guarantee you anything," said Will as he sat on the ledge of the trunk.

"So many people are doing degrees these days that they're not as valuable as they used to be," I agreed. "I enjoyed my degree, and I learned a lot, but I wouldn't say it helped me get into my field."

Will looked up at me with interest. "You're pretty up there, eh? With your job?"

I looked down and dug my shoe into the gravel. "I don't know about that. Quite a few of the people I interview don't take me seriously. I think they see me and assume I'm a young dumb blonde who doesn't have enough experience to help them."

"You're smart. I'm sure they soon realize that."

"I don't know if I even am that smart, to be honest," I sniggered. "I just worked hard in school, and teachers seemed to like me. I was a bit of a teacher's pet, I guess." I looked at Will with a scrutinizing smile. "What were you like in school?"

Will scratched his head and shrugged. "I was pretty good, actually. But there was this one teacher who just seemed to really dislike me, and I don't know why. She always seemed to single me out when people were talking."

"Maybe she secretly fancied you," I said with a smile.

"I really hope not," replied Will, wrinkling his nose. "Do you think you'll stay in your job for a while?"

"I'm not sure. I change my mind about what I want. Sometimes I like the idea of moving up and having more responsibilities, and other times I don't really care and just want to drive around the world in a campervan listening to old music." I looked at the ground in thought. "Sometimes I get Imposter Syndrome and feel like I don't deserve to be where I am, or I wonder how I came to be where I am." I gazed around at the mountains. "Like here. How did I come to be here?"

"You agreed to meet up with some weird guy from a run group."

"No regrets so far." I looked down bashfully at my tangerine and then glanced up to see Will regarding me with a soft smile.

We headed south towards Waterton Lakes. The sky grew hazier, and I began to hum the tune of a country folk song as I looked at the hot dusty road before us.

It was around one o'clock when we arrived in the park to the sight of a large lake flanked by mountains. I took in the view quietly, entranced. The view of a grand hotel atop a hill reminded me of Scotland, but the haze and the dry trees on the other side of the lake made me think of Africa.

There were only two other cars in the parking lot as we stopped at the small tourist office to learn which trails were open. The friendly lady on the front desk handed me a few elastic bands for my hair. As we studied a glass case showing a map of the park, a young girl approached us with a bashful smile and handed me a scrap piece of paper with a stamp on it that bore the park's name. I thanked her with surprise and placed it carefully in my pocket.

Many trails were closed due to smoke, but Will knew one that was partially open. When he asked how long I felt like hiking for, I said I was happy with anything. We drove back out of town and pulled over on the side of the road across from a trail entrance with warning tape stretched between two trees. I handed Will a few band-aids as he packed a small bag with our bottles and snacks. Then I looked at my camera in my hands, and after a moment's thought, put it back in the car.

We followed the trail across flat land, the grass parched yellow from the summer sun. The subject of past relationships arose, and I listened intently as Will talked about his ex-girlfriend. He shared relatable stories of uncomfortable family dinners and personality changes. There was a slight bitterness in his voice as he recalled the unexpected developments that led to their breakup the previous summer.

"That must have been hard," I said sympathetically.

"The whole relationship was hard, to be honest," he said. "She had depression, and it showed itself many times."

I watched my feet walk over the dry grass. "It seems to be on the rise, the number of people being diagnosed with it. Anxiety too. Makes you wonder if it's always been this common and just wasn't understood before, or if people are just getting worse at dealing with challenges."

Will looked down and scratched his neck. "Yeah, I don't know what it is."

Eventually, the path left the wide field to join a narrow trail that led up through a forest.

"You ran up here?" I asked in amazement as we climbed up a steepening switchback.

"Yup," replied Will from behind me. "Did another kilometre before seeing some bear cubs and deciding to turn back."

I closed my inhaling mouth and scanned the bushes suspiciously.

"Now I know why the guy is always behind the girl when I see couples hiking," remarked Will a moment later.

"So he can look at her butt?"

"Okay, yes, that. But also, because he's carrying all the water."

"I can carry it for a bit?"

"No, no. I'm only kidding."

After an hour of elevation, we left the forest and came to a clearing with a small stream. I bent down to splash my face with the cool water.

"Let me know if you want to head back," said Will.

I shook my head. "No, I'm good. How much farther until the trail closes?"

Will scratched his ear with a sheepish smile. "We already passed it. The fire is on the other side of the valley. It won't reach here."

I looked around in surprise, and my eyes fell on a mountain that rose up formidably in the distance.

"Are we going up there?" I asked in wonder.

"Only if you want to. I've been there before, so really, it's up to you."

I looked up at the grey mountain again. Suddenly, the voices of caution disappeared, and I nodded with a surge of resolve. "Yes, let's go."

"Would you like a snack first?" he asked. "Some water?"

"Nope." I set off resolutely along the trail.

The trail grew even steeper as it approached the mountain, and the terrain turned into sand and loose pieces of rock. I stopped to rest my aching calves and looked up at the mountain with a groan. "It's so far away."

"Honestly, we don't have to go up," insisted Will. "I won't be upset if you'd rather go back."

"No," I said stubbornly. "I want to do it. We've come this far. There's no point giving up now."

I blew out in determination and continued past him as a fond smile formed on his lips. The summit seemed elusively far as we began to scale the side of the mountain. Will led the way. My breath came out unevenly as I clambered over jagged rocks on all fours, sometimes slipping on the uneven surface. I ignored the protesting burning in my thighs and forced them up another step, and another. At long last, I pulled myself up onto a rock ledge and bent over with a sigh of relief that soon mixed with accomplishment.

When I straightened up, thick clouds mixed with smoke swirled around us. I looked down to see puffy beds of white-grey below us, concealing a sight of jagged peaks and turquoise lakes.

"Well, the view was worth the effort at least," I joked. I brushed loose strands of hair off my sweaty neck and sat down to rest my numb legs.

Will opened his bag and looked at me seriously. "Now, will you eat something?"

I took an apple from him gratefully and looked around at the wispy clouds. A chill suddenly shot through my legs. Will sat down in front of me and laid his head back against my stomach. I stroked his hair gently as we sat in comfortable silence, two tiny figures at the top of a huge mountain, covered in a grey cloak of invisibility.

My legs were shaky with fatigue as we began the steep descent back down the mountain. I darted unsteadily over some loose rocks and scurried precariously down the final section before ending with a giggle by Will's waiting side.

"This is definitely one of the craziest hikes I've ever done," I said cheerfully as we passed the stream. "Thanks for encouraging me."

At the feeling of a small stone pricking my foot, I stopped and bent to remove my shoe. When I straightened up, Will was looking at me intently. It was an expression I hadn't seen on him before. His blue eyes carried a look of longing that was infused with a hint of what seemed like sadness. I felt my cheeks tingle under his gaze.

"What is it?" I asked innocently, my voice soft.

Without saying a word, he stepped forward and kissed me. I opened my eyes in a daze to see him looking at me with silent pensiveness once more. Then he turned and continued down the trail.

Through the forest, we shared funny stories and quizzed each other on various preferences. Swift movements in the bushes would catch my attention.

"I'm glad the bears waited for us to complete most of the trail before eating us," I said.

"They won't like you," replied Will from behind me. "Not enough fat."

"Well, that's reassuring." My face straightened. "But seriously, what do we do if we actually see one?"

"We die."

"Oh, good."

Will's tone grew serious. "No, if one comes, you would run while I distracted it."

I snapped my head around in alarm to face him. "I wouldn't do that! I couldn't."

A silence fell around us as our eyes connected, conveying an unspoken message. Then the view behind him caught my eye and left me stunned.

"Is that where we were?"

Will followed my gaze towards a grey mountain that towered high above us in the distance, its summit hidden by swirls of cloud. "Sure is."

I continued to stare at the view with bewilderment.

It was dark by the time we reached the flat terrain. The stars in the sky were blanketed by smoke, and a flashlight guided us along the open land.

"Are you cold?" asked Will.

"I'm okay."

We walked quietly across the grass, only able to see a few feet in front of us. Suddenly, a wailing sound pierced the air. I looked around in trepidation, unsure where it was coming from. The sound repeated itself, but this time there was something majestic about the pining of it.

"Elk bugles," said Will. "Mating season."

"It's beautiful." I rubbed my arms and looked into the dark, wondering how close they were.

"You are cold," said Will with concern. He pulled a light jacket from his bag and gave it to me.

We continued on through the field, surrounded by the sounds of creatures great and small. My body was tired, but my eyes and ears were alert. As a child growing up in an isolated valley, I had been quite scared of the dark. In Will's company, I felt safe, but a part of me also resolved to put on a brave face for both of us.

"We can't be that far," I said optimistically, noticing the tiny red taillights of a car in the distance.

With a shiver down my back, I took Will's hand, and we walked quietly as the grass wisped under our weary feet. The lights in the distance seemed to remain far away, but finally, we emerged from a patch of trees to see the truck waiting for us.

"We made it." I wrapped my arms around Will with a contented sigh. "How far do you think that was?"

"About twenty kilometres."

I sat back on the trunk's ledge and smiled. "Just a casual hike, then."

"You were pretty determined," said Will with an impressed tone.

"I don't like to give up on things."

We sat sharing some bread over a pot of hummus before driving back into the town to sneak into the campground showers. Layers of dust, dirt and sweat poured off me. As I watched the murky water swirl down the drain, something told me that I would never forget this particular day.

It was eleven o'clock when we drove back to the trail entrance to avoid receiving a parking fine. My legs ached with fatigue, and I let my head hang lazily down in front of me. Will gently caressed my hair as he drove, his fingers working their way down to massage my neck. We curled up in our sleeping bags quietly, only to reawaken and move closer with curiosity.

Afterwards, we lay looking out of the window. The smoky clouds parted to show the new moon, and I instinctively covered my eyes.

"No looking at a new moon through glass," I said. "My mum always told me it was bad luck."

Will opened the door, and we sat up listening to the sounds of the night, his hand in mine. I turned to observe his face, and a warm feeling swelled up through my body.

"You're really attractive."

Will smiled to himself and held my hand a little tighter. "So are you. From every angle."

In the morning, I woke with the sombre awareness we would soon be parting. Then came a brooding wave of menstrual cramps. I emerged from the public washroom in the town and went to sit with Will in the deck chairs at the edge of the lake. Smoke continued to linger down the valley.

"This would be a nice place to work in the summer," said Will thoughtfully. "Working outside, hiking and swimming on days off."

I watched the water lap gently against the shore with a conflicted feeling as I pondered returning to work the next day.

We went for breakfast at a café with a rustic patio and a sign on the door noting an evacuation alert. As he stared at his empty plate, Will's suggestion of dessert filled me with comfort. A judgment-free zone, at last. A friendly Australian waitress brought us two plates with a large slice of chocolate cake and fruit pie.

With time to spare before my flight, Will pulled the truck off the highway and into a small park that overlooked a reservoir. The air was dry and the sky even more dense with smoke. Undeterred by the heat, we dozed in the back with arms draped comfortably over the other. Despite my own physical restrictions, I wanted to pleasure him, and his reaction spurred me on. Afterwards, we lay quietly, Will's chest rising and falling quickly.

Along the highway, I slumped in my seat, suddenly filled with shame.

"What are you thinking?" asked Will.

"That I've just cheapened our time together, and that that moment will be your main memory of me."

Will's hand reached over and rubbed my leg. "That's not true."

I looked out of the window with my chin in my hand. Suddenly, I smiled. "This definitely wasn't how I assumed the trip would go."

"Same here," said Will with a snigger. "My friends at the party were a little confused when I told them I was meeting up with a girl the next day."

I sat up in my seat. "Just so you know, it wasn't my plan for us to—"

"I know, and I don't judge you for the timing of it, if that's what you're wondering."

"Okay." I rested my head back and swallowed. "And I want you to know that it's never been my plan to use you as a band-aid."

"I know."

The sign ahead indicated the Calgary airport. I tried to ignore the sinking feeling in my stomach, the regret that I hadn't booked another day off work.

"Thanks for showing me Waterton; I really liked it," I said as we followed the exit. "This has been really fun."

"It has." Will scanned the signs and pulled into the departure terminal. "Do you want me to walk you inside?"

"No, it's okay. You'll just have to pay for parking."

Will brought the truck to a halt and turned off the engine before getting out and walking to my door.

I looked at him with wavering eyes, suddenly shy. "Well, keep in touch."

Will smiled fondly. "Do you really think I'm going to stop talking to you?"

I let my face fall into his chest and uttered a pathetic laugh. "I don't know."

He rubbed my arms reassuringly. "I'll talk to you soon."

We kissed, and after sharing a final knowing smile, I walked towards the doors with a bittersweet tugging in my chest.

THIRTY-ONE

There was a chill in the air as I stepped out of Victoria Airport's doors and walked towards the bus stop. No more airport collections from now on. A cloud of fatigue swamped me as I stepped inside the new apartment. After saying hello to Connor, I closed my bedroom door and stared dismally at the unpacked bags on my floor.

My spirits lifted when I saw a text from Will, asking if I had got home safely. I sat on the floor against my unmade bed and composed a message.

> Sorry for being all pessimistic at the airport. I really enjoyed the time with you, and I want you to know that I do trust you.

His reply came a few hours later as I lay new sheets on the bed.

> I feel like I didn't make it clear how much I enjoyed and appreciated the time with you.

A smile stuck to my face as I replied.

> Seeing you was a definite highlight of the trip. I've really appreciated your contact over the past few weeks. You've helped me feel rejuvenated.

In the morning, I woke to his reply.

> I'm happy to hear that. I pretty much feel the same way. I think you and I are a pretty good duo. It's not hard to keep you smiling, and it's equally not hard to keep smiling around you.

The words ignited a light show inside me, and I could feel the colours shine out of my skin. When Will gave me his address for sending postcards, I typed it into a search engine and saw a square white house on the corner of a leafy street. I smiled at the thought of him sitting under its grey roof, thinking of me, just as I was sitting here, thinking of him.

My new bus stop was on the same route as my previous address. It stood across the road from a white wooden house with a wild deer grazing in the front yard. I recognized the pretty woman that stepped out of its front door from previous bus journeys. The bus pulled up soon after. I stepped on with a lack of inspiration to return to a work routine.

As the morning went on, my mood dimmed with the awareness I wouldn't see Will for a few months. A procrastinating browse of the internet showed a headline that mentioned wildfires in Waterton Lakes National Park. I immediately clicked the link. The page showed a photo of the iconic Prince of Wales hotel, with a caption noting that firefighters had managed to prevent the fires from reaching the building. I read that town residents had been ordered to evacuate later in the day on which Will and I had left, as flames crept closer to the town. Another photo showed a burnt-out space. I slumped forward in dismay when I learned it was the tourist office. There was something eerie about the memory of standing inside it only two days earlier, looking at maps and asking for an elastic band.

I had been so caught up in the experience of Waterton and Will that I had forgotten to take pictures from the park. I had no physical proof to look back on to remind me of the calm lake, the smoky mountains, the deep valley. The only souvenir I had from my visit was the small piece of paper handed to me by a little girl in an office that had since been destroyed by the cruel force of nature. It was almost like the visit had never really happened and had simply been a dream.

The unsettled feeling remained with me as Jenna came into my office to hand me the resume of the afternoon's interviewee—a chartered accountant with extensive experience in various industries. I pushed thoughts of the park out of my mind and introduced myself to the man confidently. His arrogant demeanour quickly showed itself as he spoke about his experience and salary expectations. My questions drew brief responses and belittling expressions that made me feel stupid. As I explained the registration paperwork to him, he asked a tax-related question that confused me. After he repeated the question, the terminology he had used continued to whirr around my head helplessly. I took a breath and started to speak.

"That's not what I asked," the man cut across impatiently.

My throat began to tighten under the pressure of his gaze. "I'm sorry, I don't think I understand your question."

"I don't think you do either," he said sharply, his eyes fixed rigidly on mine.

Feeling my face redden, I swallowed uncomfortably and cleared my throat. "I'm afraid I don't have much knowledge of that area, so I'll ask our payroll administrator to look into it for you."

The man nodded with silent disapproval. His parting handshake squeezed the confidence out of me, and I sank back into my seat with a pounding in my temple. He had mentioned helping his daughter with the finances of her new business. She was probably around my age, and I wondered if he spoke to her with the same crushing contempt.

At home, I dumped my bag on the floor and collapsed on my bed, wishing it was already the weekend. A glance at my phone revealed that Joey and Liz had both seen the message I had sent proposing plans but hadn't replied. I stared glumly at the ceiling until the ringing of my phone broke the moping silence. With pleasant surprise, I saw Will's name.

"I wanted to call and see how you're settling into your new place," he said.

Hearing his voice over the phone had a different feel to it now that we had been intimate with each other. A different kind of excitement and comfort.

"It's okay. I still need to buy some furniture and decorate. I'll probably feel more settled then."

"Are you okay?" he asked with concern. "You sound a little down."

"Sorry, I'm just feeling a little sorry for myself. I interviewed this man today who was really intense. He made me feel kind of useless."

"I'm sorry to hear that." Will's voice perked up jokily. "But hey, you control his destiny, right?"

I smiled. "I guess you're sort of right. I've just never been that good at dealing with strong personalities like that."

When he asked about my weekend plans, my shoulders slumped. "I have a feeling my friends made plans with Harry and don't want to tell me."

"That's tough. I'm sorry."

His voice was warm and caring. I closed my eyes and remembered the feel of his hand massaging the back of my neck.

"Did you see the news about Waterton? The fires reached the town and burnt down the poor tourist office."

"I did. Sounds like we got out just in time."

I felt a sudden pinch of sadness. "How's being home?"

"I can't wait to leave," he said with a dry laugh. "I'm just unsure whether I should go to the States or New Zealand."

"New Zealand is beautiful, but going to the States would be cheaper, I guess." I played with my bottom lip. "How long do you think you'd go for?"

"I don't think I'll be back until February, just because of the delay getting there and race schedules being pushed back."

My stomach somersaulted with disappointment. "I'm excited for you."

After the call, I lay back with a sigh, wrestling with the emotions of being happy for Will but unhappy for myself. For the past several months, a firm voice in my head had vowed that I wouldn't do a long-distance relationship again. Now the voice was weakening. I closed my eyes and told myself that I wasn't in an official relationship, that I should be single for a while and use Will's time away to focus on myself. But I had caught a bug, and it was starting to show symptoms.

From my bag, I retrieved the postcard I had bought on the way home. Slightly faded, the photo showed the fins of orca whales as they surfaced from the ocean against a misty background of evergreen trees. The scene reminded me of a song, and I began to play it. As I listened, my mind created an image of a sailor returning home through the fog. At the soaring cry of the chorus, I closed my eyes and let the feeling of longing fill me up.

Joey and Liz responded to my group message on Saturday morning. As I climbed into Joey's truck, I resisted the urge to ask what they had done on Friday evening and who with. In the pizzeria, I watched Liz tease Joey about the pretty waitress giving him glances. They had become a lot more comfortable around each other since a few months earlier when I helped initiate their friendship. A friendship they would likely develop more around Harry while I was absent. The silence surrounding any discussion of Harry was glaringly obvious, and its seeming impact on limiting topics of conversation made me feel disconnected.

Connor was out when I got home. I carried my bag of dirty clothes down to the laundry room only to discover I didn't have the right change for the machines. I returned upstairs in defeat, where the sadness of my bare room called for my attention. On the wall I hung my thrifted painting of jagged grey mountains above a yellow meadow. The image reminded me of the flat, open field in Waterton and the dusty mountains rising in the distance. Then I remembered Will kissing me and the way he had looked at me, his eyes conveying a feeling I still couldn't identify. The more I pictured it, the more it seemed like a look of vulnerability.

The next morning was sunny and crisp as I got up early and ran down to Willow's Beach. Dogs of all colours and sizes tore across the long stretch of sand, splashing into the water to collect sticks and sniffing between pieces of driftwood on the shore. I followed the path around Cattle Point and down towards Cadboro Bay, turning back when I reached a viewing point that showed boats bobbing gently in the harbour. I hadn't felt this fit in a few years, and I climbed the stairs back to my apartment with an uplifted feeling.

As I took off my shoes, I remembered Tyler telling the run group about a race Tracks was hosting at Sooke Potholes. A look on the website showed it was taking place the coming Sunday. Feeling inspired, I paid the registration fee for the 5k and read the confirmation email with excitement.

I walked into the office on Monday morning with a bounce in my step. The upcoming race had filled me with a motivation to show my strength. I sat down at my desk and retrieved Friday's interview notes from my drawer. Will's words ran through my head as I read them again. Unwilling to reward rude behaviour, I wrote *Not for our agency* at the bottom and filed them away.

When Will called me that evening, my mood only lifted higher. A firework seemed to go off inside me every time my phone rang with his name. Each call was an opportunity to let the other into our life a little more. The level of trust Will showed in sharing personal details about himself with me stirred both satisfaction and surprise. There was something refreshingly authentic about his willingness to show vulnerability. There was no arrogance to him. On the contrary, he seemed almost too self-deprecating.

I welcomed Will's readiness to let me in with gratitude, but the novelty of it and the unofficial status of our relationship led me to second-guess myself. When the call ended, and I ran through our conversation, I found myself wondering if my follow-up questions had stepped into inappropriate territory, if my attempts to show support might have made him uncomfortable. I didn't want him to think I viewed him as a boyfriend I couldn't claim he was. I didn't want to be seen as too attached. I didn't want that humiliation again of realizing I had misunderstood someone's feelings and intentions.

The next morning, I dipped between work emails and my personal inbox to write to Will. I felt a need to let him know that I cared about him but was wary of coming off too strong.

Just as the email left my outbox, I received a jokey text from him about a separate topic. I closed my eyes as embarrassment flooded through me. *Why? Why must you start over-thinking things every time?*

I stepped through my bedroom door to find a missed call from Will and a text asking me to call him. I dialled his number with glum expectation.

"So, I read your email," he said with a hint of amusement in his voice.

I rubbed my eyebrows and scrunched up my face. "I'm sorry, it was silly."

"You stress too much. You don't need to worry."

"I've had a few guys go cold on me," I said feebly.

"I know, but I'm not going to do that."

My shoulders sank with relief. "Okay. I just got a little worried you might feel uncomfortable."

"Your emotional openness doesn't scare me," he said warmly. "I'm not going to cut you loose."

"Okay." I swallowed. "Your emotional openness doesn't scare me, either."

The stubborn sense of skepticism seemed to dislodge slightly from its place on the shelf as I put the phone down. It appeared that I, too, needed to have less self-criticism.

THIRTY-TWO

My alarm sounded early on Sunday. I pulled some trousers over my shorts and put my hair in a high ponytail. Connor had left a piece of paper with *Good luck, Sara!* in front of the door.

A group of people were gathered outside of Tracks, ready to take the shuttle bus to Sooke. One man, tall and lanky, spoke loudly about his training schedule to a short, stocky woman who was in the military. They chatted throughout the whole journey about nutrition, race preparation, and race time goals. As the bus approached Sooke, the man pulled off his tracksuit top to reveal a cycling jersey in Canada's colours with his name on the back. I smiled to myself in amusement. A bald man who looked to be in his early thirties then joined the conversation. I closed my eyes to ignore them and deliberated whether having toast for breakfast was a good idea.

Pumping music played from the holding area as people of all ages milled around. I collected my race bib and dropped off my bag. I felt stiff and bloated as I warmed up along the trail. A loudspeaker announced five minutes until the start of the 5k. Adrenaline began to build inside, and I shook out my arms and legs, suddenly feeling more serious. The speakers began to play an energetic song by a Canadian rock band I'd never heard of before, and the thumping tune continued to play in my head as I marched towards the front of the start line, determined to be the first female home.

At the starting gun, two men shot off ahead, and I followed to lead the women. The trail soon commenced a long drag, and I ran alone for most of the race, the eighties song playing on repeat in my mind. A few men caught up with me as I neared the halfway point with heavy legs. When I turned around to head back, I could see I had a very comfortable lead. Other women would cheer for me as I passed, and I waved back. By the 4k mark, my legs were resisting my requests to pick up the pace. I pressed on with mental grit, ignoring the discomfort in my stomach. Seeing the end in sight, I forced my legs to move faster and sprinted through the finish line in a time of 21:04, ninth place overall. I walked around in circles to catch my breath, and the post-race buzz began to kick in. I hadn't realized how much I missed it.

The 10k runners started to finish soon after. I sat quietly and clapped for the finishers. The man in the cycling jersey headed straight to the massage tent, clutching his hamstring. When the bald man finished, he came to a stop next to me and bent over panting.

"How'd it go?" I asked politely.

Upon noticing me, the man closed his mouth, straightened up, and gave a casual shrug. "Pretty good. Forty-seven minutes." With what seemed like an afterthought, he glanced at me. "How about yours?"

"Good, thanks. I was first female, so that was cool."

The man's eyebrows raised in surprise, then he mumbled a congratulatory comment before turning awkwardly for the refreshment tent.

Although I knew it hadn't been a very competitive line-up, I let myself feel proud as I walked up to collect my medal amidst applause. The smile stayed on my face the whole bus ride home during the miraculously cured lanky man's post-race routine story, during my walk through the rain, and all through my call with Will that evening.

My positive mindset carried into Monday when Will sent me a text letting me know he'd received my first postcard. I left the gym's changing room in a daydream and barely registered the male trainer flashing me a wave as he trained a client.

When I walked into Tracks on Wednesday, Zoe was stood among the runners. Seeing her made my stomach spontaneously flip with excitement, and then came the reminder that Will wasn't around. But there was something comforting about the way she gave me a knowing smile and said my name when greeting me.

After the run, I joined the group for drinks at The Anchor and took a seat opposite Tyler.

"That was a fun night when we were last here," I said as I looked around the room.

"Will's leaving-drinks? Yeah, it was." Tyler smiled cheekily as he swigged his beer. "I told him to chase you after you left, to get your number."

"You did?"

"Sure did," he said proudly. "He said he liked you, so I told him, 'Dude, go get her.' And he did, or at least, he tried."

With a fluttering in my chest, I smiled down at my drink. Then, after glancing around to check who was within earshot, I lowered my voice. "Hardly anyone knows this, but we actually met up a couple of weeks ago, in Alberta."

Tyler's eyes lit up in amazement. "Are you serious? That's wild."

He smiled mischievously as I told him about the communication over the summer and the time in Alberta.

"What's going on with you now?" he asked.

"We're talking a few times a week." I twisted my glass around in thought. "He's not coming back until February. It's a little complicated, I suppose."

Tyler smiled reassuringly. "It'll be February before you know it."

"He might have gone off me by then," I laughed. Then I slumped forward and rested my hand on my chin. "But things seem good. We seem to gel well."

"That's so great, Sara," said Tyler happily. "Will is a really nice guy. I like him a lot."

An hour later, I waved Tyler off on his bike and walked up the street from the pub in a state of déjà vu. The only difference was the sharper coldness in the air that signalled the arrival of autumn. At the top of the street, I stopped under the glow of the lamp and imagined what might have happened if I had just waited a few seconds longer on that night. A sound of running footsteps, a calling of my name, an embarrassed smile, and a ruffle of his hair. I shoved my hands in my jacket pockets with a smile and continued to the bus stop.

Will's mood seemed different from usual when he called me early the next evening.

"I have to stay in Grande Prairie for another two weeks to help my dad with something, and I'm just sick of being here," he said. "I'm having to spend money that was meant to be for my trip, and I just want to get there."

"I can imagine." My voice piped up encouragingly. "I'm sure two weeks will go quickly."

"Mm, we'll see," he murmured.

I twirled a strand of hair around my finger. "I thought about you last night. I went for a drink at The Anchor with Tyler."

"That's nice. Just you two?"

"With the other runners, and then we stayed behind and talked." I smiled into the phone. "I hadn't realized you actually did try to chase me down that night."

At Will's mumble of a response, I bit my lip with regret. A rare silence commenced. Unsure how to follow, I cleared my throat in preparation to retreat.

"Well, I'm meeting a friend in a little bit, so I'd better leave you to it."

I put down the phone and glanced at the clock on my wall that showed I still had an hour before I was due to meet Helena. I picked up a book and walked to the coffee shop early.

Maybe Will isn't comfortable with me talking to mutual friends about us, I thought as I walked.

I listened attentively as Helena told me about her new job, but in quiet moments I found myself thinking back to Will, wondering what I should and shouldn't have said. When Helena asked how I was coping with my breakup with Harry, I was caught off guard, forced to give thought to something that hadn't been on my mind.

Raindrops began to patter against the window, disrupting the topic of conversation. Helena drove me home thirty minutes later, and after waving her goodbye, I pulled out my phone and stood under the porch of the apartment building as the rain continued to fall.

Will answered with a tone of surprise.

"I wanted to clarify that I haven't been blabbing about us to people," I said. "Just in case you were concerned after what I talked about earlier."

"That thought didn't enter my mind at all," he said reassuringly.

I pulled my cardigan tighter around me and hesitated. "Okay. You just seemed a little off earlier."

"I know, I'm sorry. I promise it wasn't anything you said. It's just me feeling sorry for myself," he replied. "I'm happy to hear you've been hanging out with Tyler. He's great."

I smiled sheepishly. "Well, in that case, I'm sorry for this call."

There was something calming about the sound of the rain drumming gently on the roof as I lay in bed journaling. Through the wall into the next apartment, I heard a toddler start to cry in distress. A door opened, and I heard the inaudible soothing words of the father as he consoled his daughter. The cries soon died down at his reassurance, and all was calm again.

I picked up my phone and composed a message to Will.

> I appreciate how simply you put my mind at ease.

He responded quickly.

> Don't worry so much. You and I are good, great even.

My toes tingled with comfort just as another message appeared.

> Thank you for being patient with my crumby mood.

I turned off my light and spoke softly into the darkness. "Thank you for still being around."

News of my breakup with Harry prompted video calls and messages from my siblings on the weekend. Their criticism of Harry didn't come as a surprise. It was my expectation of this response that had prevented me from telling them his plans sooner. I nodded patiently as they insisted that I could find someone better than Harry. But after the calls, I began to feel irritated. I pondered how different things could have been if I had told them about his plans sooner, had broken up with Harry sooner, had met Will sooner and had more time together before he went away. The thoughts of an alternate reality made me curse myself, and yet a part of me wondered whether things were supposed to have worked out the way they had.

A wariness of jinxing things stopped me from mentioning Will to family and to Harry's friends. I wanted to keep the circle of confidants small. As I left to meet Carrie on Saturday evening, I was grateful to have her as one of them.

"Will seems a little pessimistic," she remarked as she poured me a glass of wine in her kitchen. "Do you think he wishes he was in Victoria with you?"

I shook my head firmly. "No, I don't think so. He's been planning this trip for a while."

Carrie shrugged. "But think of all the people that change their plans after meeting someone."

I stared at my glass in thought. "I want him to have this experience, though."

Carrie smiled playfully. "So, if he told you he'd changed his mind and was coming back to Victoria, you'd be unhappy?"

"Obviously not," I laughed. Then I leaned my head back with a sigh. "I want both situations."

"Do you know what he plans to do when he gets back?" asked Carrie.

"We haven't really talked about it. He'll go back to school, I guess."

Carrie paused and furrowed her brow with empathy. "He sounds a little lost."

I nodded with reluctance. "I think you might be right."

My phone buzzed with Will's name as Carrie and I watched an old rom-com. I smiled at his request to call me the next day. I seemed to make him happy, and I wanted to continue to do so. I silently vowed that in doing so, I wouldn't be like the clingy, irrational female character I watched on the screen.

The next evening, I stood looking at the world map on my wall as Will told me he'd mailed another postcard. He looked at his map also, and we played a game of identifying the country the other described. I caught myself getting sidetracked into a story about an experience I'd had in Portugal and apologized with a shy giggle.

"I like it when you talk a lot," he said warmly.

After the call, I peered closely at the map, looking for the name of his home. On the map, our locations were only an inch or so apart. I traced my finger over the paper with a yearning feeling. Five months. Then we would be that close in person again.

I put on my shoes and walked down to Willow's Beach. Seals popped their heads up above the calm surface, and the distant white tip of Mt. Baker poked up into the soft pink sky. The novelty of living in Victoria hadn't worn off. I felt like I had started Canadian life again, the right way.

Over the next week, the calls with Will became longer and more affectionate. There was more optimism in his voice as he discussed his trip plans, and my own optimism only increased when he made comments that seemed to convey a hope for us to be together when he returned to Victoria.

And yet, despite the promising signs, I still felt a sense of relief when the phone rang with his name. I still heard a voice of caution warning me that one day he might realize I wasn't the type of person he was looking for. I still found myself scrutinizing things I had said in a conversation, wondering if I had come off the wrong way.

Any doubts would be quelled by a response that showed our interests were aligned. I found myself continuously amazed by how in-sync we seemed to be. As the days went on, a cautious hope for the future began to develop into more of a confident expectation.

My feet would dash over the ground as I ran at dusk. All components of the body seemed to work together as allies. No stiff legs, no heavy stomach, no gasping chest. I ran like I was being pulled towards something, and it felt wonderful.

THIRTY-THREE

A cloud of vapour left my mouth as I walked to the bus stop on the first Monday of October. The resume of a scheduled interviewee caught my eye with its reference to working in Yorkshire. With her familiar accent, Florence seemed friendly and down-to-earth, and her ID showed that she was just a year older than me. She had also come to Canada on a working holiday visa, joined by her boyfriend. We chatted about Yorkshire and cultural differences between the UK and Canada, and my fondness for her grew. Then I remembered that I was in an interview and felt conflicted. My job allowed me to meet different people at a time when I was still interested in making more friends, yet the nature of it put restrictions on forming friendships with these people.

"This came for you," said Jenna chirpily in the doorway as I finished my interview notes.

I took the parcel from her hands. "Thanks, it must be my new trail runners."

I put the parcel down next to my bag. My phone was flashing with a message. Julie had invited me to Milly's birthday party on Monday's Thanksgiving holiday. Her message noted that Harry's family wouldn't be coming until the evening, so I wouldn't have to see him.

I hadn't even thought of what I'd be doing for this holiday that wasn't celebrated in England. I told Julie I would love to come along, then gathered my things to go to the gym. My right calf had started to feel a little tight. Since getting an injury in 2013, I had been cautious of overdoing it. I sat in a corner of the gym and placed my right leg straight out in front of me with my hand reaching for the toe of my shoe.

"Sore calf?" asked a voice.

I turned to see the male trainer standing nearby, holding a kettlebell. I looked back at my leg.

"It gets a little tight sometimes from running," I said.

He bent down next to me and asked where the pain was. I pointed at the inside of the lower leg and felt my cheeks go pink when he asked if he could touch. He began rubbing the spot in circles, and I made a face of discomfort.

"That's your soleus muscle." He stood up and nodded at the wall. "There's a better stretch for that. I can show you."

I stood up and quietly followed him to the wall, watching with my arms folded as he pushed the ball of his foot against a block and bent at the knee. After he finished, I copied his stance and felt a stretch where the tenderness was.

From across the room, someone called his name. Owen.

"That helps," I said before he went. "Thanks."

The large living room windows showed nothing but blackness as I cleaned my dishes at seven-thirty that evening. I looked out into the dark with a reluctant acceptance that days were gradually getting shorter. Warm water ran over my hands as Connor invited me to join his friends for a drink in Oak Bay Village. Reluctant to leave the comfort of the indoors, I politely declined.

When Connor had left, I decided to call Will. He answered quickly, but his voice sounded gruff.

"Everything okay?" I asked gently.

"I'm just going crazy because I have to delay leaving for the States yet again," he grumbled. "I have to go to Courtenay next week for a funeral."

"I'm sorry to hear that," I said. "Was the person someone you knew well?"

"My cousin."

"Oh, I'm sorry." I hesitated. "Were you close?"

"Not really, I hardly spoke to her," he muttered. "My dad's insisting that I go, though."

"I'm sure your relatives will appreciate you being there."

"I guess."

I chewed my lip, unsure how to proceed. A part of me wanted to ask how long he'd be on the island, but it seemed inappropriate given the circumstances.

"Well, I'll let you go," I said softly.

"Sorry, I'm just not feeling very talkative right now."

"It's okay."

I put down the phone and looked around the room in disappointment. Connor would be halfway to the pub by now. I picked up my book resignedly.

A few minutes later, my phone began to ring.

"I'm sorry if it seemed I was giving you the cold shoulder," said Will guiltily after I answered. "I don't want you to think I'm annoyed with you, because I'm not."

My shoulders sank with relief. "I figured it wasn't that, but I appreciate you calling anyway."

"I shouldn't act so sorry for myself," he sighed.

"It's understandable why you're frustrated. I'd feel the same."

We talked for longer, and I felt a dose of satisfaction as I heard the tone of his voice brighten.

Feeling bad for having declined his last invite, I arranged with Connor to go for a quiz night downtown with Joey and Liz the next evening. The quiz was hosted by a vivacious English man with a tongue-in-cheek sense of humour. Joey and Connor seemed to get along well, and I found myself wondering what they would think of Will.

As the quizmaster asked his next question, I felt a vibrating in my bag that rested against my shin. I picked out my phone while the others tried to decipher anagrams.

> I will, of course, be seeing you while I'm on the island.

My stomach fluttered with excitement as I replied to ask Will when he would arrive. But when he said he would fly in next Friday, my excitement changed to dismay. That was the day I was going to Vancouver to meet Amy for her week-long visit.

"Hey, Sara! How about giving us a hand here?" called Joey cheekily.

I looked up from reading Will's disappointed response and reluctantly dropped the phone in my bag. The quiz finished an hour later, and I sat restlessly in Joey's truck as he drove us home. It was almost eleven when Connor unlocked the door, but I remained wide awake, knowing another message was waiting for me.

> I'm sorry I didn't say earlier that I wanted to see you. I'd always assumed I would, but you might have thought I wasn't going to make the effort.

I lay in bed with a racing mind stimulated by the prospect of seeing Will sooner than expected. Unable to switch off, it occupied itself with ideas of how we could make a meeting work.

A dull fog hung in the sky on Friday morning. Everyone in the office was getting excited for Thanksgiving, but I found it difficult to match their enthusiasm. Eva's gaze seemed to linger on me when she asked about everyone's plans. I listened quietly as Jenna and Paige described the dinners they had arranged with their family or that of their partners. The ringing of the phone saved me from having to admit that I had no specific plans, and I returned to my desk with a sudden glumness.

At two o'clock, Eva suggested we close early and head home to start the holiday. Jenna and Paige skipped animatedly out of the door together as I finished writing an email. As I approached the stairs, Eva came out of her office to wish me a nice weekend. She carried a sympathy in her eyes that only made me more aware of my circumstance, and as I walked home, I was hit with a pervasive feeling of loneliness. At home, I closed my bedroom door and slumped on my bed in a state of self-pity.

Will answered quickly when I called.

"How are you doing today?" he asked brightly.

I looked down and fiddled with a loose thread on my leggings. "I'm feeling a little weird, to be honest. Everyone at work was all excited about Thanksgiving, and it just reminded me how I don't have any plans, or any family here. Made me kind of sad."

"I'm sorry," he said tenderly.

"Nothing for you to be sorry about. I'm just being silly."

"Well, I hope you feel better."

I rested my head back against the wall and uttered a dry laugh. "On a scale from one to ten, how uncomfortable would you be if I joined you in the US for a few days?"

Will cleared his throat. "Uh...probably a four?"

I swallowed with regret.

"I kind of want to do my own thing when I'm there," he continued. "It's not that the idea freaks me out."

I closed my eyes and pinched my forehead with embarrassment. "I totally understand. I don't want to impede your personal trip; I'd just like to see you."

"I know," he said gently.

"I don't really know why I said that. Now I feel embarrassed."

"There's no need to be embarrassed."

I pushed my hair back from my forehead and sighed. "I don't know if we'll be able to see each other when you're here."

"We'll work something out."

He sounded so sure of it that it boosted my optimism.

"What are you going to do tonight?" he asked encouragingly.

I glanced at the clock on the wall. "My friend Liz invited me over to play board games, but I don't really feel in the mood to go."

"You should. You'll feel better for keeping busy."

I boarded the bus an hour later. Liz greeted me at her door with a prolonged "hey." I had never seen her drunk before. I shared amused smiles with Joey as Liz confused herself and giggled over card games. The evening proved a temporary distraction from my earlier woes.

"Would you like to meet in Sidney on Monday morning?" I asked Joey as he gave me a ride home. "I'm going to Harry's aunt and uncle's house at noon."

"Sure." After a pause, Joey cleared his throat. "Do you think you'll meet up with Harry anytime soon?"

I glanced out of the window at groups of people walking towards the bus stop, ready to go out downtown.

"I'm not sure. I've realized that I don't have a particular interest in working to keep a strong friendship with him."

"Why's that?" asked Joey casually.

"In the time I've had to reflect on things and talk with family, I'm just annoyed and disappointed with how he acted," I said.

Joey nodded. "Fair enough."

At his invitation to have Thanksgiving dinner at his house on Sunday, I politely refused. He ridiculed my reason that I didn't want to intrude on his family time, and I would later realize how self-perpetuating my decline of the invite was.

The sound of my phone ringing cut through the silence of the apartment the next evening. Will said he planned to be in Victoria until October 20th. The day Amy would be leaving. The chances of seeing each other seemed narrow.

"It's too bad about the timing," I said.

"It'll be nice for you to see your friend again after so long," he said pointedly.

"I know, I know. I'm excited."

"I'm looking forward to leaving Grande Prairie for a few days, that's for sure."

"Sorry I can't offer you a place to stay," I said.

"I wasn't asking," replied Will with a tone of confusion.

"I know, I was just making a proactive comment." I wrinkled my face with self-annoyance.

Will cleared his throat. "I saw that photo you had shared online, for your brother's wedding anniversary. They're a good-looking couple, geez."

He asked how he had met his wife and when they got married.

"And here I am at the same age, unhitched," I joked after telling him.

"Twenty-five is still young," said Will.

"Oh, I know," I said hurriedly. "It's not that I'm in a rush to get married."

"I wasn't thinking that you were."

I rubbed my warm neck and laughed weakly. "I feel like this conversation has been filled with misunderstandings."

"It's all good," said Will. He seemed distracted, and I chewed my nail.

"I like you," I said with playful softness.

"I like you too," he said warmly. Then he exhaled with irritation. "My dad keeps trying to call me. I should probably go."

I put the phone down with a dissatisfied sigh, only to pick it up again and write a message.

I stood motionless in the shower while warm water poured over me. I felt disappointed at the prospect of not seeing Will and guilty that I felt this way when I hadn't seen Amy in a year. I knew she should be my priority, but I also knew that not seeing Will when he was in the same location for a week would leave me with regret.

My phone showed a missed call from Will but no message. I called back but the phone continued to ring with no answer. Droplets dripped from my wet hair and glided slowly down my back as I put the phone down with unresolved curiosity.

Another call came the next morning as I finished speaking with a friend in Denmark. Will's voice sounded croaky, as if he'd been crying. The unfamiliarity of it made the hairs on my arms stand up with apprehension.

"I just wanted to say not to worry, in terms of that text you sent last night," he said with a muffled voice.

"What do you mean?" I asked gently.

"You don't need to worry about what I thought you were thinking," he said with a sniff. "It must be mentally exhausting, all that worrying."

I chewed my lip. "Will, what's wrong? You sound really upset."

"I'll be fine."

"Are you sure? What happened?"

Will sighed into a moment of silence. "I'll call you later."

He promptly ended the call, and I stared at the phone with unease. A few unsettling minutes passed as theories began to race around my mind. I took a breath and went to dial his number, only for the phone to start ringing again.

"That's freaky," I said upon answering. "I was just about to call you."

Will attempted an amused snigger that came out weak. "Why were you about to call?"

I swallowed the lump in my throat. "Because I sense something's wrong, and I can't move on from it."

There was a thudding in my chest as I waited for him to answer. After a moment of silence, he choked up and spoke.

"I don't think we should do this anymore."

The small surrounding sounds of the room went silent as I processed his words. Each word seemed to come out heavier than the last.

"Have I done something?" I asked faintly.

"No, it's not you." He sniffed and paused. "I'm just not in a great place right now."

I listened to the uneven sounds of his breath with an ache in my stomach.

"Okay." I hesitated. "Would you like to stay in touch at all?"

"I don't know," he said drowsily. "I just...I don't know."

I closed my eyes and let us fall helplessly into a moment of silence.

"Please talk to someone," I said. "I'm here if you ever want to talk."

His response was inaudible, but it carried a heavy weight that made me acknowledge defeat.

"I'm really thankful for the time you've invested in me," I said.

I waited for him to hang up, and the flat tone made my ears ring. I held the phone in my hand and stared at it numbly.

After a moment, my fingers slowly rose to my face, and I realized I wasn't crying. The confusion that spiralled around my head was suddenly overshadowed by a strange sense of calm, a soothing voice of wisdom that told me it wasn't the end.

I gazed around the room in thought, unsure what to do but wanting to help in some way. With a dose of inspiration, I opened up social media and typed Zoe's name into the search box. I ended my message with a request that she not tell Will I had contacted her. Then I gathered my notepad and walked calmly down to the beach.

The sun was out, and its heat pierced through my scruffy jeans as I scribbled down thoughts that entered my mind—the recent signs that suggested something might be going on behind the scenes, the things I wanted to say to him. Then a solemn voice reminded me that he might not want to hear from me, and my first tear fell and splashed onto the paper.

Zoe had replied by the time I returned home. She said she was equally concerned about Will and was checking in with him regularly. Then she told me how nice it was to know how much I cared for him. Filled with uncertainty, I told her that I didn't know what to do. A part of me worried contacting Will might cause stress, but another part of me yearned to make him feel valued. Something told me he didn't feel that enough.

> I know he knows you value him. Reach out to him if you want to, but also trust that he knows you care.

The words brought some comfort, but as the day turned to dusk, the sense of unease began to build once more. The sky darkened and the view outside the window became less clear.

THIRTY-FOUR

Dashes of gold glimmered from the trees as the bus headed towards Sidney. The man in the seat in front of me raised his hand to gently massage the back of his wife's neck. I watched with a bittersweet tug in my chest.

Joey was waiting by his car near the bus stop. As we walked past the boutique stores and bookshops, he asked how I felt about starting to date other people. I looked down at my boots and suddenly felt too tired to pretend any longer.

"The truth is, I've actually sort of been seeing someone."

Joey whipped his head towards me in surprise. "You have? Since when?"

"I met him in July when I started doing the runs at Tracks. He went off on a road trip, and we kept in touch after he'd gone, and then we met up when I was in Alberta."

"Huh." Joey looked away, seemingly stunned. "When's he coming back to Victoria? Do you think things will get serious?"

I pushed my hands deeper into my pockets and cleared my throat. "I don't know. We haven't really talked about it. He's… working through some stuff."

Joey bowed his head in thought before shaking his head and smiling. "Why didn't you say anything?"

I shrugged. "It just felt weird, given how close you are with Harry. I thought people might judge me."

"Judge you?" chuckled Joey. "I don't care. I think it's awesome."

"You do?" I asked uncertainly.

"Yeah, it all sounds really refreshing."

I nodded. "It has been."

We stopped at a junction and waited for the pedestrian light. Joey turned and regarded me seriously. "Well, I hope it works out."

"Thanks. Me too."

When we got into his car and drove towards Ted and Julie's house, a thought crossed my mind.

"You're the only friend of Harry's I've told about Will," I said. "Let's just keep it between us for now, please."

Joey shrugged. "Okay."

The sound of children's party music increased after I waved him goodbye and walked the gravel path towards the wooden cottage. I passed through the open door to see a group of children in princess and spiderman costumes playing musical chairs. In the corner sat Jean, clapping her hand on her thigh to the music. Upon seeing me, her eyes widened with surprise. I smiled and braced myself for the inevitable.

The party moved outside as the children requested to play on the small zip line Ted had built between two trees. I sat on the wooden steps to watch and thought about the email sitting in my drafts folder.

"Harry's family isn't coming over later after all," said a voice to my left. I turned to see Julie standing on the step, holding a tray of plastic cups. "We'd love to have you stay for Thanksgiving dinner."

I smiled gratefully. "That would be lovely."

Suddenly, a squeal erupted from the zip line area. Milly sat howling in tears about not getting the next turn. Sensing that Jean was approaching me, I went inside to help Julie prepare the cake.

"Have you been in touch with Harry at all?" she asked as she spooned icing onto the sponge.

I played with my ear. "I haven't really felt a need or desire to speak with him, if I'm honest. I don't know what I'd gain from it."

Julie nodded. "I understand."

An hour later, the house was quiet once more as Milly's friends left with their goody bags and a slice of cake. The kids sat dozily at the dinner table, slowly coming off their sugar high. Jean took a seat next to me and regarded me solemnly.

"Now, how are you getting on, dear?" she asked as she patted my leg.

"Fine, thanks, Jean." I cleared my throat and looked around the table. "I saw some photos Hannah had shared from Austria. It looks like she's having a great time."

Jean nodded, her eyes still solemn. Then she leaned towards me intently. "You know, William and Kate broke up before getting back together again. Now they're married with children!"

"Okay, Mom," said Ted with a roll of his eyes. "Let the girl eat in peace."

After collecting everyone's plates, Julie began slicing up a pumpkin pie. As I watched her explain to her son that he didn't need a bigger slice, I realized that I was most thankful for her family on Thanksgiving.

The bus to Victoria was packed with people returning from their weekends spent with family on the mainland. I stood leaning against a railing and shared in the mood of fatigue that seemed to hang in the air as everyone anticipated returning to work or school the next day.

In the warmth of my bedroom, I noticed a flashing light on my phone. I willed it to be a message from Will, telling me he was feeling better and took back what he'd said. Instead, the message was from Harry. I read his name with a mixture of disappointment and suspicion.

> Hey! I seem to recall that Amy is visiting soon and was wondering if you still wanted me to meet her? If so, perhaps you and I should meet up before?

His message came like an irritating drip of water after the tap had been turned off. Right now, I only wanted to focus on one thing and one person.

I dropped the phone on my bed without replying and opened my laptop. My fingers played with my lips as I read over my draft email to Will. I hovered my hand hesitantly over the mouse pad, and then with a deep breath, I pressed the send button.

> It's been 24 hours since we last spoke, and you've been on my mind this whole time. It's hard to contemplate letting you go when all I want to do is help you in whatever small way I can. I've come to care about you a lot in the past few months. In the short amount of time that I've known you, you've brought me a lot of happiness when I really needed it, and I've wanted to bring the same to you. But we met at a time when you were looking to focus on yourself, and the last thing I want is to be a distraction from your goals or make you feel pressured to enter into something you're not ready to.

> I hope you're not choosing to hide from me because you think you'll be a burden or disappoint me in some way. Your well-being is more important to me than a relationship. Any personal issues you're dealing with don't scare me, tarnish my view of you, or stop me from wanting to invest time in you. You have so many great qualities that I admire and that you should admire in yourself. There are a lot of people who value you and have time for you. I hope you'll open up to someone, because I want you to feel better about yourself. And I hope that you'll eventually let me back in, even if in a different form from before. Either way, I'm thinking of you and willing you to pick yourself up.

The clock on the wall said it was almost eleven. I rubbed my tired eyes and turned off the laptop.

As I looked through the bus window at the grey sky, the realization that I might never speak to Will again began to set in. It seemed incomprehensible and unnerving in its likelihood at the same time. As much as I reminded myself that I was seeing my best friend that Friday and should feel excited and happy, I couldn't shake the dejected feeling.

Feeling the need to talk to someone, I messaged Tyler. Having previously told me of his former struggles with his mental health, I believed I could trust his confidentiality, and I hoped he could give me some insight. We met in the pub that evening. I played pensively with my beer glass, pondering my words.

"If someone is going through a bad episode, is it common to push a partner or close friend away?" I asked.

Tyler leaned forward. "If Will is dealing with some depression, it's very likely that he's trying to stop you getting hurt, or trying to stop himself getting hurt."

"What do you mean, stop himself getting hurt?" I asked.

"Some people fear that their illness will drive others away, once they learn about it or are exposed to it."

I told him about my email.

"It's good you did that," he said. "He might have needed that assurance."

I looked out of the window with a sigh. "It's selfish of me to keep thinking of how I'll feel if he doesn't talk to me again."

Tyler smiled. "I find it hard to believe he wouldn't want to see you while he's in Victoria."

My mailbox in the apartment building showed a sliver of white. I unlocked the door to see two letters. As I retrieved them, a postcard fell from between them. I picked it up with a sinking in my stomach. *Hey blondie, I miss your face.* There was something cruel about its upbeat and affectionate tone. Sent over a week ago, it promised a future communication that was no longer certain.

Heavy rain drummed off the pavement as I exited the bus the next morning. I interviewed a polite man with a weak command of English and went on to face one of a recruiter's most difficult challenges of being objective and not letting a candidate's likeability govern a decision. I decided to come back to it after lunch and logged into my personal email to finish a message to Amy.

The inbox showed a reply from Will. The sight of his name sent butterflies rippling through me.

> Sara, I really appreciate this email. I'll be in Victoria next week. I want to see you. Let's talk then.

An immediate rush of relief was slowed by a warning voice that reminded me not to get my hopes up.

Underneath Will's message was an email sent by Harry the evening prior. It had repeated the text message I had forgotten to reply to. I clicked the reply icon with a deep inhale and wrote with a building sense of empowerment that had been missing earlier in the year.

> Hi, sorry for the delay. Amy and I are going to be quite busy while she's here, and to be honest, it's not a priority of mine to see you at the moment. I'm happy, and I hope you are too, and I'm sure I'll eventually see you.

THIRTY-FIVE

Sun rays sparkled on the water as the ferry cruised past the Gulf Islands towards the mainland. I stood in the crowd in the arrivals lounge at Vancouver International Airport and waited with anticipation for the doors to open. Amy's slim frame and bobbed brown hair came into sight quickly, and upon seeing my frantic wave, her face burst into an excited smile. We boarded the SkyTrain and Amy proceeded to tell me about her experience of repatriating in England.

"Thanks for being okay with me seeing Will next Thursday," I said as we walked along West Broadway towards our Airbnb.

"Of course," said Amy as her suitcase rattled over the ground. "I hope you know that you're not to blame for what happened."

The Airbnb was an old house with flakey white paint, a stiff door lock, a messy kitchen, an awkwardly timid Irish tenant named Amber, a quiet French tenant named Alexander, and a nosy cat that seemed to have a fetish for the blanket on the mattress of our small box room. It had been the cheapest option close to the water in the trendy Kitsilano neighbourhood.

We walked down the leafy street towards the beach and followed the path round to Granville Island. As runners passed by, Amy asked if I would ever consider moving to Vancouver. I looked up at Granville Bridge and the cars rushing towards downtown with its collection of glass skyscrapers. I had thought about it before, but now it just felt like another big city that lacked Victoria's charm.

I had forgotten how much I loved Amy's laugh. It felt like it had only been a matter of days since we had last seen each other. I had missed her company more than I realized, but as we walked through Stanley Park the next day, I knew I couldn't see myself living in London again.

We spent Saturday evening having dinner in Chinatown and watching a movie before wandering along the cobbles of Gastown. It was just after ten when we approached the Airbnb. Pumping music and drunken shouts blared through the window. We entered the living room to see five girls in cropped tops and leather leggings throwing back shots while Alexander sat amongst them looking like an overwhelmed teenage boy. At the opening beat of a raunchy pop song, an emancipated Amber stood up with a whoop before downing a shot and pulling a petrified Alexander up from his chair. Amy and I exchanged amazed looks before withdrawing unnoticed to our room.

I collapsed on the mattress and opened the pack of Cherry Bakewell tarts Amy had brought me from England. "I'm so glad you're boring like me."

We returned to Victoria the next afternoon. Amy was sniffly and assumed she'd caught something from the plane. On the ferry, I messaged Will with a proposal that we meet at Willow's Beach on Thursday evening. When he confirmed, I once more felt the mixture of relief and apprehension.

I had booked two days off work, and on Monday morning, Amy and I headed downtown for breakfast. As I pointed out a notable building to her, I recognized a man walking in our direction. He had a lean frame and dark hair, and his spectacled face looked at the ground with a pensive expression.

A few moments after he passed, I grabbed Amy's arm in shock. "That was Harry."

Amy stopped with intrigue, and we slowly turned to look behind us. Now twenty metres away, Harry had also turned. He wore the beige pants I had frequently folded from the laundry basket. He raised his hand to wave, and I returned it with a surreal feeling.

"Now I feel bad," I sighed as Amy and I continued down the street. "He looked really sad."

"No, do not feel bad," said Amy firmly. "Do you not remember how crappy he made you feel?"

"I know, but still…"

"You shouldn't feel bad for saying you don't want to see him. It's perfectly reasonable. Things change."

"You're right." I scratched my head and glanced behind me once more. He was no longer in sight. "What are the chances I'd bump into him on this street? He hardly ever goes downtown."

"It is a pretty strange coincidence, I'll admit."

"I wonder if he's feeling bad about things," I said.

"I should hope so," said Amy sharply.

Brooding clouds gathered in the sky as we walked along Dallas Road, and in the afternoon, it began pouring rain. We ran into a bookshop for shelter before catching the bus home. Amy pulled from her suitcase our favourite brand of hot chocolate that wasn't sold in Canada. My phone buzzed on the coffee table as we watched a movie. I had a new email from Harry.

> I hope you're having a great time with Amy. I'm emailing you because I'm not very happy at the

> moment, and it's because I'm not letting you go. I wanted you to know in advance that I'm going to block you on all social media. I'm also going to delete your number and unsubscribe from your blog.

Stunned into silence, I passed the phone to Amy. Her response was unsympathetic, as I expected. I closed the message and typed his name into my social media connection list. Nothing appeared, and all our messages had vanished. He felt the remorse and regret I had hoped he would feel, but now that it had happened, it didn't bring me the satisfaction I'd expected. Instead, I felt a tug of pity as I pictured him sat solemnly at his computer in the barn, listening to a song about a guy who broke up with a girl, but there was a part of him that still loved her.

On Wednesday morning, I woke to a text from Will.

> I did a poor job of responding to your email. We'll talk on Thursday, but I want you to know that I definitely care about you, and I feel awful about the whole situation. You've been a casualty of a really weird, confusing time for me, and I'm really sorry for it, for my own sake, really, as you're a strong person and are probably getting along fine.

The message made me want to say all kinds of things, but I told myself to wait until we were in person. Amy and I walked through Oak Bay Village before wandering down towards Fairfield. At the top of Moss Rock, I closed my eyes and remembered the warmth of the evening sun on my back when I had stood up there with Will. Now there was a chill in the air, and my back instead prickled with nerves at the thought of seeing him the next day.

It was already dark when we walked alongside the harbour towards the IMAX. A group of runners wearing headlamps approached, and I heard Tyler shout my name excitedly in a way that filled me with warmth. It was hard to imagine such an encounter happening in London.

In the ticket queue, Amy laughed at the irony of yet another familiar encounter after I recognized Helena and her friend. They were going to see the same movie, and their seats happened to be right next to ours. After the film ended, Helena offered to drive us home. When I asked about her plans for the rest of the week, she said she was seeing Harry the next day. I felt a sudden tightness in my chest and coughed.

"I really hope he's doing okay," I said.

At the sound of my alarm the next morning, I heard a gentle pattering of rain against the window. My stomach swirled as I dressed in my favourite work outfit. I left some bus money and a note with recommended places on the bedside table, and Amy woke to wish me luck before I closed the door.

At the bus stop, I ran scenarios through my head. What we would talk about, what we would do if it kept raining, whether he would cancel. The bus rolled into view, and the woman that lived across the street dashed across the road, kicking up droplets of water with each step.

Throughout the day, I glanced at my phone expectantly, waiting for the text from Will telling me he'd changed his mind. It didn't come. By two o'clock it was still raining, so I suggested we meet indoors somewhere instead. He replied quickly with an offer to give me a ride from work. I re-read the message with intrigue. *I thought he said he was flying?*

At twenty past four came the text saying he was parked down the street. I looked in the washroom mirror with a flurry of butterflies and ran a brush through my hair while taking deep breaths. Jenna was putting on her coat as I walked down the stairs with shaky legs.

"I'm meeting a guy," I blurted out. "Do I look okay?"

Jenna looked at me in surprise. "Yes, great."

A navy-blue car was parked on the other side of the street with its lights on. I licked my lips and crossed the street before clearing my throat several times.

Will was looking at an album cover when I opened the passenger door. He gave a quick smile in my direction and held the cover towards me, making a joke about the musicians' moustaches. I glanced shyly at him, trying to read his mood.

He pulled away from the curb, and we chatted with calm ease about the weather, my workday, Vancouver. I kept my gaze forward or through my window, wondering if we were both faking our confidence. The car park at Cattle Point was empty, the heavy rain having driven everyone indoors. There no longer seemed to be any point in being there, but I still stepped out into the downpour and walked towards the water. When I looked back at Will, he watched me quietly with his blue eyes. We shared a knowing look. Suddenly, I felt less nervous.

"Had enough?" he asked.

I nodded and followed him back to the car, wiping my nose. My trousers were stuck to my legs as he turned the heating on. The music immediately turned on with the ignition. Will switched it off and sat back in his seat. I looked down at my boots and rubbed my hands together.

"I didn't think your response was poorly done because I hadn't expected you to reply to my email."

My voice came out softly, just audible above the hum of the heater. Out of the corner of my eye, I noticed Will looking at me.

I cleared my throat and continued. "I also don't know that I'm necessarily a strong person. I just think you act strong for someone if you care about them."

After a pause, Will spoke. "I should have made it clearer that what happened wasn't because of you. I'm sorry."

"You don't have to be sorry." I turned my head to look in the direction of his feet. "How are you feeling?"

"I'm much better than I was in Grande Prairie," he said.

I brushed a wet strand of hair off my face and hesitated. "I get it if you'd rather not say, but what happened?"

Will looked down at his lap and shrugged. "Around three years ago, I started feeling down about small things. I just don't seem to have a middle level."

I gazed across the dashboard. "So, what are your plans now?" I asked tentatively.

Will dropped his head back against the rest. "I'm not going to the States anymore. There's too much snow where I want to be. I'm going to look for a job in Victoria."

I tried to conceal my impulsive relief. A weight seemed to fall off my shoulders as I silently recalled the series of emotions I'd been feeling since we last spoke.

"Why do you look sad?" asked Will gently.

"Because I wasn't sure if I was going to see you again."

Finally, I let my eyes focus directly on his face, just over a foot away from mine. As he took in my gaze and my words, his face seemed to soften, but his eyes flickered with sadness. Then he smiled tenderly and placed his hand on my leg. I covered it with my own.

Moments later, Will started the car and drove us to a teahouse on a quiet street in Oak Bay. Soft piano music played as I browsed the display of teas. Will took a seat opposite me, and a voice in my head giggled like a teenage girl when he looked into my eyes.

"I'm a lot less tanned than when we last saw each other," I joked.

"Your hair is just as blonde." His eyes fell over it admiringly as he spoke.

Once again, we entered our private bubble, the music in the background drowning out as we focused our attention wholly on the other. Everything seemed to fall gently back to where it was, and when we clasped hands over the table, Will's face carried a content look that assured me everything would be okay.

An unclear amount of time later, the bubble was interrupted once more as the waitress approached to let us know it was almost nine and the café was closing. I suddenly remembered Amy at home, entertaining herself. Will knew the way to my street, and as the car approached my building, I looked across at him.

"Would you like to meet Amy? Or would that be weird?"

"No, I'll come say hi."

He pulled up past the corner, and I unclipped my seatbelt before reaching for the door.

"Wait," said Will with a mixture of shyness and urgency. I turned to see him looking at me. "Could I kiss you first?"

His lips were warm and soft and sent tingles through my body. I lingered close to his face, reluctant to stop.

Amy answered the door with a knowing smile before standing back. There was a warmth in Will's voice as he asked about her visit. From an unseen place in the kitchen, I quietly observed the surreal scene of two different worlds coming together in one room.

Following their goodbye, I walked Will downstairs. Outside of the building, he turned to face me and pulled me close.

"Can I see you tomorrow night?" I asked quietly, my face in his neck.

He slowly released me with a smile. "That's not so bad."

I studied his face curiously. "What do you mean?"

"I don't have to wait too long."

I walked back inside feeling like I was floating on air. Amy sat in my bedroom with a grin on her face as I sank on the bed and recollected the evening. When I had finished, I lay in a daze, still comprehending the fact Will was back in Victoria.

"Just think, you could have a boyfriend soon," said Amy encouragingly.

I smiled. "It's still early days. But yes, maybe soon."

THIRTY-SIX

Amy caught the bus back to the ferry early the next morning. I waved her off from my doorway with tears in my eyes and wondered how long it would be before she noticed the letter I'd placed in her bag. When I opened the bathroom cabinet, I found her letter for me propped against my moisturizer.

As the day went on, the sadness was gradually balanced with anticipation for the evening ahead.

"You're rushing off," said Jenna with a playful smirk as I ran down the stairs. "Got another date?"

"Yes, he's coming over. I offered to make dinner. Wish me luck!"

I paced around the living room as the clock approached six, finding items on the coffee table to rearrange. A moment later, the intercom rang, setting off a pounding in my chest. I listened by the door for footsteps coming up the stairs. Will stood with a fresh loaf of bread in his hand.

"An ode to your love of 'caaabs,'" he said in a mimicking accent as he handed the loaf to me.

After dinner, Will stepped through the open doorway into my bedroom and gazed at the pictures on the wall. We stood side by side, inches apart, looking at the world map. Then we shared a lingering look, and I closed the door.

His skin was still smooth like I remembered, and I shivered with excitement as he moved down my body. In the light, we seemed more nervous as it began, our eyes catching briefly like two teenagers having their first time.

Afterwards, self-consciousness about my skin made me cover my back with the duvet before I laid my arm across Will's chest. His left hand gently slipped the duvet down and caressed my shoulder. Minutes later, he proposed we go for a walk, and I trod daintily among the clothes scattered across the floor.

There was a dampness in the air as Will nodded in the direction of our route.

"You know your way around here better than me," I remarked as we passed a small wooden cabinet on a corner, filled with books for public use.

Will scratched his head. "I used to spend quite a bit of time in this neighbourhood."

We walked down Estevan Avenue past the windows of cafes and boutiques. From behind a dark tree came an inquisitive purr, and a black cat approached with languid steps.

"Black cat at night," I said with a smile. "Isn't that supposed to be bad luck?"

Will bent down and let the cat rub itself against his leg before he scooped it in his arms and held it on his shoulder. The cat sat peacefully for a moment before growing restless and jumping down, and then it disappeared once more into the night.

Willow's Beach was deserted except for a group of teenagers drinking together. A chilly breeze blew off the water, and I linked my arm through Will's. As we walked back in the direction of home, he seemed quieter, as if deep in thought. At my street, he began to cross the road towards a path between two houses.

"Where are you going?" I called with amusement.

"To your place?" said Will with a blank look.

"It's this way." I pointed down the street.

"Oh, I'm sorry." Will shook his head and smiled. "What time is it, anyway?"

"Almost eleven." I looked down and shrugged. "You could sleep over if you like."

Will rubbed his eyes, and under the light of my porch, he suddenly looked tired. "I should probably head home. I'm getting up early tomorrow to run with a friend."

He kissed me goodnight and looked me warmly in the eyes, but as I walked through my door, I couldn't help but feel slightly disappointed. My vision of the evening had looked different. Instead, it seemed to have come to a sudden ending, the warm candle inside me blown out sooner than I'd hoped. But as I brushed my teeth, I reminded myself it was still early days. Running was important to Will, and I didn't want to get in the way of his interests.

Rain fell in intermittent showers throughout the next day. An exchange of texts with Will gave me reassurance, and when he asked if I'd like to do something on Sunday afternoon, my disappointment on Friday seemed foolish. I put on my favourite hand-me-down sweater and watched from the living room window for his car. He showed up on a yellow mountain bike that was too small for his tall frame. I watched with amusement as he wheeled it through my door and sheepishly explained that Zoe had lent it to him. He was renting her spare room.

"I think I might have seen your friend on the way here, on his bike," he said as he took off his helmet. "Nathan? That one that lives with Tyler."

"If he was tall, probably." I sat down on the couch with a smile. "I enjoyed watching you arrive on your little bike."

"Creeping on me from your window, eh?"

"I know. Almost as bad as looking someone up online and contacting them on their blog."

"Touché." Will scratched his ear and chuckled. "That's probably the creepiest thing I've ever done."

"I'm sure you've witnessed some creepy behaviour from girls before."

Will leaned his head back against the cushion and sniggered. "The same day I first met my ex, she followed me on social media and sent me a song about growing old together."

I regarded him thoughtfully. "You must have made a good impression on her."

"It didn't last." He blinked out of a thought and patted my leg. "What about you? What's the creepiest thing you've ever done to a guy you liked?"

My mind immediately played a scene that made me blush with shame. I rubbed my thigh hesitantly. "It's part of a wider story."

"I'm all ears."

I bit my lip and played with a tassel on the cushion. It took the focus of my gaze as I began to tell him the story of the man at my workplace in London. An evening when I had grown insecure after seeing him with a woman in the on-site bar.

"Later that night, he sent me a text asking if I'd been checking up on him. As much as I tried to deny it, he wasn't convinced. And so, he just shut me off, dropped all contact. Then I found out he'd been sleeping with other women all along. He had every right to, but I felt like such an idiot. I'd thought he genuinely like me, but he was playing a game all along, and now he thought I was some weird, clingy girl. And on top of that, he told some of his male colleagues too. So, he was the cool guy that got claps on the back, and I was the crazy slut."

By now, I had tears in my eyes. I glanced up at Will and shrugged with an embarrassed smile. "So, there's my story."

Will observed me quietly. Then, without saying a word, he leaned over and wrapped his arms around me in a long hug.

When I looked out of the window, the clouds had parted to reveal splashes of blue. We walked into Oak Bay Village and into a small grocer where I pointed out popular British brands in the World Foods section. Will's mouth curved into a smile whenever I got excited at the sight of an item I hadn't seen in a while.

Sharing my story with Will had seemed to deepen my level of comfortability around him. There was something reassuring about his acceptance of my mistake. It reinforced a belief that I could be my true authentic self around him and that we could be vulnerable with each other without fear of judgment.

"So, what's the worst thing you've ever done to a partner?" I said dryly as we passed a row of bramble bushes on the way back from the teahouse.

Will shook his head. "I don't judge you for what you did. I can see your reasons. You were lonely and unhappy. It sounds like the relationship with your ex was pretty difficult at times."

"It was, but without him, I suppose I might not be here right now." I kicked a small rock over the ground. "I obviously wouldn't have done it if we'd lived in the same place, and I'm not planning to do anything like that again."

Will laughed gently. "Don't worry, I know." He took my hand and looked at it in surprise. "Your hands are freezing."

"Cold hands, warm heart."

He placed my hand in his pocket and wrapped his own around it. I walked with him along quiet pathways with a lightness in my step. The sun seemed to follow us wherever we went.

As we climbed the stairs to my apartment, a sweet soulful song from the teahouse entered my head, and I instinctively began to hum it. Seconds later, Will said its name.

I turned in surprise to look at him, and something swelled inside me as our eyes met. The sudden and dizzying wonder of having perhaps met that person, the final missing piece in the jigsaw.

Connor was in the kitchen, and I left Will to chat with him as I used the bathroom. Beaming eyes looked back at me in the mirror. Outside, Will looked in my direction, and I pulled him away with my eyes before quietly closing my bedroom door.

It was dark by the time we said goodbye downstairs. In the cool air, I watched with a warmth in my bones as he cycled away on his small bike into the night.

THIRTY-SEVEN

On Wednesday morning, Eva called to the team from her office with a question of preferred dates for the office Christmas party. I looked up from writing a congratulatory email to Florence, who had been hired directly by a client. It was hard to believe that Christmas was already approaching.

"Hey, Sara, bring your boyfriend if he's in town," called Eva cheekily.

"I think he might be," said Jenna in a sing-song voice.

A goofy grin took over my face at the sound of their giggles. I looked at my phone and re-read Will's proposal to meet that evening for a run. The mild soreness in my calf had made me hesitant to compete in the next Tracks race that coming weekend, but Will's encouragement and comment that he would be there running the half marathon had changed my mind. When registering online, I had wondered how he would act with me around others, around his friends. The same question had entered my mind when he mentioned he would eventually return to lead the run meet-ups.

After work, I walked down to Centennial Square. With a fluttering in my chest, I spotted Will sitting on the ledge of a fountain, looking into the distance.

"That's a pretty blonde," he said with a smile as I approached.

In his hand, he held an envelope. He had been dropping off resumes at a few high-end outdoor clothing stores. We walked up the street in the direction of Zoe's apartment. While Will changed in his room, I stood looking around the living room with its piano and abstract artwork. The envelope was on the dining table. I quietly pulled out a resume for a curious peek. As I scanned the Times New Roman font, I bit my lip with the question of whether I should tell him that he'd made a typo on some dates.

Suddenly the door opened, and I turned to see Zoe step through the door, talking on the phone. Upon seeing me, she looked surprised, only to smile and flash a wave. Will and I left for mine shortly after. After noticing Connor wasn't home, I gazed at Will invitingly.

"I took a test recently, and it was all fine," I said later as I pulled on my sports bra. "I was thinking of going back on the pill, just as an extra precaution."

Will nodded. "Whatever you're comfortable with."

I took my headlamp from the drawer, and we set off in the dark at an easy pace towards Cadboro Bay. From the village, we ascended the hill towards Arbutus Road, and through the wealthy neighbourhood I had passed on runs months earlier. Clouds blocked the moonlight, but I could just make out the dark outline of tall bushes hiding the mansions behind.

"I used to do landscaping for this woman," said Will, gesturing at a large iron gate. "We weren't allowed to look at her if she walked past us."

I remembered running this route those months ago before I even knew Will existed and before I would ever have imagined dating someone new.

"How far have we run?" I asked as we turned back the way we had come. It seemed to have been a while, and I was impressed that I had maintained the same pace.

"It'll probably be seventeen kilometres by the time we get back."

"Seventeen?" I said in amazement. "I don't think I've ever run that far before."

"There you go," said Will. "You're capable of more than you think. You just need someone running with you."

As we ran up the drag from the village to join Beach Drive, my legs began to complain, and mental willpower started to take up the reins. A desire to impress Will spurred me on. We crossed the road towards the pavement and joined flatter ground. From in front of me, I heard the sound of rustling leaves and Will cussing.

"You okay?" I called.

"I didn't see a branch, and it hit me right in my eye," he said grumpily. "Fricking hurts."

"Do you want to stop?" I asked.

"No."

"I could see if there's something—"

"It's fine."

I closed my mouth, feeling the skin on my neck prickle at his unfamiliar tone. We ran in silence, hearing only the sound of our feet on the ground. A tension seemed to fill the air as I ran behind him, uncertain what could be said.

A few minutes later, Will's steps began to slow, and he let himself fall in line with me.

"I'm sorry. I feel like an idiot."

"It's okay. It sounded painful."

"I shouldn't have let it bother me."

"It's fine. Forget about it."

When the lights of my apartment building came into view, I felt a mixture of relief and disappointment. His keys already on him, Will gave me a hug and walked off to his car. By now, my calves were pulsing with soreness. I walked up the stairs with a grimace and ran a bath. Something told me Will would contact me to apologize again. I sank deep into the tub and closed my eyes.

From the bedside table thirty minutes later, my phone flashed.

> Do you feel like I'm a bit of a dick to you? I feel like I'm a bit of a dick to you. I'm going to work on that.

I let my hair fall out of its bun and down over my shoulders before I replied.

> I don't think you're a dick to me. I think you're a dick to yourself, and you should probably work on that first if you're concerned about hurting other people.

The next morning, Will asked if I could meet him on my lunch break. Assuming he wanted to apologize in person, I told him to meet me at noon in a café down the street. But as I put on my coat, I felt clouded with doubt about the purpose of the meet.

From my window, I saw Will walk down the street with his cool, calm gait. I jogged down the stairs, wincing at my sore calves. Will didn't seem hungry, and I had food in the office fridge, but I ordered soup as a courtesy to the café staff. With a tired warmth in his eyes, Will rested his cheek in his palm and asked how my day was going.

"The others have been talking about their relationships all morning," I said with amusement. "I think they like having a safe space to vent about their partners."

Will looked down with a smile, and then his eyes rose to meet mine. "So, what are we?"

I swallowed a mouthful of chilli and looked up at him, suddenly uncertain. A voice told me to be casual. I shrugged and smiled coyly.

"Hanging out."

Will kept a calm gaze on my face. "What would you like us to be?"

I wiped my hands with my napkin, pondering my words. "I'm not sure. I enjoy spending time with you, but I don't know where you're at."

Will began to fiddle with the salt and pepper on the table. "I'm not sure I should be in a serious relationship right now."

I instinctively folded my arms on top of the table and nodded. "I don't know if I want to be in a new one so soon."

Will's eyes locked on mine. They seemed to look searchingly, as if penetrating my soul. I looked down at my phone to avert giving the truth away.

"I should probably head back to the office soon. We have a business mixer this afternoon, and I need to make a few calls before."

Outside of my office, he smothered me in a playful hug. It made me laugh and blush at the same time, but when I walked inside, I felt confused and unsatisfied. The conversation had been rushed, and questions lingered in my head. I sat at my desk in a daydream and thought of my message to him the night before. I had meant what I said, but in saying it, had I shot myself in the foot?

My hands impulsively reached for my phone. At my request to talk, Will replied quickly to say he would stop by mine in the evening.

The business mixer at the local employment centre was attended by a few different employers and consultants from around Victoria. I smiled and made small talk, but networking wasn't a natural skill of mine, and my head wasn't in the right space. As a man began his presentation on the state of the labour market, I thought of Will dropping off resumes.

Compared to Harry, Will didn't seem as set on following a specific career path and having a certain title. Drained by the behaviour that had resulted from Harry's pursuit of his ambitions, I welcomed this approach. It appealed to the adventurous part of me that dreamed of a life spent roaming the world without responsibilities. Wealth and accolades weren't what I looked for in a person. I hadn't asked Will what he wanted to do for a career, partly because I wasn't sure he knew.

Connor had some friends over when I arrived home. They left for the pub just as Will arrived at the door in his running clothes, with a slight sheen on his face. I placed a glass of water in front of him on the table and took a breath.

"I feel like my text last night might have seemed too presumptuous about our status," I said.

"I didn't feel that," said Will reassuringly.

"Okay, well, that's good." I twisted my mug around in my hands in thought. "It's just a weird situation because I hadn't expected to see you until February, and now you're back—and that's great—but things are happening faster than I initially expected. And I like you, and I like spending time with you, but I'm not sure I should rush into another relationship."

"That's okay. Like I said, I don't think I'm in that place either."

I played with my ear. "And why do you feel that way, exactly?"

Will looked down in thought. "I think I should work on myself and my identity before sharing that with someone else."

My mind flashed back to my message. I nodded slowly before resting my elbows on the table.

"So, how do you want to move forward?" I asked hesitantly. "Are you happy seeing me like this? Do you want to keep sleeping together?"

"I am, and I want to continue that." He looked at me with a smile. "But I also like spending time with you for reasons other than that."

I rubbed my lips together, suddenly timid. "What about other people? Because personally, I don't want to see anyone else."

"I don't either."

"Okay." Relieved, I sat back in my chair. "I'm fine not putting a label on things, but I want to ensure we communicate openly with each other about how we're feeling. I don't want to be taken for granted like I was in my last relationship. And I don't want to just be some secret…call girl."

Will's face wrinkled into an amused smile, and then his face grew serious. "That's not how I see you."

We cuddled quietly on the couch as a reggae song played softly in the background. Will's neck smelled like sweat infused with coconut shower gel.

"Do you want to spend Halloween with me?" he asked, his chin resting on my head.

I felt a sprinkling of happiness. "I'd like that."

When he left, I closed the door and leaned against it with renewed optimism. *I can wait.*

Carved pumpkins sat on display in a local coffee shop as I waited for Liz after work on Friday. At her invitation to join her and some friends for dinner, I pushed through the introverted voice that was resisting and accepted. My legs were still sore as we walked into the Irish pub where fake cobwebs hung from the banisters. A local band played the fiddle as we walked upstairs to meet Liz's friends. They were very different from her with their girly appearance and loud voices. When I removed my coat, my collared dress shirt contrasted with their low-hanging tops. I pictured my quiet living room and felt my jaw ache with forced smiles as I tried to keep up with their energy. An hour later, I made my excuses and asked a waitress in a short tartan skirt for my bill.

The lights in the apartment were off when I unlocked the door. Everyone was out celebrating their Friday night, but I was happy to be alone. I changed into my pyjamas and settled on the couch with a new book. At ten o'clock, a buzzing sound disrupted the silence.

What are you up to?

Just at home reading. You?

It was a few minutes before Will replied.

Getting chocolate and picking you up.

I sat up with intrigue and felt my body begin to tingle with excitement. Ten minutes later, there came a knock at the door. Will's eyes took in my pyjamas with mild surprise.

"You'll need some warm clothes for where we're going," he said.

I pulled on a hoody and some tracksuit bottoms and followed him downstairs to his car.

"Do I get to know where we're going?" I asked as I snapped off a piece of chocolate.

"You'll find out," he said with a smile.

I sat buzzing with anticipation as we headed towards the highway.

"Is this where your stalking goes to another level, and you leave my remains in a forest somewhere?" I joked.

Will sniggered. "Not quite."

As we joined the highway, he grew quieter. I looked out of the window, trying to guess where we were going. At a junction, he turned right onto a windy road I didn't recognize. Then we joined a narrower straight road that was flanked between flat farmland. In the headlights, I saw a scarecrow standing in one of the fields, and a lightbulb sparked inside my head.

"I think I know where we're going," I said brightly.

I looked through the window at the starry sky, expecting a sign for Island View Beach to appear any second. Then the car suddenly slowed to a halt. Seeing nothing on the road, I looked at Will questioningly.

"Actually, I think I'm just going to take us home," he said quietly. He put the gear in reverse and proceeded to turn around.

"Why?" I asked in confusion. "What's wrong?"

"I don't really feel like being around people right now."

My heart sank as I watched his eyes focus on the road ahead.

"Have I done something?" I asked faintly.

Will's hand reached across and laid on top of mine. "It's not you."

I looked down at his hand with a spinning head that wanted to ask more questions but felt unsure where to begin. After a moment, he took his hand away, and I stared out of the window with a ringing in my ears. We drove in silence until we reached my street. Will brought the car to a stop, and the silence suddenly seemed deafening.

"Do you want to talk about it, or should I just let you go?" I asked gently.

Will laid his head against the rest, his eyes still focusing ahead. Then he turned to look at me, and his big eyes were sad with hopelessness. "We need to stop doing this."

The words came out pained but with a lack of conviction. As I took them in, I felt strangely calm. Without another word, I leaned across to give him a hug, then I opened my door and slipped out quietly. I walked towards the building without looking back, and the car pulled away behind me with a groan of the engine.

I undressed quietly, trying to understand why I wasn't crying. In bed, I sat up, unable to fall asleep. Just as I reached for my phone, it began to ring.

"There's something wrong with me," came a voice of despair. "I can't control these mood swings, and it's not fair to you."

My shoulders sagged with pity. "It's okay. I'm not mad about what happened."

"I fuck up relationships because I just can't seem to do them."

I played hesitantly with my lip. "Do you know if something specific triggers the mood swings?"

"They just come out of nowhere." Will took a few breaths, as if gathering his thoughts. "I'm full of self-loathing and can't stop dwelling on the aspects of my character that I find negative."

"Aspects like what?" I asked delicately.

"I just see myself as selfish and greedy, insensitive, uncaring, narcissistic."

"You're not those things, Will. You're not."

Will's voice began to shake. "There's this voice that comes in my head sometimes and tells me I don't deserve to be alive."

A shot of fear ran through me, and before I knew it, there were tears streaming down my face. I began to speak, but my voice crumpled under the sobs.

Will said my name, his voice filled with guilt. I gulped for air and began to speak.

"Please don't—"

The line cut. I stared at the phone in anguish and called back. No rings. I began to sob once more. Then the phone lit up with an incoming call, and I gasped with relief.

"I'm sorry, my phone ran out of battery," he said.

"Please see a counsellor," I said desperately. "Just talk to someone."

"I know, I'm going to."

"Okay, good." I took a breath and wiped my eyes.

There was a pause on the line, followed by a solemn sigh. "I don't know why you like me."

I felt a pulling in my chest. "You're not a bad person, Will. You're not all those things you say you are."

Will sniffed. "I should let you sleep. I'm sorry for keeping you up."

"You don't have to be sorry." I swallowed. "I care about you."

The line went silent. I put the phone down and sat still, reeling from the unsettling realization that someone so calm and confident on the surface could be concealing so many dark thoughts.

When I woke in the morning, events of the night replayed in my mind. The sight of Will's pessimistic and despondent eyes as he committed self-sabotage. I knew he expected me to give up on him, but I wouldn't.

Soon there came a text.

> Could I see you this morning, or would that be too much? I want to apologize, to your face. Last night was a mad shit show on my part, and I feel horrible about all the things I said. But if you want space, I get it.

I glanced across the room at my laptop and hesitated. I was supposed to call a friend that I had already rescheduled with last weekend. I told him it wouldn't be too much to see him but that I had plans all morning. He called soon after the message, and his voice was filled with shame.

"I'm really sorry. I really care about you, Sara. I wish I could control these feelings and not take them out on the people I care about."

"Don't be so hard on yourself," I said. "Don't create a self-fulfilling prophecy."

Will mumbled inaudibly.

"Girls in the past might have got angry or upset and ditched you in these situations, but I'm a mature person, and I'm not going to do that," I said.

When the call ended, I reached forward to touch my toes and felt an uncomfortable stretch up my leg. The tightness in my calves hadn't eased. I glanced at my trail running shoes in the corner and tried to imagine how things would go the next day. I still had to work out how I was going to get to Elk Lake for the race. My fingers hovered uncertainly over the contacts in my phone before selecting Neil's name to request a ride.

I stepped out of my room after my call to see sunlight filtering through the big living room windows. Carrie had suggested we go for a walk, and I welcomed the idea. As we headed towards the beach, I told her what had happened with Will. At the mention of his words in the car outside my house, she stopped and said my name with a worried tone.

"It's okay," I insisted as I took in her concerned face. "We spoke after. He felt really bad about it, and he opened up about his feelings. I really feel for him."

"I get that, and that's sad for him, but this sounds stressful," she said. "I know he can't necessarily help it, but all this sudden changing of his mind doesn't seem fair to you."

I shrugged off her words. "I don't mind. It was obviously a shock at the time, but I know he cares about me."

Carrie looked unconvinced, but then her face softened. "It sounds like you've been really patient with his mood changes. It's admirable of you; I couldn't do it."

I looked down at the orange oak leaves crunching under my feet. "I just want to be strong for him. I feel like he isn't used to being with emotionally mature people and having difficult conversations." I looked up with furrowed brows. "It felt like he was trying to protect me from himself, from a person he doesn't like."

"You might be right. He might feel like he isn't good enough for you, or for anyone, even."

I looked up determinedly. "I want to help him feel better about himself."

Carrie folded her arms. "Well, I guess you just have to be a listening ear and let him know you're there to talk," she said. "Just make sure you look out for yourself too."

THIRTY-EIGHT

A beautiful pink sky spread above the road to Elk Lake. The parking lot was already filling up as Neil pulled his car into a space. Through the window, a car like Will's caught my eye. My stomach somersaulted when I saw him emerge from the driver's side. As Neil and I walked down to the race area, I reminded myself to wait for Will to come to me and tried to ignore the voice that suggested he might not. We passed a group of males and females in matching branded jackets stood holding various stretch poses. Their presence and that of the soreness in my calf made me feel pessimistic.

Neil spotted some fellow Tracks runners, and we went to chat. Moments later, Will passed in front of us nonchalantly before stopping to pin on his bib. Then he turned and walked slowly towards us.

"Will!" exclaimed Neil in surprise. "I wasn't expecting to see you here for a while."

Will scratched his head and sniggered. "Same here. I decided to come back early." He looked at me with a hint of uncertainty. "Hey."

"Hi." I smiled normally and let the gaze linger.

"How did you get here?" he asked.

"Neil gave me a ride."

A look of guilt briefly crossed Will's face.

"I guess I'll have to settle for second place today," joked Neil.

Will shook his head with a smile. "There are some semi-pro runners here today. An elite team travelled up from Washington."

I glanced in the direction of the group I had passed earlier and observed their fit, lean physiques as they removed outer layers of clothing.

The half marathon started first. I paused my warm-up to watch from a distance as Will dashed away from the line. Jogging was painful, and I began to wonder if it had been wise for me to have run as far as I had on Wednesday.

When the announcer called the 5k runners to the start, I stood back slightly from the line. The adrenaline I had felt ahead of the last race seemed to have been replaced with apprehension. At the buzzer, I sprang away with a grimace. The course started with a gradual incline, and I forced my stiff legs up it before a group of women overtook me on the flat, chatting to each other with ease. I helplessly watched them run away from me. Today wasn't going to be a winning day. The course was tough, and each step left a wincing pain through my calves. A mental marathon commenced as I tried to persuade my protesting legs to oblige. More people passed, and I looked on powerlessly. After managing to convince my legs to do a final sprint towards the finish line, I crossed it with a mixture of relief and disappointment. The clock showed a time of 21:25, and I was surprised I'd only been that much slower than the last race.

I stood with some people that had finished before me and watched the other runners come in. Will finished his race twenty minutes later, coming in third place. A smile played at the corner of my lips as he approached.

"Did you win?" he asked me with a grin.

I felt a dull thud of disappointment, knowing I couldn't give him the response I wanted to. "Not even close."

A fellow runner began to talk with him intently about technique and pacing. I listened politely, wondering if I would get a chance to speak with Will alone. His eyes tended to catch mine, as if he was wondering the same thing.

"Hey Sara, would you like a ride home later?" he asked when the person had finished speaking.

I felt a ripple of excitement as I answered. When the man asked if anyone would like a coffee, there was something satisfying about the way Will told him I didn't drink it and gave me a knowing smile, and the way this prompted the man to look between us quizzically and ask how we knew each other.

I clapped from the side as Will walked up to collect his medal thirty minutes later, looking happy and relaxed. As I watched the top three women from the 5k have their picture taken, I wished they could have skipped the race so that I could be standing in their place, seeing Will clap for me.

We left shortly after the ceremony. Will called goodbye to his friends while I tried to conceal the satisfaction of not being hidden away. At the teahouse in Oak Bay, we were greeted by a waitress that recognized us from our previous visits. I surveyed the pastry counter and suggested sharing a slice of pumpkin pie.

"We should try something else," said Will. "We'll have pumpkin pie on Halloween."

At my expression, he feigned insult. "You forgot we're hanging out that evening?"

"I wasn't sure you still wanted to." I avoided his eyes and focused on the cake display. "Let's get a slice of the German chocolate cake."

As we sat out on the patio in the sun, it was hard to believe that only two days earlier, Will had told me we should stop seeing each other. Now his foot rested gently against mine, and he smiled affectionately as we spoke. I'd walk with painful calves for the rest of the day, but it seemed worth it for the way I'd felt under the focus of his gaze.

In the evening, the sky turned a gentle mauve colour that seemed to say that everything was at peace once more.

I walked into the office on Halloween to see a box of candies on the front desk. When Will texted at four-fifteen to suggest a meeting place, I looked at the empty candy wrappers in my hand with regret. I'd spontaneously taken a handful out of a sudden worry he was going to bail on our plans like he had on Friday. I found him sitting on a bench outside a local market store, looking deep in thought.

"I haven't celebrated Halloween in years," I said as we walked. "Not since 2013."

"My last time was 2015," said Will. "My ex and I dressed up as lifeguards."

"That doesn't seem very scary."

"Nobody really dresses scary. It's more of a jokey thing." As he spoke, he seemed subdued, as if caught in the memory. Then he sniggered. "I actually saw her recently."

"Your ex?"

"I drove past her on the way to yours once. She was walking up her steps. Thankfully she didn't see me."

"She lives close to me?"

"Just two streets up."

"Oh." I brushed a strand of hair out of my eyes as a memory entered my mind.

On the corner of the block was an old video store. We rented two DVDs and drove back to my place with a pumpkin pie from the market.

My bedroom was toasty from the heater, but I kept my t-shirt on, embarrassed by an outbreak on my back. Will kept his on too. His face seemed serious, and his movements less relaxed. I wanted to reach up my hands and pull him down to kiss me, but something stopped me. We watched the two terrible movies on my bed with a space between us that I felt shy to close out of a sense he didn't want to.

From the beach, we saw fireworks shooting off in the distance, bursting into streams of gold, red, and purple. I watched them quietly, pondering why Will might be holding off physically.

Outside my building, he hugged me before walking away. Something hurt about the way he didn't look back, and I exhaled with offence as I turned around. Then I heard my name. I turned to face him, and my shoulders sagged.

"Are you uncomfortable around me?" I asked.

Will stepped closer. "No, not at all."

"Are you sure?"

He reached a hand across and stroked my hair. "Don't worry so much. You and I are good."

In the kitchen, I looked on the counter at his plate, sprinkled with pie crumbs and flecked with bits of cream. Tiny pieces of evidence that he had been with me when in reality, it almost felt like he hadn't been present at all.

The next afternoon, hundreds of job-seekers filled the room at a hiring fair to speak with various employers and give out resumes. Some employers had bowls of candy on their tables, as if hoping this would entice applicants to their organization. A handsome man with glasses and a Spanish accent approached our table and spoke with me about his engineering background. I turned around from shaking his hand to see Eva and Paige giving me cheeky smiles.

"Will your friend be in Victoria around the time of the Christmas party?" asked Eva teasingly as the crowd began to disperse.

I looked down at the collection of resumes in my hand. "I think so. I'm not sure I'll bring him, though. It might be a little soon."

By the time I returned to the office, my inbox was flooded with emails from people submitting resumes. Many of the messages noted being desperate for work. There were mentions of struggles to pay bills and concerns about employment insurance benefits due to end. I began to feel overwhelmed. Suddenly, I found myself carrying a sense of responsibility for strangers' financial circumstances and wellbeing.

When I walked to the bus stop the next day, many leaves seemed to have vanished from the trees overnight. I stumbled my way through an interview, unable to think straight. At Tyler's invitation to go to a kayaking group at the university that evening, I replied with an excuse. It masked the simple fact that I was shy about getting in a kayak for the first time in years and surrounding myself with people I didn't know. He said he'd send me a link to an event on Saturday instead, only to text again moments later saying not to mind—Harry was going.

I looked up the event online out of curiosity. It was a Motown-funk party at an arts venue downtown. My spirits rose at the idea of dancing to the music of groups I'd grown up listening to. The event page showed Joey and Liz's names in the 'Going' section. I sat back with a frown, wondering why they hadn't mentioned it. Minutes later, I pulled out my phone and texted Joey.

> I heard about that music event you're going to on Saturday, and I'd like to go. Do you know how Harry is doing?

A reply came swiftly.

> I think it's best that you and he don't see each other yet. He's been pretty emotional.

My temple pulsed with annoyance as I put the phone down. I felt a threat of angry tears at the unfairness of it, but I held them back.

I looked at the pile of resumes on my desk with an inward groan. The gym beckoned me as an outlet for my frustrations, but there were too many deadlines to reach. Instead, I sent Will a text asking if he'd like to go for a run the next evening.

Moments later, the phone rang, and Jenna called my name. A candidate I had met at the job fair said his first name expectantly, but my mind drew blanks.

"In order to hear about available jobs, you first have to register with our agency," I explained after he asked about opportunities.

"I thought I already had at the job fair?"

"No, the process involves having an interview and completing our screening procedures," I said patiently.

"Okay, can I come in this afternoon?" he asked hopefully.

"I'm sorry, we're fully booked this afternoon. We're currently reviewing all the resumes. We received a lot, so it may be a couple of days until you're contacted. We appreciate your patience." I quickly typed his name into my inbox and scanned his resume.

"What about this weekend? I'm free then."

"We're closed on the weekend."

"I really need a job," said the man pressingly.

"I understand that, but like I said, we have a lot of resumes to go through. Some applicants have specific experience that our clients need urgently."

"What kind of experience?" he asked.

"Well, we have a need for a bookkeeper and—"

"Bookkeeper?" the man repeated. "I worked as a night auditor in a hotel for a few months. I could do that."

I wrinkled my nose uncomfortably. "I'm afraid we need people with more experience. We need people who have done accounts payable and receivable, and—"

"Can't they provide training? I'm a quick learner."

"Not for this position, I'm afraid. It's to cover a sick leave. The client needs someone who can hit the ground running."

"I really think I'd be fine. I'm a great worker. All my colleagues would tell you so."

I gripped the phone tighter. "I appreciate that, but we still need people with experience in that job. I don't see any relevant experience on your resume."

The man ended the call with a sulky goodbye, and I put the phone down with a sigh.

Next door, Paige was wrapping up an appointment with a woman. Through my doorway, I saw her walk the woman to the stairs and wish her luck in hearing back from her other interviews.

The woman scoffed. "Thanks, I'll be upset if I don't. I mean, I am *from* Victoria."

With a prickle of discomfort, I watched her walk down the stairs in a pair of dark jeans. She looked to be a few years older than me. I pondered how she would have acted with me had I interviewed her with my foreign accent.

I pushed aside the guilty voice that suggested my status as a newcomer meant I didn't deserve my position. Realistically, nobody deserved a job. A job had to be earned.

There seemed to be an increasing sense of entitlement among job-seekers—an expectation of reward for minimum effort. In an increasingly digitalized world, it seemed that some people had forgotten the importance of attitude, work ethic, and manners.

A buzzing sound distracted me from my thoughts. Carrie let me know our evening plans would now involve more people. Suddenly, I no longer felt like being sociable, and I made an excuse once more. After sending the text, I rose lethargically from my desk. The Halloween box had a few candies left—the reject flavours that nobody wanted.

It was ten o'clock that evening when Will replied to agree to do something the next evening. There was a vagueness to his message, one that stirred a sense of disappointment at the memory of days when he had seemed more responsive.

In my kitchen, we chopped vegetables for ratatouille, our shoulders brushing. Will had had an interview the previous afternoon with the owner of a boutique outdoor clothing store and would be going in for a trial on the weekend. I silently scolded myself for having assumed he was ignoring me.

When Connor arrived home, the three of us chatted animatedly at the table. I enjoyed living with Connor, and I appreciated him even more as a roommate for the way he seemed to fit so easily into the dynamic and add to the conversation. When Connor left to meet some friends, Will and I sat on the couch at opposite ends, our feet touching. At my playful suggestion that we go to my room, he shuffled down further into the couch.

"I'm a little sleepy."

My stomach swelled with a feeling of rejection. "Okay. I'm just going to do some dishes."

"I'll help."

I dragged the sponge over the plates quietly. When my hand brushed his, a playful smile instinctively crossed my lips. "Sorry, I know you don't want me to touch you."

"I just don't feel like making out right now," said Will with a hint of defensiveness.

When he left at ten o'clock, his mood was bright, but I slumped on the couch and tossed the cushion away from me with frustration. I was frustrated that he didn't seem interested in being physical, and I was frustrated that my initiations seemed to contradict my request to be regarded as more than just a physical companion.

THIRTY-NINE

With the changing of the clocks came the onset of glumness that always seemed to come knocking when the days shortened. I sat at my kitchen table on Sunday evening, reading over messages I'd received the night before.

> Harry is actually fine with you coming to the dance event now.

I had first read Joey's message in Tyler and Nathan's living room. An afternoon of standing in the freezing rain watching Nathan's cycling race had inspired me to stay in their warm space and forgo the event. But the feeling of exclusion had remained with me.

I flicked through my phone to my most recent message—a text from Will asking after my evening. Tyler's words from the day before ran through my head.

"He must have a deep attraction for you if he's letting himself see you in spite of any issues he's dealing with."

The words had given me a surge of optimism, a sense of hope that Will felt he could trust me.

A glance at the clock showed that Will would have finished his job trial. His phone rang as I watched the sky begin to dim.

"I think it went well," he said after I asked about his day. "Everyone I met seems nice."

"I'm glad." I let out a laugh in an attempt to disguise my curiosity. "I've heard that everyone who works at that store is really good-looking."

"Oh, I don't know. I didn't really pay much attention."

I cleared my throat. "Are you free tomorrow night? I thought we could go up to Gonzales Hill and see the sunset. I've never been."

"I think I might be working tomorrow. Seems like they need the evening hours covered."

A flicker of disappointment trickled through me. "All good. That's good."

I hung up the phone with a daunting sense of realization. My happiness for Will having a job was only confused by the barrier it would potentially create in seeing each other. I sank my elbows onto the table and told myself not to be so selfish. Outside, the sky had turned pitch black.

You said you wouldn't do this, a voice said sharply. *You said you wouldn't be clingy and dependent.*

Will messaged the next afternoon to confirm he was free after all. I found him in the history section of the local bookstore, studying the inside cover of a military hardback. We drove down to Fairfield and up the steep road to the observatory at Gonzales Hill.

The sunset was just reaching its final stages, warm colours blending into one. Dots of light shone from the houses below us. Will sat quietly on the rock, a few feet away from me. I glanced across at him, wondering why he hadn't sat closer. He was quiet, and it made me uneasy. I wanted to reach out and touch his arm, but the prospect of him resisting dissuaded me. I looked at the sprawling view in front of me once again. Suddenly, it seemed anti-climactic.

"Would you like to be alone?" I asked.

Will stirred slightly. "Why do you ask that?"

"You don't seem too happy."

"What makes you think that?"

I pulled my knees up to my chest and shrugged. "You're just… it's like you don't want to be here."

Will said nothing, and I found myself growing deflated. I stood up and brushed off my coat. "Let's just go."

We drove in silence. There wasn't even any music to drown out the awkwardness. I swallowed the lump in my throat, determined not to cry.

"I need to get some groceries," said Will quietly. "Should I drop you off first or after?"

"I need some too, but I can just walk home after."

I got out of the car and walked ahead without him, prepared to leave without saying bye. In the candy section, I saw from the corner of my eye that he was approaching.

"Yes, I'm buying chocolate because I'm upset," I said sullenly.

"What's wrong?" he asked softly.

I turned to look at him with a sigh. "I don't know what's going on. You seem unhappy, and I don't know how to react. I'm scared to touch you because of how resistant you seem." I shrugged helplessly. "Am I coming on too strong?"

Will smiled. "Don't worry, Sara."

"No, it's not funny, Will." My voice broke, and my eyes began to well with tears.

"Everything's fine," he said soothingly. He came forward and pulled me in for a hug. I fell into him limply. Then he pulled his head back slightly and looked at me warmly. "Would you like to make dinner together?"

I regarded him uncertainly through teary eyes. He led the way to the cheese section and picked up a slab of mozzarella and some salad. A renewed energy seemed to radiate from him.

In the car, I reached for my seatbelt hesitantly. "Do you definitely want to hang out? We don't have to."

Will's hand patted my knee gently. "What should I say to make you not worry?"

"That you're happy around me?"

"I am happy around you," he said sincerely.

I tried to hide my puzzlement as Will made a salad dressing while chatting jokily with Connor. He was like a different person. *Surely he wouldn't make this much effort with Connor if he didn't want to keep seeing me?* I thought as I went to my room for a moment of privacy.

Moments later, I heard soft footsteps entering the room. Will took a seat on the green rug next to me.

"What's in the box under the bed?" he asked with gentle curiosity.

I slid the box towards me with a smile. "Mementoes."

Will watched inquisitively as I took out letters, medals, small notes and cards, a race bib, plane tickets, and the scrap of paper from the little girl in the tourist office in Waterton. He smiled when he saw his postcards, placed neatly on top of each other. How long ago it seemed now since the first had arrived in my mailbox. As I looked fondly at the four-leaf clover my mum had drawn for me on a scrap of paper, Will reached carefully into the box and removed a small yellow post-it note. His eyes narrowed as he tried to read it.

"What's this one?" he asked.

I took it from his hand and immediately pulled it to my chest with an embarrassed laugh. "You probably shouldn't read it."

Will leaned forward with a smile and tried to take it from my hands. As I leaned back, he moved closer and tickled my arms. I lowered to the ground with a giggle as he hovered over me, and my fingers loosened their grip.

"It's a list of baby names," I said with a bashful smile. "Amy and I randomly made a list one day at work."

Will laughed and gave the note one last look before placing it back in the box. I pulled out an album of photos and handed it to him. He turned the pages delicately, studying each picture with a fond smile. My parents, my nephew, our house, our dog, the sheep, the orchard. I watched him quietly, wondering what he was thinking.

At his car, he hugged me tightly. "I appreciate you," he called after me as I walked away.

I turned with a playful smile. "I appreciate you making me cry in the candy aisle."

Will's brows furrowed. "Hey, wait. What was that about?"

Instantly regretting my attempt at a joke, I approached him shyly. "I wasn't sure if it was to do with me. It was hard to read your mood earlier."

Will scratched his ear. "To be honest, I haven't been feeling great, but hearing that doesn't make me feel better."

I bit my lip and looked down. "I'm sorry. I'll try to stop worrying about things." I looked at him with eyes that asked for a hug, and my lips softly brushed his cheek.

From the porch, I looked back at the empty space where his car had just been. There was something surreal about the evening—the way it had ended so differently from how I thought it would. The deflated feeling was replaced by a sense of accomplishment. A restored belief that I could turn things around.

Despite my renewed optimism, a voice of caution told me to take small steps with Will. At Connor's proposal that we host a gathering at our apartment on the coming Sunday, I agreed enthusiastically. But when he suggested I invite Will, I concealed my hesitancy. Wary of any pressure a group setting might create, I instead proposed to Will that he and I see each other on Friday evening.

I sat around at home restlessly until a text came from Will at six o'clock proposing we meet for a drink downtown. I jumped in the shower with a buzz of excitement and rummaged through my makeup bag for my favourite lipstick. My shoes tapped on the bus floor, anticipating the evening to come.

Will was stood on the corner of the main street leaning against a lamp, his eyes on the ground. I took a breath and walked over with a spring in my step. But when he looked up and saw me, my heart sank. A limp smile, big sad blue eyes, no energy.

"How are you doing?" I asked gently, already knowing the answer.

Will looked back at the ground. "Sorry, I don't really feel like drinking right now."

"Okay." I looked around uncertainly, hearing faint music from inside the various pubs and bars. "We could go for a walk?"

We walked aimlessly up the street in what gradually seemed to be the direction of Zoe's apartment. I tentatively asked about his day.

Will snorted. "I'm earning peanuts in a company owned by a millionaire. It's ridiculous. I'm worth more than that; everyone is."

"You're right."

"I could earn more money working at a fast-food joint in Alberta," he grumbled. "It's a bullshit system."

I dug my hands further in my coat pocket and rubbed my coloured lips together. He probably hadn't even noticed that I was wearing mascara in front of him for the first time.

"You get a commission from sales, right?" I asked.

"Yeah, but not that much. They have a confusing way of doing it."

"You're a likeable person. I'm sure you'll make a lot of sales," I said encouragingly.

Will huffed at the ground.

"Is everyone else on the same wage?" I asked.

"No idea."

"Because if they're not, you should—"

"I don't know what the others make."

I clamped my mouth shut, feeling my cheeks grow warm. His street was approaching. I regarded the sign resignedly.

"Would you just like to go home?" I asked gently.

"Yeah."

At his response, I came to a halt and gestured limply to my right. "I can take the bus."

"I can give you a ride." His eyes met mine briefly before falling back to the ground.

I followed him quietly to his car. We drove without speaking until the dark windows of my apartment came into view. I unbuckled my seat belt and turned to face him.

"You are valuable. You'll work it out."

The car tires screeched as he pulled away. I walked silently past the two residents smoking outside on the porch before I let out a sigh. In the bathroom, I slowly removed the new blouse I had worn for the first time and watched scented bubbles froth in the bath as I removed my makeup.

My phone sat on the floor mat, ready for the call that something told me was looming. It came twenty minutes later as I lay rubbing my feet over the tap in a daze.

I found Will outside, perched on the wall with his hands in his pockets. He looked up at me with a mixture of despair and shame, and we began to walk quietly down our usual route. His breathing was heavy, as if preparing himself. I waited patiently.

"I don't know how to talk to you," he said with a disgruntled tone.

"What do you mean?" I asked delicately.

He ran a hand through his hair and sighed. "I don't know how I can explain my feelings to you so you can understand."

"You can talk to me."

I reached out for his arm and went to hug him. He pulled back uncomfortably and walked away. I watched him helplessly. At the end of the road, he stopped, as if waiting. I followed tentatively, and we walked side by side down to the beach. It was deserted except for a man walking his dog. We sat silently on a log, a few feet apart from each other.

Suddenly, Will turned to me with a look of bewilderment. "Why are you here with me now?"

"Because you asked to talk to me, and I want to be here with you," I said calmly.

Will scoffed with derision.

"You're not selfish and uncaring like you think you are," I continued. "I know there is a good person inside of you because I've experienced it myself."

Will remained silent, staring moodily at the ground. I wrapped my jacket tighter around me and looked at him hesitantly. "Do you know where these feelings come from?"

Will sniffed. "They're pretty constant. I just hate people. I hate society."

I nodded. "It's understandable to feel that way sometimes, with everything going on in the world."

Will continued to stare at the ground, consumed by thoughts. Then he looked up with frustration.

"I'm twenty-six, and what the fuck am I doing?"

I watched his head fall into his hands, his breathing becoming heavy once more.

"You're working it out," I said. "Everybody's different; everyone's at different stages. It's okay."

"What's the point of it all?" he asked bitterly. "Life is just meaningless. I'd be better off not being here."

The skin on my back prickled with fear. "Please don't say that. It's not true."

"You don't understand. I just hate myself." He ran his hands through his hair and sighed with aggravation. "I wish I could get away from myself."

"I want to understand," I said pleadingly.

Will looked at me with a disbelieving scowl. "Why?"

"I want you to feel better about yourself."

Will scoffed and turned away. We sat in silence for a few minutes. My mind raced with ideas of things to say to brighten his mood. But in his state, it seemed he would resist any form of positivity.

Eventually, Will stood up with a gloomy sigh. "Let's go."

We walked in silence along a narrow side path that passed a playground.

"I really just want to kick something," said Will.

He turned his head around, and before I could say anything, he was running back the way we had come. I watched with alarm as he launched a kick at a real estate sign and sent it flying in the air. It landed on the ground with a sharp clang that made me shiver.

When Will returned, his face was less tense, relief oozing out of him. "That's better."

I walked quietly, stunned into silence.

"Can I sleep on your floor?" asked Will with a touch of timidity.

"You don't have to sleep on the floor, Will."

"Zoe has a friend visiting, so I'm basically homeless for a few days."

I looked at him with concern. "You should have said sooner. You can stay at our place. Connor won't mind. He really likes you."

Will walked on with his head bowed in thought. A humble softness seemed to have taken over his body, and he looked up into the sky with a solemn sigh.

"I wish I could focus on the ninety-eight percent of things in my life that are awesome and not on the two percent that are shitty."

"You'll get there."

Will's shoes scuffed over a pebble on the ground. "I feel like you always see me at my worst."

"It must be a sign," I joked.

"Probably," he sniggered. Then he lowered his voice. "I'm kidding."

I glanced behind us at the sign lying in the middle of the path and licked my lips daringly. "I can tell you used to play soccer."

Will's face relaxed into a smile, and I willed the feeling to continue.

The lights in the apartment were off when we walked through the door. We brushed our teeth together quietly, and then Will lay down in my bed facing me. When the light was off, I reached over slowly and stroked his hair.

"I'm sorry," he said softly.

"It's okay. Thank you for letting me in."

I woke to the sound of Will rustling. The clock showed it was seven-thirty. He sat up and rubbed his face with a look of discomfort.

"Did you sleep okay?" I asked.

"Yeah, I just have a headache." He closed his eyes and hesitated. "Sometimes I'll bang my head on the wall when I'm feeling pent up."

I felt a pinch of panic. "Please don't do that."

"I can't always control it."

We walked down to the laundry room, him carrying the basket with his clothes lying on top of mine. The machine began to spin, mixing the clothes together. When we returned from getting breakfast an hour later, our wet clothes were intertwined. Will had shared more of himself with me, and as I watched him place the clothes in the dryer, I hoped that his demons had been washed away.

Connor entered the living room in his gym gear as Will and I sat on the couch.

"Hey, Will, are you coming over tomorrow night?" he asked cheerily.

Will looked between us with confusion. "What's tomorrow?"

"Sara! You didn't tell him?" scolded Connor playfully.

A sinking feeling of shame consumed me as he told Will about the gathering.

"I wasn't sure if you'd want to come," I said quietly.

Will laughed it off, but in his eyes, I saw a sadness that made me wince inside. Minutes later, he rose to his feet and said he was going for a run.

I stood up with concern. "Is that a good idea? What about your headache?"

"It's fine now."

I went to my room while he used the bathroom, pretending to tidy things that didn't need tidying. In my mirror, I saw him approach my doorway timidly.

"See you," he said.

I turned to face him, and his blue eyes met mine with a look of uncertainty.

"Here." I held out my keys. "To let yourself back in."

At the sound of the door closing, I sat down on my bed and chewed a nail.

Maybe he'd hoped you'd join him, a voice pondered.

But he might have wanted space, said another.

What if you just made him feel unwanted? What if he's feeling worse about himself? asked the first voice with worry.

I scrunched up my face in annoyance. *Idiot. Why didn't you just tell him about the gathering?*

Half an hour later, the door opened, and in stepped Will carrying our bag of dry laundry. He put it in the bedroom without looking at me. Still reeling with guilt, I handed him a towel for the shower and sat in the living room with a book. The pages turned, but the words didn't seem to go in. Minutes later, Will walked into the living room sluggishly and looked out of the window with a heavy sigh.

"Would you like to talk about anything?" I asked gently.

"No, it's all right."

I sat up in my chair. "If you want to come tomorrow night, I'd obviously like you to."

"It's all right."

My shoulders sank slightly. "Well, you're welcome to crash here again anytime."

"Thanks, but it's fine."

I walked him downstairs to his car.

"See you," he said glumly, his eyes glancing at my feet.

I moved closer to hug him. He looked at me blankly, as if confused by the gesture. Then he looked down with a sigh and rested against his car bumper.

"How the hell am I supposed to go sell t-shirts?"

I shrugged with attempted optimism. "Better to be doing something than nothing, right?"

He stared at the ground sourly, and I impulsively tapped his knee. "I appreciate you."

Will scoffed at my words, his moody eyes still on the floor. Then he walked towards his door without another word and drove away.

Upstairs the apartment was cold and silent. I collapsed onto the couch with a sudden feeling of exhaustion. The cushion took my weight and with it the strength I had been holding onto for the past twelve hours. With the armour now removed, I let myself cry.

At four o'clock came the text.

> Sorry for having to deal with me last night and this morning.

I told him it was fine and not to talk himself down that way. But part of me wanted to tell him off for leaving the way he had, for refusing my affection so coldly. A fear of reinforcing his perception of himself stopped me.

A lack of energy made me resign myself to my room the next morning. When I emerged from the bathroom in the afternoon, I had a missed call from Will. *Perhaps he'll ask to stay the night, after all,* I thought as I got dressed.

He called once more after I had returned from the grocery store. There was an uncertainty in his voice, as if he had forgotten what he wanted to say.

"Did I leave my toothbrush at your place?" he finally asked.

"I haven't seen one."

"Okay. No worries."

An awkward pause ensued. I bit my lip, debating whether or not to ask him about his counselling sessions. His vague response to my question made me suspect he hadn't sought any professional help. In some ways, it wasn't surprising. How could a minimum wage job with no benefits pay for counselling?

I took a breath. "I need you to tell me what to do and say when you look at me the way you do when you're sad, because when I try to comfort you, you seem to close off, and I just want to hug you."

There was a sigh, followed by a pause. "I feel like a failure for not having done my trip."

"You're not a failure, Will. It's not your fault that things kept getting delayed." My voice picked up with enthusiasm. "You can always go back one day."

"Maybe," he said unconvincingly.

My stomach rumbled in protest at the lack of food I'd eaten all day. "I don't really feel like having people over and being sociable."

"I genuinely would have come. I just didn't think I'd have a great time, given how I'm feeling."

My face flushed with another shot of guilt. "I'm really sorry I didn't mention it. I just thought about what we talked about in terms of being in a serious relationship and, well, I didn't want to make you uncomfortable."

"It wouldn't have bothered me, meeting your friends."

I bit my lip with regret. "Maybe another time, then."

Guests would be arriving in thirty minutes. I rose to my feet reluctantly to brush my hair. Connor's three female friends were friendly and energetic, and I had to force myself to match their level. Joey and Liz sat on some cushions next to each other. I pictured Will sitting by them, laughing politely at their jokes and dropping teasing comments about me with an affectionate smile. The thought of it gave me a sad, aching feeling.

FORTY

For Monday's statutory holiday, Joey and I arranged to go for a hike. On the drive to Thetis Lake, I looked out of the window quietly and thought about my mum's latest email in which she'd said she hoped being with Will wasn't too draining on me.

"How was the soul night last weekend?" I asked with a hint of bitterness as we commenced the trail around the lake.

Joey shoved his hands in his pockets. "It was fun. Harry actually ended up bringing a friend."

"A friend?"

"Her name's Alina. They met at squash club."

"Harry joined a club?" I asked in surprise.

"He's been making more of an effort to be sociable in the past few weeks."

"Good to hear he's finally realized there's more to university than getting straight A's," I said dryly.

Joey scratched his head. "To be honest, I think it's been more about trying to distract himself from you."

A twig snapped under my foot, and with it, my temper.

"I see. So, for months I'm told that Harry wants to be more independent and not commit to one relationship. Then, I'm essentially punished by being excluded from an event because his poor soul is feeling upset and doesn't feel ready to see me, only for me to be told it's fine to come after all, because he's got some new girl to go with him and boost his ego."

Joey bowed his head with guilt. "I'm sorry, I just felt it was best you don't see each other yet."

"It was selfish of him and unfair to me."

Joey sighed. "You don't understand, Sara. He's been really struggling. I'd go to his place, and he would cry about you the whole time, saying he regretted everything and wanted to take it all back. And then when I told him about the new guy—"

"You told him about Will?" I asked sharply.

Joey shrugged. "I had to. It was the only way to make him realize he had to move on. And don't get me wrong, he's happy for you, but it was hard for him to hear. That's why I didn't think he should see you."

"But he ended up bringing a girl anyway!" I crossed my arms. "So, what, are they dating?"

"Not officially. I think it's just casual. We were at a friend's place on Saturday, and she was there, and he stayed at hers after."

I looked at the soil under my feet and once again cursed my reluctance to invite Will to the house gathering.

"How do you feel about Harry seeing someone else?" asked Joey tentatively.

I picked up my pace to stride up a small hill. "It doesn't bother me if he's seeing someone else. I just don't like feeling left out."

As we stood looking out over the lake, Joey cleared his throat to break the silence. "How's it going with Will? I was hoping to meet him last night."

"It's good. He just had something else on yesterday."

"You should invite him on a hike with us sometime."

I nodded and looked away. Little did Joey know about the challenges that had surfaced over the past few weeks. Part of me desired to talk about it, but it was outweighed by a desire to protect Will's privacy.

And then there was the part of me that didn't want to hear the concerned tones and suggestions that I step back. I thought of Carrie's worried face a few weeks earlier. She was overseas on vacation for the next few weeks, but I knew what she would say about it all. Things that came from a place of care but seemed so easy to say from an outside perspective.

It didn't seem right, the idea of giving up on someone when the very thing they needed was support. How could I just drop someone I had become so invested in?

When I arrived at work the next day, I decided to talk to Paige and Jenna about Will.

"I guess you just have to be there for him if he wants you to be," said Paige sympathetically.

If he wants you to be. The words ran through my head with an unsettling presence.

Moments later, I picked up my phone and asked if he wanted to do something on the weekend or if he would prefer some space.

The team had agreed to go to the gym together, having been too busy to go the previous week. As I emerged from the washroom in my gym kit, Eva looked at me curiously.

"I think you've lost weight," she remarked.

I looked down at my shirt in surprise, unable to tell.

"You do look very slender," said Paige in agreement.

"Must be all the running I've been doing," I said.

My calf had been sore for the past three weeks, and I felt it throb during certain movements in the class. I walked slowly back to the office with the reluctant acceptance that I should avoid running for a couple of weeks.

A triumphant sound came from Paige's office before she told us a client had emailed her to say they wanted to hire a candidate. I read the forwarded email and recognized the candidate as someone I had interviewed and submitted. A feeling of dejection landed heavily in the pit of my stomach when I saw the client's thanks go purely to Paige.

At Jenna's appearance in my doorway, I forced a smile.

"Harry dropped this off for you," she said, handing me a letter.

I stood up in surprise and looked out of my window to see the backs of Harry and Joey walking down the street. Harry's shoulders were hunched against the cold. I looked down at the letter in my hands and opened it. It was from the student loans company, informing me that my overseas income was due for assessment. I had forgotten to notify them of my new address.

As I sat back down in my chair, I began to wonder what Alina looked like. Harry had never really had a specific type. Then the buzzing of my phone distracted me, and all thoughts of Harry promptly left my mind as I read a message from Nathan.

> Will came into my workplace for coffee last night! We had a good chat. I look forward to getting to know him more.

Intrigued, I asked how they had got talking.

> I'd seen his picture on social media, and I initiated the conversation. He did seem a little surprised when I said, 'And you're seeing my friend, Sara.'

My eyes widened in alarm.

> You're joking about saying that to him, right?

No?

I put my head in my hands with a groan. In my mind, I pictured a worried face, its owner concerned at the thought I had been giving people the wrong impression, and embarrassed at the prospect I had shared sensitive details.

> I don't want him to think I've been suggesting to people we're more serious than we are. We've just been taking things slow.

Suddenly, I felt a piercing in my temple, and then dots began to appear in my eye. I reached for my water bottle and gulped down a few mouthfuls.

> It wasn't weird at all. We chatted for fifteen minutes after that.

I closed my eyes and inhaled deeply. As I rubbed my temple, a voice of reason gradually appeared, reminding me of the time Will had told me he'd seen Nathan on his bike. The only way he would have recognized him was by seeing a photo of him online. Looking up people on social media was the way the modern world worked.

Maybe Will was happy to hear you told friends about him, said a reassuring voice. *Maybe it made him feel uplifted, knowing you weren't trying to hide him away after everything you've witnessed.*

My migraine slowly subsided. I walked home in the cold November rain, and once there, made a point of hiding my phone away. When I checked it before bed, Will had replied to my message about the weekend.

> I'm not sure. I'll let you know how I'm feeling, but right now, I kind of want to do my own thing.

My shoulders slumped with dismay. Suddenly, my earlier concerns seemed valid.

Then my phone buzzed again.

> Sorry, it's not that I don't want to see you or anything like that.

I closed the message with a faint sense of relief and turned off the light. But as my eyes looked into the darkness, I wondered if his desire for time alone was just a reference to the weekend.

A dull cloud seemed to hang over me the next day, following me wherever I went. The lethargy that ensued conflicted with the fierce gale that had been blowing all morning. Wind whistled between the cracks in my office window. I turned and looked out through the glass in a daydream. Another sudden gust sent the branches of the tree outside flailing backwards. The branches wobbled weakly, overcome by the power, unable to resist. As they continued to struggle against the gusts, it seemed like at any moment, they might snap and fall to the ground.

I pulled my eyes away and turned slowly back to my computer. I would finally address my mum's last email. I'd tell her, with a sinking in my stomach, that I was going to try to start viewing Will just as a friend and nothing more.

I tried to boost my spirits by planning some time off with my remaining vacation days. I had already decided I wouldn't be flying home for Christmas. It was a lot of money for only a few days, and a part of me worried that spending time outside Canada might hinder my chances of being invited to apply for permanent residence. But with the prospect of spending Christmas alone came a melancholy feeling, a feeling I was reluctant to admit to anyone else. I decided to book the three days after Christmas off and left them in my calendar with a question mark hanging over them.

A woman sang with wistful tones as I sat alone in the apartment on Friday evening, writing down a timeline for starting the residency application. I had spoken with a few people I knew that had gone or were going through the process, and all seemed to provide conflicting information. I picked up my notepad and scanned over the next steps I had set for myself. But the singer's sorrowful words distracted me. I dropped the notepad on the table with a sigh.

It's not that you won't see him again. It just might be a while.

A moment later, my phone buzzed from across the table.

Actually, what are you doing tonight?

My body froze, stunned by the bizarre coincidence of two people thinking about each other at the same time. When I told Will I understood if he wanted space, he insisted he was fine, and thirty minutes later, I greeted him at the door.

His mood was jovial as we walked down the street, my arm linked through his in the cold. At his mention of meeting Nathan, I acted like it was new information. But when he spoke positively about their interaction, I began to believe that the reference to our relationship might have been beneficial after all.

We drifted back to my apartment comfortably. I carried no expectations as we lay side by side on my bed watching a documentary. Then, Will's head gently fell onto my pillow with closed eyes. Calm and peaceful, all troubles locked away.

I turned the laptop off before quietly placing it on the floor. At my movement, Will stirred and sleepily asked if he could stay. I turned off the light, and the room became silent except for the soft sounds of our breathing. My eyes began to droop contentedly.

But some time later, I woke to the sound of rustling, and then there were gentle footsteps on the floor. I rolled over and turned on the light to see Will holding his coat.

"Are you leaving?"

Will glanced back at me and nodded.

"Are you okay?" I asked uncertainly.

"Yeah." He reached behind him for the door. "Night."

I stared at the closed door in astonishment. And then, for the first time, I felt angry.

> Even if your mood suddenly drops, please don't ask to sleep over only to up and leave without saying anything. That hurt.

I sent the message at the kitchen table the next morning with a firm nod. A reply came quickly.

> My mood didn't drop. I just wanted to go home and sleep in my own bed.

At Will's proposal to meet in the afternoon, I sat up with satisfaction. When I opened the door, he came forward and gave me a long hug that made the hurt feelings melt away.

We left the building and walked down past the creek, having a light and easy conversation. But as we approached our usual teahouse, I couldn't hold my feelings in.

"Do you still want to sleep with me?" I asked quietly.

"I don't want to sleep with anyone at the moment."

I nodded at the ground. "I understand. You just have to appreciate that I had wondered if it was because of me or something I'd done."

"It's not you, Sara."

We sat outside under the hanging plants. Will left a milky stain on his top lip and looked at me with big eyes. "Do you still think I'm pretty?"

My lips curved into a smile, and then our eyes locked together with an intensity that made everything around us disappear. I wanted to tell him that I got goosebumps every time he looked at me a certain way. That I would inevitably think of him every time I listened to a certain song. That I daydreamed of us driving around in a truck and hiking more crazy mountains together. That he'd made me feel alive again at a time when the future seemed grey. That I was scared I'd wake up one day and realize it had never happened.

"Yes, I do."

He smiled, his eyes still on mine. "Thank you. I think you're pretty too."

I looked down with a bashful smile. "That's a relief."

Will stroked my hand tenderly. "What do you mean?"

I traced the pattern on the tablecloth with my finger. "I've sometimes felt like you're uncomfortable around me because you don't seem to like affection from me."

Will's finger moved up my skin until his hand was resting on my arm. "I'm sorry, I don't want you to feel like that."

Upon seeing my face, Will's eyes softened.

"Don't give those sad eyes," he pleaded gently. "You make me feel bad."

He raised his hand and gently squished my lips into a smile. As my face goofed up, I took his hand and moved it down to the table with mine.

"Did you and Harry argue this much?" Will joked as we walked back.

"Way more." I stuffed my hands in my pockets. "He often won. And now he seems to have won the loyalty of our friends, at my expense."

Will looked at me. "How do you mean?"

"Because I'm being left out of social things." I kicked at a stone on the ground. "I guess I should have expected it would happen, but it still hurts a little."

"I can imagine. I'm sorry to hear that."

I uttered a dry laugh. "Even at work, there are some clients who don't seem to remember me. I'm starting to wonder if I'm invisible."

"I can tell you for sure that you're not invisible," said Will warmly.

As we walked on, our roles seemed to reverse, and Will was consoling me. At my porch, he wrapped his arms around me and looked down at me with caring eyes.

"You should do something fun with Connor tonight."

I looked up at his encouraging smile, and in an instant, my plan to view him as a friend no longer seemed possible.

FORTY-ONE

Although I was taking a break from running, Tyler encouraged me to come for a drink at The Anchor on Wednesday evening. I invited Will to join, and he said he would come along.

"You look nice," remarked Connor as I emerged from my room that evening.

I gave a twirl and laughed, but as I caught the bus downtown, I reminded myself not to go in with high expectations. A few other runners remained at the table as I walked into the pub at seven-thirty and sat with my back to the door. When Tyler smiled and waved his hand in someone's direction thirty minutes later, my chest fluttered with hope. I turned to see Will take the empty seat next to me with a relaxed smile.

Tyler's girlfriend appeared ten minutes later, and soon it was just the four of us. The dynamic clicked comfortably, and light-hearted conversation flowed. A cycle streamed between Will and me—his teasing comments and affectionate smile followed by my rolling eyes and playful touches. When Tyler went around the table asking for rejection stories, Will looked down with an embarrassed smile.

"I don't really have any, to be honest. I haven't asked many girls out."

I raised my eyes to see Tyler regard Will with a knowing smile. There was something elevating about the sight of it.

Later on, we were greeted by a few more of Tyler's friends. He went around the table giving introductions.

"Sara runs with Tracks, which is how Will met her." He flashed a cheeky smile at Will before proudly adding, "And I was there."

When I spoke, one of the friends looked at me curiously and asked where my accent was from.

"Oh, I thought it was Australian," he remarked in surprise when I told him.

"It takes a while," joked Will.

The man proceeded to talk about a business he had recently set up. His pride came across as boastful, and as he continued, I sensed Will's energy start to fade. He drank his beer quietly, his eyes on the table. I observed with silent dismay as the evening's joy began to fade away.

Minutes later, Will gathered his coat from behind him without saying a word. I swallowed and looked at Tyler.

"I should probably get going too. Busy day tomorrow."

With a look of disappointment, Tyler nodded and took the unfinished beer I passed him.

Once outside, Will seemed chirpier again. Reluctant to make him dwell on negative feelings, I decided not to share my opinion of the man. At the top of the street, we hugged goodbye with a silent denial that anything had just occurred.

I hadn't lied when I told Tyler I had a busy day coming up. The next afternoon, Eva, Paige and I had lunch with a client that was visiting from Vancouver. In the sushi restaurant, I ate slowly, wary of looking clumsy with my chopsticks. The man was English, and he took an interest in where I was from and why I had moved to Canada. I began to relax as we talked about our home country. The conversation then moved onto business and the upcoming contract renewal bid. At Eva's request for feedback, the man noted how pleased he was with the agency's work.

When we said our goodbyes and returned to the office, Eva took off her coat and looked around at us with a mixture of relief and doubt.

"Do you think that went well?" she asked. "I thought it seemed okay, but now I don't know."

"You sound like me after a date," I joked.

A few minutes later, a new email titled *Thank You* arrived in my inbox. Eva noted how quickly I had caught on to the nuances of the client's needs and commended the quality of candidates I had presented. Then she highlighted how valuable my contributions had been to the team and the community in general since I joined the agency.

Recent insecurities about my work being recognized began to fade as I read the email, and Imposter Syndrome took a sidestep. I let myself believe the words and believe that I was responsible for the accomplishments that had been referenced.

Long ago seemed the days when I had wondered if I would ever find a job in Victoria. I had found more than just a job; I had found something challenging and fulfilling that allowed me to continue the career path I enjoyed. I had found something meaningful that allowed me to help and empower others. I had found what seemed like my calling. I began my reply with a smile still glued to my face.

And then the memory of Will's dip in mood the evening prior entered my mind. It was followed by the memory of him on the beach and the words that had left his mouth that night.

The words of someone who seemed to view himself as a failure when he compared his life with that of others. My fingers paused their typing as I pondered the possibility that I was inadvertently adding to the problem.

When Will responded to my text the next day to say he wouldn't be able to hang out on the weekend, I tried not to overthink it. But the quiet emptiness of the apartment gave me space to reflect. Doubts began to filter through my mind as I sat in the bathtub and considered recent events. When the water turned cold, I pulled out the plug and watched the water slowly spiral and sink lower and lower until it drained away.

By Monday afternoon, something told me the end was coming. Then Will texted me, and I left the office in the direction of his house. We walked towards Fernwood Square where a large Christmas tree stood decorated with lights and fake candles. We took a table by the window in a café on the corner and sat across from one another as Christmas music played in the background. The lingering of Will's eyes and fondness of his smile made me question my doubts yet again.

"When do you think you'll next see him?" he asked after I showed him a video of my toddler nephew chattering away with incomprehensible noises.

"Hopefully next summer. I'm not going home this Christmas."

"Duly noted," said Will, his mouth curving into a smile.

Connor was eating dinner when we arrived at the apartment an hour later. From the bathroom, I faintly heard him asking Will about his Christmas plans. Then Connor mentioned my name. I leaned closer to the door curiously but their conversation was muffled. When I emerged, Will asked if I wanted to go for a walk.

On the empty beach, he chased me playfully with a piece of kelp, but on the way home, he quietened as we passed a small public garden. I glanced over the hedge nosily and spotted a bench on the other side.

"That's the spot where my ex and I broke up," said Will, nodding in the bench's direction. He sniggered dryly. "And then the six months of feeling like shit began."

His head was bowed after he spoke, eyes studying the ground. Something stopped me from asking if he was truly over her. Perhaps my intuition knew the answer would be hard to hear. Restraint fought against the urge to discover why exactly the relationship had affected him the way it clearly had.

A pile of leaves stood a few metres away. As we passed, Will gently moved his body into mine, and my legs wobbled towards the pile. With a giggle, I grabbed his jacket with my hand and regained balance.

"Meanie."

Will placed his other hand on my waist and pulled me towards him with a playful smile. "It's because I like you."

I looked up at him inquiringly. "Do you?"

Will studied me carefully. I glanced at his lips, but sudden shyness stopped me, and I slowly unlocked my arms from around his waist.

"How frustrated are you with me?" he asked as we walked on.

"What do you mean, frustrated?"

"Because we haven't been sleeping together."

I shrugged awkwardly. "I miss it sometimes."

"What do you want to do about it?" he asked.

I looked at him quizzically. "Does this mean you want to sleep with me again?"

When he said yes, the surprise was swiftly replaced by a mixture of relief and excitement.

It was late by the time we reached my apartment.

"You could come by tomorrow if you like," I said with a hinting smile.

Will ruffled his hair and nodded. "That should work. I'll text you."

I climbed into my bed feeling optimistic.

Visualizations of the evening ahead bounced around my mind as Paige and I headed to a local post-secondary college to help at a mock interview workshop for students. At her mention of the office Christmas party, I decided that I would propose an invite to Will that evening.

I walked home fervently, running a list through my mind of things to do before Will arrived. By the time I got home, he hadn't texted. As I stepped in the shower, a pit of uncertainty began to form in my stomach. Connor played his guitar on the couch with blissful unawareness while I drummed my fingers restlessly on the kitchen table. Sometimes I got up to look out of the window, as if hoping I might see Will approaching below. I would then sit down again, fiddling with my hands as I tried to think of possible reasons for lateness. The clock seemed to tick louder than usual. As I watched its hands move, the pit in my stomach grew deeper and deeper.

By eight-thirty, I had accepted Will wasn't coming. I closed my bedroom door and called him to check he was okay, but there was no answer. I looked around the room, unsure what to do with myself.

At ten-thirty, my phone began to ring. I sat up to see Will's name.

"I'm sorry, I totally lost track of time," he said.

"It's okay." I chewed my lip, and then my shoulders sank. "Just tell me next time. It's okay if you don't want to hang out, but let me know. Don't leave me in the dark."

A message arrived shortly after we hung up.

> I'm sorry, it was really selfish of me not to contact you.

I played with a strand of hair, pondering what to say. I was getting tired of saying it was okay.

> I'm just a little confused by everything.

I turned off my lamp and pulled the duvet over me.

Sometime later, I was woken by the sound of ringing. My hands fumbled through the dark for my phone. Through squinting eyes, I saw that it was twelve-thirty.

"Is everything okay?" I asked with concern.

"We need to stop doing this."

The words came out more convincingly this time. This time, I knew he meant it.

In the darkness of the room, my skin began to prickle with dread.

"Why?" I asked faintly.

"I don't see us working out long term. Our personalities just mean it won't work."

My fingers loosened their grip around the phone as his words sank in.

"But you're giving up on us when we've barely begun."

"It's not that I'm not attracted to you," he said. "I just don't see the point of carrying on when I know it won't work. I'd rather tell you now instead of later."

"But you don't know that." I clenched my jaw, trying to fight back tears. "You don't know it won't work."

"I do," he said sadly. "It won't work. We're not right for each other."

My voice began to shake. "I don't understand. You said you were happy with me."

"I am," he said. "It's not that I don't have romantic feelings towards you, Sara. I just can't be in a relationship right now, and we seem to want different things."

I chewed my cheeks determinedly. "But just last night, you said—"

"I know. It was stupid of me to say that."

"So, you didn't mean it?" I asked uncertainly.

"I did mean it, it's just…" His voice trailed off with a sigh. "We can't do this anymore. I hate telling you like this, but I know it's just going to get dragged out if I don't. It's the right thing to say it now."

By now, my eyes were able to make out the faint outline of my bed, but everything seemed blurry as Will's words resounded in my head. Then I felt a painful wrench inside. Suddenly, my shoulders crumbled, and everything seemed to break down uncontrollably.

"What's wrong with me?" I sobbed. "I just scare everyone away."

"No, you don't—"

"I scare everyone away. I always do something wrong."

"You haven't scared me away, Sara." Will's voice was soft and pleading. "You're a great person. You don't need to change; you've done nothing wrong."

"I haven't done much right either."

"That's not true. I enjoy spending time with you, and I care about you. I just don't think this will work. We see the world in a different way. I can't be a good boyfriend to you right now."

"How?" I said desperately. "How do we see it so differently?"

"I can't explain." He hesitated. "I just can't seem to communicate with you in a way that helps you understand how I'm feeling."

"But you can with others?"

"Yes, with some of my friends, I can," he said gently.

My face flushed with shame. "So, I have messed up."

"I really appreciate you trying to help, Sara, but it's not your responsibility to make me feel better."

My sobs came out unevenly as I stared down at my lap.

"How long have you felt this way?" I asked.

There was a pause on the line. "I've been thinking about it for the past couple of weeks."

My mind flashed back to his big blue eyes, looking at me hopelessly in my doorway before he left for his run. The random call the next day before our house gathering, his awkwardness on the phone. I closed my eyes and winced at the memory.

"This is so embarrassing. I've made a fool of myself this whole time."

"You haven't, Sara," insisted Will. "There's no reason to be embarrassed. This isn't about anything you've done. You're a great person."

I rubbed my forehead and exhaled wearily. "I'm tired of being told I'm a great person. It never makes any difference; people still walk away."

"I'm sorry, Sara. I'm just being honest."

I bowed my head with shame. "Why didn't you just tell me?"

"Because I wanted it to work. I like you, and I'm happy when I'm with you. I just don't think it's a good idea for us to be together."

"I feel like I've just been an inconvenience once again."

"That's not true," said Will. "I still want to hang out with you. I want you to be in my life, and I want to be in yours. I want to be there for you when you need it."

My eyes filled with fresh tears. "I feel so stupid. All this time, I've been telling myself to stop worrying and that everything is okay, and clearly it wasn't."

"It's not your fault, Sara." There was a pause and then a drawn-out sigh. "I'm sorry, I really feel awful for calling you and doing this right now. I just had to."

I remained silent, sniffling in between uneven breaths.

"Would you like space?" asked Will hesitantly.

I wiped my nose. A cloud of fatigue fell over me, and my shoulders drooped.

"I think I just need a friend right now."

"Okay, and I want to be that," he said. "Honestly, I think I can be a better friend to you if it's established that we're not in a romantic relationship."

My lip wavered. "I feel like you're just saying that because you know I'm upset."

"That's not true. I mean it."

I closed my eyes and pictured him sat in his room. "I wish you cared about yourself more."

There was a silence on the other end of the line. I slumped lower into the bed resignedly.

"I should go to bed."

"I'm really sorry I woke you, Sara. I really regret doing this over the phone."

I swallowed the lump in my throat. "Well, good night."

"Good night. I care about you."

"I care about you too."

At the sound of my alarm, I woke with a dull ache in my stomach. A weight seemed to lie on top of me, forcing me to stay down. Slowly I resisted. My feet shuffled into the kitchen, and my eyes squinted with discomfort as I turned on the light. Outside it was still dark. I sat at the table and stared at my bowl of cereal, holding the spoon limply in my hand.

In the bathroom mirror, a tired face with pink, puffy eyes stared back at me. I dabbed concealer over my bags, but as I did so, the memories of a few hours ago came back, and once again, I began to cry.

I walked into the office quietly and managed a weak smile at Jenna. Moments later, she and Paige were standing in my doorway, asking what was wrong. I slumped my elbows on my desk and told them.

Paige's sympathy was followed by a hesitant shrug. "I will say, it is admirable of him to end it now rather than stringing you along. He clearly needs to work on his own issues before being in a relationship, and he obviously didn't want to hurt you."

I let my cheek fall into my palm with a sigh. "I know. It still just hurts."

"That said, if he shows interest again, you have to say no," added Paige firmly. "Otherwise, you'll just get caught in a cycle, and that could really screw up your self-esteem."

I gave a reluctant nod, and then I uttered a pathetic laugh. "I think I repel guys."

Paige raised her eyebrows. "I really don't think so."

"Definitely not. Every time we go to the gym, that trainer Owen is staring at you or trying to talk to you," said Jenna playfully.

I rolled my eyes and shook my head. "I don't think he is."

When Eva arrived at the office, I smiled and made small talk, but when she was out of view, the smile left my face. My mind kept going back to Monday evening and conversations from days in the past. It questioned little details, the way Will's words and actions seemed to clash so sharply with the words he'd said last night. I stopped typing and wiped my eyes.

How am I supposed to trust people's intentions and feelings?

I glanced down at my bag, and after a moment's hesitation, picked up my phone to send a text.

As the end of the day approached, talk of the Christmas party began. What was on the catering company's menu? What were we thinking of wearing? I closed myself off in my office, unable to share in the mood. At four-thirty, I gathered up my things quietly, hoping to leave unnoticed.

"Sara, are you still bringing Will?" asked Eva as I walked towards the stairs.

With a panging in my chest, I turned to look at her expectant smile, her twinkling eyes.

"No."

The word came out faintly, choked by the realization of it. My eyes fell to the floor, and I walked down the stairs in defeated silence, feeling the eyes of everyone on my back.

At home, I lay on the couch in a daze. My stomach rumbled but I lacked the energy to make dinner. When Will texted to say he was ten minutes away, the rumbles were replaced by a series of somersaults.

He sat calmly across from me on the couch in his jeans and plaid shirt. I looked down at my hands, unsure where to start and too embarrassed to look at him.

"So, what's on your mind?" he asked gently.

I scratched my neck. "I guess one thing I don't understand is how you couldn't say anything sooner."

"Because it was contrary to how I was feeling," he said. "I like you. I just don't think a relationship is a good idea. I don't think we're right for each other."

A tear fell slowly down my cheek as I took in his last sentence.

"I feel like I screwed things up."

"You didn't, Sara." Will shifted in his seat. "What do you want to hear me say?"

I forced myself to look him in the eye. "That you had genuinely cared about me."

"I wouldn't be here right now if I didn't care about you."

There was something bittersweet about the comfort of his words.

I slowly nodded my acceptance. "I'd like to be friends with you. But if you change your mind about your feelings, you can't come to me, because I know I'll let you."

"I'm not going to do that," he said with an assurance that was almost cruel to hear.

The front door opened and in walked Connor, whistling a tune. I wiped my eyes and cleared my throat. Conversation was light and easy-going, like it had always been, as if nothing had changed.

As Will and I left the apartment, I noticed a Christmas wreath hanging on my neighbour's door.

"Maybe I'll ask them if they want to invite me over for Christmas dinner," I said dryly.

Will cast an eye at the door and then looked ponderingly at the floor. "I think I'm going to be here for Christmas."

I snuck a curious glance across at him. "You don't want to go home?"

"Not really. I'd rather save the money."

At his car, he gave me a long hug. "Are you okay?"

"Yeah." I swallowed, trying to resist the feelings that were building up.

Will pulled his face back to see me, his hands still on my arms. They squeezed me a little tighter. "You sure?"

I nodded, and then I walked away with a twisting feeling in my chest.

FORTY-TWO

How are you doing today?

I read the text with a mixture of gratitude and sadness. What even was today? I looked at the calendar on my wall and realized I had forgotten to flip the page.

It was December 1st, three days since the call. Three days in which I had been struggling against a drowsiness that made me want to hide away in a hole and enter a deep sleep. Three days in which I had watched with resentment as couples walked hand-in-hand down streets I had walked with Will. Three days in which self-pity had mixed with self-criticism as I recalled things I'd said and done. Stupid attempts at jokes, pathetic requests for reassurance of his feelings. In wanting to be there for him, it seemed I had only sabotaged my chances and made him walk away.

I looked at the calendar again. How had December come around so quickly? My mind flashed back to sitting across from Will in The Anchor in the summer, him telling me with lingering glances that he planned to return to Victoria this month.

I sat back in my chair and pondered how things might be if he hadn't come back to Victoria sooner but had continued with his trip as planned. Perhaps the dark feelings wouldn't have returned to haunt him, and I would instead be sat in this chair with flutters of anticipation as I counted down the days until I was due to see him again.

The sound of the phone ringing brought me back to reality. I picked it up with a continued reluctance to deal with people's questions. A woman with a dainty English accent explained that she was lost on her way to the interview. I gritted my teeth at the impression I was already forming of her in my mind: vacuous woman, raised with wealth, in control of her husband's credit card.

Then I sat down with the woman and learned she was from a town an hour and a half away from where I grew up, and she had decided to move her family to Canada because her bi-racial child was being bullied. I learned that she had been conned by an immigration scheme that had requested thousands of dollars in advance, only to offer no further assistance. I learned that the only way her husband could get a work permit and help support the family was if she became a permanent resident. I watched her grey-blue eyes shine as she tried to remain strong, and I felt awful for my initial judgment.

When the woman had left, I looked at Will's message again. Tyler's words from our meeting the night before ran through my head.

"It's a shame that Will is so self-destructive. We all think highly of you, Sara, and I imagine he does too."

I looked at the calendar mournfully, and then I told myself that after I responded to Will's message, I wouldn't contact him for another week.

Christmas lights twinkled off balconies and over door frames, in trees and around bushes as I walked home. Their brightness inspired nothing in me except the melancholy tune of a love song cynical about the supposed joys of this season. The song went on to play on repeat in my head like a soundtrack, just like all the other songs that had suddenly taken on new meanings.

As I stared at the ceiling of my bedroom, the song in my head changed to one cynical about love and romance.

Maybe you got him completely wrong, said a voice. *Maybe you were just deluded this whole time. Maybe he never saw a future with you.*

With a sudden surge of frustration, I pulled on my running shoes and sped down to the beach. As much as I'd had my own moments of self-doubt, I knew Will hadn't lied to me about his feelings. I knew his breakdowns and moments of vulnerability hadn't been an act. I knew there was a time when he had wanted things to last and had battled with his own enemies to make it work.

My throat grew tight with the cold breeze. I came to a stop by the water, gasping for breath. My body felt weak from a lack of sustenance. I looked up into the dark sky at the stars that twinkled from far away, out of reach. My lip trembled. *I know there was a time when he did want to be with me.*

The glum fatigue carried into the next week. It hung over me as I followed Eva and Paige into a meeting with a potential new client in Langford. I sat silently through the meeting and contributed nothing. I didn't have the energy to talk about receptionists and servers. As much as I told myself to focus my efforts on helping other people, helping them gain happiness only seemed to bring me so much of the same.

The apathy remained with me when I returned to the office to discover a candidate's job offer with an insurance firm had been rescinded. It turned out she had lied to me about her driving record. The extra time and effort I'd put in to help someone I had believed to be kind and sincere had been wasted. I got up and walked sluggishly to the washroom. *Why bother getting expectations up so high?* asked a voice. *You'll only be disappointed.*

Helena and I had arranged to see a play at the local theatre that evening. I resisted the desire to cancel and left my apartment early. There was a frosty tingle in my cheeks as I walked towards Fernwood Square. The night was quiet, and even though I didn't want to feel alone, I enjoyed being alone.

The only table available in the café on the corner was the one where Will and I had sat just a week earlier. I regarded it with a lump in my throat and took the seat next to the window. I remembered my growing reassurance that things were going to be okay. How naïve it seemed now.

Another unwelcome ring of my alarm the next day, and I looked up into the darkness with a lethargic sigh. Each morning, the view from the kitchen window seemed a little darker. My toast fell clumsily to my plate as another sudden round of sobs began. No morning breakfasts. No camping trips. No future together.

I stepped onto the bus reluctantly, trying to find some motivation for the day ahead. The labour market was loose, and time passed slowly as I waited for someone to contact us about a vacancy. I filled time by browsing flight search engines absent-mindedly.

As fortunate as I felt, the reality of having a permanent job in Canada suddenly seemed confining and exhausting. I thought back to what I had envisaged for myself before moving overseas. It was hard to remember because so much had changed from what I had assumed Canadian life would look like. For so long, my priority had been to find a job and continue a career overseas, but now I found myself longing for a free schedule and a road that had no end.

I went to the gym for the sake of doing something, hoping the loud music would give me some energy. Instead, it seemed to go right through me. The class left me light-headed, and as I walked out of the changing room, the sound of someone saying my name startled me. I turned to see Owen waving at me as his client sat on the rowing machine. Surprised he knew my name, I gave an inaudible reply before walking on with my head down.

At my desk, I opened my inbox to find an email from a candidate. She noted how unimpressed she was that she hadn't received any job leads since registering with the agency a month earlier. I closed my eyes and exhaled slowly, trying to stop the stinging of what felt like yet another jab. *You can't help everyone. Don't take it personally.*

At four-thirty, I wrapped a scarf around my neck before leaving the office and walking downtown. A desire to make new friends had inspired me to email Florence, the Yorkshire woman who had been hired by our client. I'd felt quite shy contacting her given the context of how we met, but her agreement to meet for tea had given me a boost. I usually tried to avoid English people when abroad, but there was something comforting about talking to a mature person who understood my colloquialisms and could relate to the realities of living overseas.

I was grateful for the distraction the evening offered. I made evening plans for the entire week for that purpose: a Zumba class, a run through Beacon Hill Park, a reunion with Carrie following her return from vacation. Each distraction was helpful, but it was only temporary, and soon again, I would return home with a dull ache and lament over what could have been.

My one-week vow of silence passed. I lay in the bathtub on Friday evening and wondered if Will would respond to the message I had sent earlier in the day. I'd come to expect a slow response from him. No longer would my contact elicit the same excitement that it had a few months ago.

His final words on his call entered my mind. *I care about you.* The words had seemed genuine at the time, but once again I began to question their sincerity. Perhaps he didn't truly care about maintaining a friendship. He had said things before when he knew he wasn't able to follow through on them.

I'm a fool to keep waiting, said a voice in my head.

At eleven o'clock, my phone began to ring. I sat up from another failed attempt at sleeping and turned on the light. I tried to meet Will's apology for his late call with nonchalance. When he said he would be free to meet on Sunday evening, I told him to text me a time and place. Then, I put the phone down and exhaled slowly. I hadn't realized how fast my heart was beating.

Excitement turned to pessimism with the absence of any messages on Sunday afternoon. By six o'clock, pessimism had shifted to annoyance. I spontaneously grabbed my phone off the coffee table.

I guess I'm being flaked on again.

Ten minutes later, the phone beeped.

Or I'm at work.

I scowled at the phone, now annoyed with myself. I didn't want to sink to that level.

I had Monday off work, and we agreed to meet in the afternoon. When I offered to meet Will at his suggested place of the teahouse, his counter-proposal that we walk from my apartment made me happier than I knew it should.

At the ringing of the downstairs buzzer, my body tensed. Upon opening the door, I could only look quickly in Will's face before lowering my eyes self-consciously.

As we walked down the street, Will's mood was light and playful. I tried to think of witty comebacks, but they didn't seem to come as easily anymore. I looked desperately at the ground, willing myself to find something funny to say. My hands stayed in my pockets as I silently scolded myself for not coming off the way I wanted to. In our new status, Will seemed so relaxed and content. I wished I could feel the same. There was something wounding about the way he seemed so comfortable with the change.

"Together?" asked the familiar girl on the till with an expectant smile.

"Separate, please." I looked down bashfully at the counter before taking my cup.

As we approached the beach, I stopped trying so hard.

"I've realized I'm feeling discontent with the idea of being confined to a full-time job and not able to travel as much," I said. "To travel, you need time and money, and to get the money, you need to work, which takes away time."

"I feel the same," said Will. "I'm back in Victoria doing a low-paying job that doesn't interest me and spending all my money on rent when the whole point of me taking a year off school was to travel."

From then, his mood seemed to dim. I cursed myself for letting the conversation turn negative. Hoping to turn things around, I looked at him brightly.

"There's still time for you to travel. You have the whole spring."

Will made a skeptical expression. "I'm hardly saving anything while living here."

"It doesn't have to be really expensive." My eyes widened with an idea. "You could do WWOOFing, and get food and accommodation in return. On all the help-exchange sites I used, people were always looking for people with horticultural experience. And you could run in your free time."

"I'd still have to get there, though," he said pessimistically.

"True, but after that, it doesn't have to be super expensive."

"I guess."

I gently punched his arm. "You should just do it. Don't think about it too much. So many people don't do things that they want to because they spend too much time thinking about it. Sometimes you just have to take the plunge, and sure, there may be challenges along the way, but overall, you'll be glad you did it."

Will mumbled inaudibly and scratched his head.

"Now is the time to do it, while you don't have many responsibilities," I said encouragingly.

"Yeah, maybe."

We walked on quietly. I had ideas, but something told me not to share them.

Outside of my building, Will closed his eyes and rubbed his head. Suddenly, he looked exhausted, as if all energy had drained from him. I let him go without approaching for a hug and walked inside with disappointment. From the living room window, I watched longingly as he lingered in his car, looking at his phone. Then, unaware he was being watched by yearning eyes, he closed his door and drove away.

> I'm sorry if I said something that bothered you.

His response came quickly.

> No, you didn't say anything. Just the same old stuff.

I put the phone down on the table sadly as Connor walked through the door.

"How's your day off going?" he asked cheerfully.

"It's okay. I was just hanging out with Will."

He smiled. "Will's great. I like him."

I smiled painfully as he took a seat on the couch and popped his feet on the coffee table. Then I cleared my throat.

"Will and I are just friends now."

Connor looked at me with surprise. "How come? You seemed good."

I rubbed my neck. "He's working through some stuff and doesn't feel he can be a good partner right now."

Connor's face softened with sympathy. "I'm sorry, that's a real shame." He scratched his arm thoughtfully. "I can see his point of view, though. I've made that call before when I was in a state of flux."

I regarded him curiously, hit with a sudden realization that I knew nothing about his relationship history. He had never brought a girl home, never mentioned going on dates.

Connor sat up perkily. "Why don't you ask Will if he'd like to spend Christmas with you?"

I laughed awkwardly. "I don't know about that."

"He might want to, but he might feel weird asking in case it seems misleading or hypocritical."

Will's previous words as we left the apartment entered my mind, but I looked at Connor unconvinced. "Maybe I'd invite him if you were going to be here too. But just him and me? I don't know."

Connor shrugged. "Just an idea." He opened his satchel and took something from it. "I forgot, there was some mail for you downstairs."

His suggestion stayed in my mind as I took the small envelope with Amy's neat writing on the front. Inside was a Christmas card. The first sentence noted how excited she was getting for the holidays.

I placed the card on the bookshelf by the window and looked out at the darkening sky. And at once, I was consumed by a piercing sense of unhappiness. An unhappiness that spurred a desire to get away from a place of familiarity and wander at my will.

My words of travel encouragement from earlier in the day ran through my mind. Words that I needed to apply to myself too, for my own happiness. Without further thought, I booked myself a flight to Kelowna for Boxing Day.

FORTY-THREE

A star-lit sky looked down on me as I crossed the bridge over the creek and continued towards Oak Bay Village. It was Thursday evening. Tyler had proposed we meet for a drink, and I had responded gratefully. We found a table in a room decorated with holly and mistletoe.

"Sorry that I was late to confirm a time," said Tyler as he took off his jacket. "I saw Will at Tracks earlier, and we were saying how bad we are at responding to messages."

"Oh, you saw him?" I folded my arms on the table. "I invited him to join tonight, but I don't expect he will."

"That was nice of you to ask him."

"I figured he might be more willing to come if it wasn't just me." I twisted the stem of my wine glass between my fingers and sighed. "I feel like I always say the wrong thing to him."

"What makes you think that?" asked Tyler with a smile.

"I'll say something to try and make him feel better or help him work through something, but it only seems to make him more down."

Tyler rested his chin on his hand in thought, as if considering how to express himself. "For people going through depression, receiving advice is sometimes unhelpful because it seems to simplify their problem and their feelings. Counsellors rarely ask questions or offer advice; they just listen."

At his words, I grimaced with realization. "All this time, I've been trying to offer solutions. I thought I was being helpful."

"It doesn't mean he didn't appreciate you trying. It just won't necessarily have any impact on his feelings."

Smothered in regret, I took a long sip of wine and slumped my elbow onto the table.

Tyler regarded me with sympathetic eyes. "Are you still a little hung up on Will?"

I nodded solemnly at the table.

"It'll get easier."

"Maybe he's been seeing someone else this whole time," I said dryly.

Tyler smiled. "Definitely not."

My eyes stared into space. "But he might meet someone else."

"It sounds like that's not a priority of his right now." Tyler shrugged. "But if he does, it's not a bad thing."

My eyes snapped back to him. "What do you mean, it's not a bad thing? How can it not be?"

"If his experience with you helps him become a better partner to someone, how can it be a bad thing?" asked Tyler optimistically.

My voice trembled. "Because it would mean that I wasn't good enough."

Tyler shook his head calmly. "It wouldn't take away anything from you, Sara. It would just mean he was in a better place mentally for a relationship."

"A relationship that could have been with me."

Tyler studied me quietly, as if accepting he wasn't going to convince me otherwise.

A moment later, I rubbed my forehead with shame. "I sound so selfish."

"Don't worry yourself with thoughts like that. You don't know what will happen."

As we left the pub, I felt a vibrating from my bag. I read the delayed apology and excuse with a sigh and walked home in the still of the night.

Tyler's words ran through my mind as I walked home under my umbrella the next afternoon. We had spent the morning setting up tables for the Christmas party, before Eva insisted that we leave early to relax and get ready. When I got home, I hung up my coat and called Will.

"I just wanted to apologize for the other day—how I kept going on about you travelling. It's ultimately your decision, and I'm sorry if I sounded a little pushy or, you know, wasn't very understanding."

Will laughed gently. "It's fine. I wasn't bothered by it. But thank you, anyway."

"Well, you know yourself best, so…" my voice trailed off awkwardly.

"Are you not at work today?" he asked.

"We got to leave early." My lips wavered with hesitation. "We have our Christmas party tonight."

"Ooh, that sounds fun."

My heart sank at the irony of it all. I pictured walking into the office in front of him, him shyly running a hand through his hair, me trying to conceal the goofy smile forming as I introduced him to my colleagues, the knowing smile on their faces.

"It'll be nice."

We spoke for a few more minutes until he had to leave for work. I ended the call to see a new message with Harry's name.

> Hey, I was wondering if you'd be free to meet this weekend? I have a gift for you, and I thought it might be nice to catch up.

I put the phone down with a groan. Not him. I didn't want it to be him contacting me.

At six-thirty there was a knock on my door. I forced the alternative scenario out of my mind and opened it to greet Joey with a smile. We walked into the office to the sound of Christmas music and chatter. Eva's husband, David, poured us a drink as we joined the others at the table. In the kitchen, there were trays of turkey, potatoes, vegetables, and stuffing.

Later in the evening, David asked if I wanted to stay in Canada.

"I'm definitely going to apply for permanent residence," I said. "Hopefully, it works out."

"We wouldn't let you leave," said Eva with a warm smile.

I met her eyes with a lump in my throat.

"Thanks for coming along," I said with a yawn as Joey pulled up outside my apartment shortly after midnight. "I hope you had a good time."

"Thanks for inviting me to be your sloppy second," he joked.

"I didn't have to invite you," I insisted. "Consider it a token of my gratitude for your friendship this past year."

Joey chuckled. "Well, thanks." He turned to look at me. "By the way, my mom said you're welcome to spend Christmas Day at ours."

I smiled faintly. "That's nice. I'll let you know."

"What are your plans for tomorrow?" he asked.

At the trigger of the reminder, I looked down at my bag with acceptance.

"I'm going to Sidney."

I looked through the window in thought as the bus trudged miserably through the rain on the familiar route to a less familiar person. I was unsure what to expect. All I knew was that I didn't want to cry.

Harry and I had agreed to meet in one of the local bookstores. My eyes glossed over the back covers of history books, and then at the sound of footsteps, I turned to see him. He looked good, with new trousers and a fresh haircut. We hugged briefly before walking across the road to a café. I could tell he was nervous because he kept talking about himself—exams, music, his plans for after graduating. I sat subdued with my chai latte and nodded at the right moments. But as he continued speaking about himself, I began to lose patience.

"Was there anything in particular you wanted to say?" he asked, his eyes searching my face uncertainly.

I looked down at my mug with a cool shrug. "I think I'm more annoyed with myself than I am with you. For having stayed for so long in a relationship I wasn't content with."

Harry sat back. "I would have understood if you'd wanted to break up sooner."

"I was too stupid and loyal to do so."

Harry pushed his glasses up his nose in thought before linking his fingers together on the table. "While I regret the way that I communicated my feelings at times, my reasons for thinking we should break up were still valid."

"I'm not talking about why you wanted to break up. I'm talking about the fact that I should have left sooner when you were making me feel so unwanted."

Harry looked into my eyes imploringly. "I really did want to be with you, Sara. I wish you could have seen me during the couple of months after we broke up. I was crying every night."

At his words, I felt the hot pricks of tears begin to form. "For you to stand there at the airport and tell me to be more selfish and not weigh others against you...do you have any idea how arrogant and patronizing you sounded?"

Harry looked at me blankly, as if he'd forgotten the very conversation. By now, tears of frustration were streaming down my cheeks. I wiped my eyes and took a determined breath.

"This is the first time I've cried about it since we said goodbye. I wasn't thinking about it at all before. I've been happy."

Harry's face softened. "I'm glad you're happy. Despite how I was feeling, I was happy to hear you were doing well."

"And yet, I was left out of going to things all because you were suddenly feeling sorry for yourself." I shook my head crossly. "That was so unfair, Harry."

"It wasn't my intention for it to be that way. I didn't want you to feel left out."

"You always think about yourself before others," I said with a snort.

A look of irritation crossed Harry's face.

"I don't think that's fair. There were times I thought about other people when we were apart, but I didn't pursue those feelings because I was with you," he said. "But you did, remember?"

His eyes flashed at mine accusingly. My mouth snapped shut at his words, but I returned his gaze fiercely. The cold silence lingered for a while until I crossed my arms and cleared my throat.

"I think we've just grown out of each other."

"I agree."

I looked up, and our eyes met. I felt nothing, and in that moment, I wasn't sure what I had to be annoyed about anymore. He still had his mannerisms that had annoyed me before, but no longer did they instil the same reaction. It didn't seem to matter anymore.

Harry cleared his throat and smiled faintly. "Anyway, I heard you're seeing someone. I think his name is—"

"We're just friends."

Harry studied me with a look of surprise. "Oh, I'm sorry. I—"

"It's for the best."

I kept my gaze down and tightened my jaw, desperate to disguise my real feelings.

After a moment, I looked up. "Joey said you met someone."

Harry nodded and smiled. "Alina, yeah. It's pretty casual, but things seem good."

I nodded, trying to ignore the jealous voice in my head. *Of course it's worked out for you.*

"You decided against the whole polyamorous thing, then?" I asked casually.

"I'm still thinking about giving it a try."

I scratched my neck uncomfortably.

"How is your family doing? How's Hannah?"

"Hannah is doing awesome. She was in France for a bit, but now she's in Austria, with Jonas." He smiled fondly. "I'll miss seeing her at Christmas. We're leaving for Hawaii in a few days."

"Ah, of course."

"Jake and I are flying together. Hopefully, we don't cut it so fine this time." He grinned at me pointedly, and I remembered the three of us dashing through Vancouver Airport two years earlier.

"Well, I hope you have a nice time."

Harry gestured his hand at me courteously, the way someone would if they were conversing formally with a stranger. "What are your plans for Christmas?"

I shrugged and picked up my mug to finish its contents. "I haven't decided yet."

The door opened behind us, and I felt a whoosh of cold air on my back. I put my empty mug down on the table and sat back in my chair, unsure what to do next.

"Would you like a ride home?" asked Harry.

"It's okay. I can take the bus."

"I really don't mind," insisted Harry. "I've been driving downtown quite a lot recently. I practise piano at the Conservatory of Music."

I looked at him hesitantly. "Okay, if you're sure."

We placed our mugs on the counter and walked quietly through the door towards his car.

"I see you finally bought yourself a proper winter coat," I said, nodding at his black jacket.

Harry laughed as he unlocked his car. "I'll need to upgrade when I move east."

"You're still planning to go to grad school there, then?"

"Definitely."

We held a mild conversation throughout the journey. Harry talked mostly about himself, but I let it wash over me. It didn't matter anymore.

Outside of my building, he brought the car to a stop and furrowed his brow. "I think I still want to keep you blocked on social media for a bit longer."

I shrugged awkwardly. "Okay."

"I am glad we met today, though."

"Yeah." Unsure what else to say, I opened my door.

"Don't forget your present," came a cheerful tone behind me as I stepped out. I turned to see Harry exit the car and walk around it towards me with something wrapped in a paper bag. He handed it to me with a smile. "You know how Nana loves to collect things. I thought you'd like this."

I pulled out a laminated poster from the bag and turned it over to see a photo of an iconic band from the seventies.

"Thanks," I said with a smile. "It's great."

"You're welcome." Harry's face turned serious, and then he came forward and hugged me for a long time.

In his hold, a kaleidoscope of memories from the past six years shot through me and left me standing with a heavy feeling that I couldn't explain.

I pulled away and swallowed before looking up at him sincerely. "I truly do appreciate what you and your family have done for me over the years."

Harry nodded, his eyes warm and knowing at the nostalgia of it, and then with a final smile, I walked into the building.

In the still quietness of the apartment that I would solely occupy for the next three weeks, I pinned the poster against the wall in the living room. I looked at it carefully, and then came an onset of sorrow as a song began to play in my head—a promise of happiness, but no warning of the obstructions.

I lay on the couch and silently reflected on the meeting with Harry. Seeing him had confirmed the closure I had felt, and I realized I was glad if I had helped him discover a desire to be more generous towards others.

And yet, the more I thought about it, the more my resentment seemed to grow when I compared his circumstances with mine. Him, feeling stable in a relaxed relationship that met his needs, about to go on a tropical vacation of waterfall hikes and ocean swims with his family. And me, mentally preparing myself to go to work the next day and for the ongoing future, as I found myself still reeling from the reality that the man who had appeared out of nowhere a few months ago and made me feel revived didn't think we were right for each other.

Thoughts of Will suddenly seemed more potent than ever. A part of me clung to a hope that he would change his mind in time, that through the non-pressures of a platonic friendship, feelings would be rekindled, that he would let go of the self-loathing and decide he wanted to let a relationship work. The hope battled devotedly against a voice that told me to concede defeat and let go.

With a deep breath, I sat up and made a vow to myself. I would have one last try. If Will didn't respond to my run proposal, I would take it as an indication of his indifference, a sign that I should give up trying, and I would no longer reach out to him.

FORTY-FOUR

Two days passed with no response. I let the weight sink in for a moment before looking out of my window at the sleet outside. I had never liked sleet. It had always seemed like an indecisive form of snow and rain, one that only left a slushy mess behind.

That evening, I ran a bath and texted Joey to accept the invitation to spend Christmas Day with his family. Then I put the phone down with a dull sigh of acceptance and stepped into the warm water.

A few minutes later, my phone beeped. I picked it up expecting Joey's response, only to see Will's name on the screen.

> Yeah, sorry, no can do, clearly…

The phone slipped out of my fingers as I recoiled with shame. I clutched my shins, holding onto the remaining pride that was crumbling away at his words. Words that had been delivered with such unfamiliar carelessness and insolence.

As I sat motionless, past scenarios began to run through my mind. Short tempers. Sudden changes of plan. Aloofness. The patience and understanding I had shown as I tried to conceal what I had regarded as my selfish feelings of worry and disappointment.

Suddenly infuriated, I rose from the tub, resisting the voice that told me to ignore the message and forget it. I had tried to ignore past behaviour. I had tried to forget the impact it had had on me. I was tired of accepting it as it quietly tore away at me.

> I know I have my own faults, and I've tried to accept yours, but after essentially being strung along the past few months and dealing first hand with your mood swings, your aloofness and insolent messages are the last toll I can take. You needn't worry about being bothered by me again.

The reply came thirty minutes later as I lay tossing and turning, unable to switch off.

> I'm not going to respond via a series of knee-jerk texts. I can either call you tomorrow to have a legitimate conversation, or we can leave it as it is. I'd prefer to continue forward on better terms, but if you'd prefer this route, that's your call.

Feelings of regret immediately filtered through my mind. Then another message appeared.

> Truly though, I get why you feel that way. Generally, spending time with you doesn't make me feel great. It's largely an issue of my own personality not meshing well with yours. We communicate and understand things in different ways, and it leaves me frustrated. It's not an issue with you. It's an issue with us.

Generally, spending time with you doesn't make me feel great. The words hit me like a stab to the chest. I told him he could call me the next day and turned off my light with a restless mind.

In what felt like a short time later, my alarm rang. I woke with groggy eyes. A re-read of the messages spurred a groan of remorse, followed by a rush of worry as I pondered the potential impact. At the bus stop, I saw familiar faces, but I couldn't seem to take them in. All thoughts were consumed with trying to decipher the meaning of Will's message.

The day passed by in a blur. I dressed for bed early, waiting for the call I'd been told would come. Time passed by, and I let myself drift off into a light sleep. Then there was a beep, and I opened my eyes to see that it was just before midnight.

> Sorry, I got distracted. To be honest, I'm not sure what else we have to say to each other anyway. I've pretty much said all I need to say. I don't think you have a realistic idea of who I am or how I think at all. Frankly, I can't muster the mental energy or patience to care about this situation. I'm not saying this to hurt you, I'm just being honest. Sorry if it's brutal. It's not meant to be.

After a momentary grip of cold, there followed a strange sense of peace. A calm after the storm. Without another thought, I deleted all our messages and removed Will's number from my phone. Then I turned off the light and said "Good riddance" into the dark.

But as my alarm sounded on the shortest day of the year, I woke with a hollow feeling inside. A brief question of whether it had been a dream, and then Will's final words ran through my mind and left a throbbing pain.

In the bathroom mirror, a pale, gaunt face looked back at me. I brushed my lifeless hair with limp hands. Every part of my body seemed to feel numb. I cast an eye indifferently at the cereal box on the kitchen counter before pulling on my coat.

On the bus, I stared blankly out of the window. The bus went to depart, only to suddenly halt again. I heard the doors re-open, and then, from my daze, I felt someone sit down next to me. A glance to my side showed the woman from the house across the road, brushing her hair out of her eyes and catching her breath after dashing across the road.

"Oh, sorry," she said as her bag slipped onto my lap.

"That's okay." I flashed a brief smile in her direction, and then, before I knew it, I was speaking again. "You live just across the street, right?"

The woman turned to smile at me. "That's right. And you're at the same stop as me."

Her name was Melissa, and she worked in the provincial government. We chatted all the way until we reached my stop, and I stepped off the bus with some restored energy.

The morning was quiet, with few emails coming in. Mum had sent me an email thanking me for the Christmas card I had sent. When I read the line asking if I was going to Kelowna with Will, my throat tightened as another wave of reality hit. I told her we had had an argument and asked that she not mention him again.

I waited for tears to spark, like I had waited all morning. They still didn't come. It was almost as if I'd exhausted myself of the ability to cry. All my tears had been used up in a year in which I'd expended so much effort trying to win the commitment of two hearts with different souls but the same resisting mind.

It was pitch black by the time the clock reached four-thirty. I grabbed my bag from the corner of my office and walked to the gym. I had been meaning to go to one of the evening classes for a while, and today was a day I needed the distraction. On arrival, I didn't recognize any of the trainers or other attendees. I sat shyly at the side as I waited for the class to start, but I left the building an hour later with a stronger mindset.

"I am not a bad person. I did my best. I tried to be supportive. I will get over this. It will get better. I am going to continue having a great life here."

In the silence of my apartment, I repeated the words out loud, willing myself to believe them.

On Friday, we closed the office early, ready for the holidays. I took the sunshine as an incentive to go for a long walk. A cool wind whipped around my ears as I walked along the coastline. I reflected on Amy's latest email and the way she had suggested I should be angry with Will for his recent communication. For brief moments I could be, but it never seemed to last. Regardless of things said and done, I didn't want things to be this way between us.

Across the ocean, the snow-capped mountains of Washington rose high in the sky above swirling grey clouds. I reminded myself how lucky I was. No matter what happened in life, the mountains would always be beautiful.

My walking route led me past Melissa's house. I regarded the Christmas tree in her window with a smile as I recalled the day before when she had taken the bus seat next to me again. All those months of not saying a word, and for what reason? A fear of looking silly? A fear of rejection?

I meant to get your number but foolishly let the opportunity pass.

I swallowed uncomfortably at the memory of Will's first written words. How did two people get to this point? How did they go from a profound attraction and a deep feeling of care to an explosion of angry and incoherent text messages?

Street signs and pathways brought back memories that left a lingering ache. I couldn't wait to get away from the island for a few days.

Christmas Eve morning carried a sharp chill. I sat with Joey's dog by my feet as we drove to Gowlland Tod Provincial Park. When he told me he was seeing someone, I tried to resist the self-pitying sense that everyone I knew was having more luck in their relationships than me.

"How are things with Will?" he asked as we turned onto West Saanich Road.

I looked out of the window. "We're not actually talking anymore. We had an argument."

"Oh, really? About what?"

"Stupid stuff. It was just a stupid, unnecessary thing that happened over text. I lost patience with him. It escalated, and he ended up saying that he doesn't feel good when he's with me and that he doesn't have the mental energy to care about us anymore. And that's the last thing that was said."

"Yikes. I'm sorry."

"Me too."

We parked off the side of the road by the forest, where a snow-covered trail led us down to McKenzie Bight. Billy trotted off into the distance, wagging his tail with glee.

"It sounds like you both reacted angrily in the moment and misinterpreted each other," said Joey. "I'm sure Will still cares."

I looked down at Billy's prints in the snow. "I don't think so. He basically said I make him feel worse about himself."

"I'm sure that's not what he meant," said Joey reassuringly. "He probably feels bad because you witness his mood swings, and he's unable to give you the relationship you'd hoped for."

I gazed up solemnly at some icicles hanging off a branch. "I don't know. He just sounded fed up and really cold, as if he truly didn't care one bit anymore."

"Why don't you call him after Christmas and see if you can talk things over?"

I shook my head in defeat. "I doubt he'd pick up the phone or call back. Honestly, I think he hates me."

"I'm sure he doesn't, Sara," replied Joey with a smile. "Not after a couple of silly texts."

"Sometimes I wish I could hate him. But I can't."

The trail led onto a small pebble beach. Calm ocean water lapped gently onto the shore, and across the inlet, the evergreen trees were sprinkled with snow. Joey picked up a pebble and sent it skimming across the surface six or seven times. I reached down with my gloved hand and followed suit. My pebble flicked the water daintily for two jumps before sinking under the surface.

"Maybe just having a friendship with Will is for the best," said Joey gently as we stood looking out at the view.

The frosty air pricked my cheeks and made my eyes sting.

"I don't know that I could ever just see him as a friend."

Snowfall spread to downtown Victoria that evening as I prepared to pack for my trip to Kelowna. I looked out of the living room window to see flakes falling gently on the ground, and at once, I felt sombre again. Across the street, the space where Will had tended to park his car was empty.

In my bedroom, I reached under my bed and retrieved the holdall I had brought to Alberta. Dust fell off the sides as I shook it. Happy memories now reduced to tiny particles sprinkling onto the floor. Flat open plains, smoky mountains, lingering blue eyes, soft moonlight, gentle hands. *It's equally not hard to keep smiling around you.*

I picked out clothes from my drawers and folded them carefully into the bag. Woollen socks and thick gloves, leggings for layers, a large fleece. Clothes for a new season.

Through the living room window, the snow was falling heavier, covering the ground in a white rug. Children walked hand in hand with their parents, sometimes pulling free to kick up a pile of snow and twirl around amongst the falling flakes.

Across the street, the parking space had been filled by another car.

EPILOGUE

And so, I find myself staring at the ceiling of a small box room in Kelowna. The events of the past year suddenly seem like a blur. My mind is fatigued, drained by weeks where the days have all seemed to muddle into one. And yet, it was only yesterday that I called my mum to wish her a happy Christmas and heard the sadness in her voice at the reality of it being her first Christmas Day without kids around. It was only yesterday that Joey's family kindly hosted me for dinner, and Joey blushed as his mum insisted that he give her the address of his friend's cabin up island and call her as soon as he arrived. My mum has no idea where exactly I am right now; in fact, nobody does. It's quite freeing.

After taking a deep breath, I sit up and open my holdall to find another sweater. City Park is just across the road that leads onto the bridge over to West Kelowna. Canadian geese fly in formation above me as I tread along the icy path through the park in my snow boots. The surface of Okanagan Lake is silver and smooth. I feel the chilly air pinch me through the two layers on my legs. The path leads past an ice rink where families laugh with each other and giggling girls hold out their arms towards their boyfriends. Further on, there is a sharp slicing sound as I walk through a quieter park. Two teenage boys skating over a patch of ice by what looks like a senior residential home swing a puck towards each other.

I return to my building an hour later after having found a grocery store and survived multiple slips on the icy streets. The doorknob doesn't turn at the twist of my hand. I remove my gloves and blow on my tingling fingers and try again, to no avail. After another unsuccessful try, I turn around helplessly. No lights show from the windows down the balcony.

Behind me, across from the parking lot, I notice a large wooden house. Through the French windows, I see a long wooden table with candles on it. I step carefully down the stairs and prepare my strongest English accent before knocking on the door. An elderly lady with pink lipstick opens the door.

"I'm so sorry to bother you. I'm staying in the motel across from you, and I can't seem to unlock my door." I roll my eyes and laugh. "I wondered if you might be able to help."

The woman smiles warmly and beckons me in. "Certainly, dear. Come in from the cold, and I'll get my husband."

I stand in the hallway, looking at photos on the wall of various grandchildren at differing stages of tooth growth.

"Gerald, you'll help this sweet young girl, won't you?" the lady calls into the living room. She then turns back to me with a smile and asks me where I'm from.

"Yorkshire, England."

Her eyes widen with pity. "Oh, so far from home!"

Her husband follows me across the parking lot and up the narrow steps. On his first try, the door opens.

"More power," he says with a strong Quebec accent.

I wave him off with several apologies.

Snow is falling when I wake the next morning. My plans to hike are instantly revealed to be naïve. Instead, I have a look at my basic city map and decide to head south. Today the lake is choppy under the blustery winds. After a while, I find the entrance to Mission Creek Greenway and join its wide path flanked by a frozen river and tall fir trees.

I have no plans for where I'm going or how far; I just want to aimlessly wander in a new place where nobody knows my name. A couple of walkers pass me heading in the opposite direction, but otherwise, I am alone on the trail. Fresh flakes of snow quickly cover the prints of those before me.

As I walk, I wonder how different things would be if I had joined the run group earlier and formed a connection sooner. I wonder if I should have seen Will in person the day before the race at Elk Lake instead of just talking on the phone. I wonder if it would have made a difference if I'd invited him to the gathering at our apartment. And I wonder if we'd still be talking had I known the right things to say.

A glum voice of reason tells me to stop and accept that it wouldn't have made any difference. An expiry date was set as soon as the demons came back and told Will he was unworthy.

An unknown amount of time later, there is an option to leave the trail. I find myself walking along the side of a busy road that is marked with swerving tire tracks. Minutes later, there is an ambulance siren. Perhaps a car crash.

My feet eventually find their way back to where I began, and I sit in City Park looking at the snow-dusted hills across the lake. Elderly women in big winter coats say hello, and a young man jogs past with confident feet that are used to the icy conditions. From the back, he could be Will. The question crosses my mind of whether he would stop if we crossed paths in the street or out on a trail.

Minutes later, the negative temperatures cause me to retreat to my room. I change out of my damp clothes and play some music.

The first song that comes on shuffle is the one that Will had identified from my hum weeks earlier. A snort leaves my mouth at the irony of it, but I manage not to cry.

I think back to the twisting tire tracks on the road, and then I think about Will and me. Two vulnerable souls that had collided, creating an impact that caused gradual damage—a crack in a mirror, a scratch on the surface. And then, finally, we had broken into fragments that couldn't be glued together again.

And yet, I had tried to glue things together. I had tried to fix Will's problems. Foolish naivety had drowned out the voice of reason telling me I could not do such a thing, that only Will could free himself. I had ignored the reality of needing to heal my own wounds before trying to heal someone else's. I never did let go of the possibility of a serious relationship with Will. I never did respect the need to let go of romantic feelings. Neither of us did.

Why did you hold on for so long? asks a voice. *Was it love, or a longing to be loved?*

I lie back on the bed and recollect the day I first met Will. A day my ego had been deflated from another relationship. *Did I only like him because he was interested in me? Would any new man have seemed better than Harry at that time?*

Part of me wishes it was that simple. Will had ticked so many boxes on my list of desired qualities. I had become blissfully tangled in a whirlwind romance that sent me swinging high then swooping low. And now I had landed with a crashing thump, bruised from the painful lesson that seeming perfection on paper doesn't guarantee a perfect partnership.

In Will, I had seen a picture of someone I had hoped he might be. I had found someone with so much promise, someone I felt I could truly be compatible with. But the colours had painted over a stain that hadn't been removed.

I run the shower and stand still while the warm water pours over me. The more I force myself to think about it, the more I know he's done me a favour by cutting ties. What we had wasn't sustainable. *You can't love someone if you don't love yourself.*

He's been cruel to be kind. But right now, it just feels crueller than it feels kind.

Snow is falling heavily as I call a cab on the morning of my departure date. The weather has prevented me from doing much in Kelowna, but having the privacy to stop and reflect is what I've needed.

The cab driver mentions that flights have been getting cancelled. I think nothing of it and stare out of the window at the distant, snowy hills.

There is a large queue leading to security after I've checked in. The departures lounge is packed with people, and the tensions in the room rise as airline agents announce delays due to weather conditions. Then the cancellations begin, followed by the irrational complaints. I sit calmly amongst it all, remaining hopeful. Fifteen minutes later, my flight is announced as cancelled.

"What will you do?" asks the middle-aged woman next to me with concern.

"I'll just sleep in the airport and get a flight tomorrow," I say with a shrug.

"I'd offer you to stay at my house, but I live in Summerland," she says apologetically.

At the check-in desk, the agent tells me that the next available flight isn't until Sunday. I sit back down and consider my options. Going back into Kelowna seems pointless. I check on my phone for buses to Vancouver, but they are all sold out. With an accepting sigh, I ask the lady to book me a seat on Sunday's flight. Then I pick up my bag and walk into a general lounge area to find a place to charge my phone. Boredom leads me to make a witty post on social media about my situation, and it's met with sympathetic comments from friends, many of them people I didn't know this time last year. It's a bizarre thought.

By ten o'clock, the airport is much quieter, as local residents have returned to their homes. I establish my sleeping spot for the night and lay one of my sweaters down on a seat as a pillow. My eyes stare up blankly at the squares on the ceiling. In the background, a janitor whistles to himself as he goes about his duties. The idea of staying in an airport for two nights suddenly seems less bearable. I spontaneously pick up my phone to look up the airport hotels and book a room for myself for the next day. The price is exorbitant, but privacy and a comfortable bed are better than a row of stiff chairs in an open space.

By eleven-thirty, I'm still wide awake. A stodgy sandwich from an airport deli sits uncomfortably in my stomach. I've spent the past hour thinking about Will, and now I remember the email sitting in my drafts folder—one I had started a week ago but with little intention of sending. With a long sigh, I sit up and open up the email.

My message is brief—an apology for my part in the texts, an expression of regret for our circumstances, a thank you for his friendship over recent months, a statement of my care, and well wishes for his future.

I watch the email send before lying back down again. I don't expect a reply, but I feel better if these are the last words that will be exchanged between us.

In the morning, I wake to the sound of announcements over the PA. I open my eyes to the sight of a large advertisement on the wall in front of me, showing a smiling family on their skiing holiday. A digital clock behind me tells me it's seven o'clock. I've somehow managed a few hours of sleep. I sit up and stretch my stiff back before lying back down lazily and watching people pass by.

At three o'clock, I walk outside into the fresh air gratefully. It's sunny but sharply cold, and the roads are extremely icy. I slowly make my way up the hill to the hotel, where a woman with a thick eastern European accent checks me in. My room has two queen beds and a large TV. I dump my bag down and gaze out of the window at the snowy hills looking over the valley. Planes are taking off and landing, but snippets of conversation overheard inside the airport suggested more snow is forecasted.

As I watch a small plane soar into the sky, I'm suddenly reminded that it was a year ago today when I boarded a small plane from Seattle and landed in Victoria airport.

"Happy anniversary." The words leave my mouth dryly.

I run a bath and think over the past year. It's been the most challenging year of my life, one that has left me questioning my abilities at various times and on various fronts. With all the struggles that took place, it's hard not to feel like it was a year filled with failures.

On New Year's Eve morning, the view from my window shows falling snow and a white fog that hides the hills. My shoulders sag with pessimism.

When I turn on my phone, there's a message from Hannah. It's the first I've heard from her in a while, and given the time difference, I expect it to be a "Happy New Year" message. Instead, she tells me that Jonas has just broken up with her. The image of her in my mind makes me ache inside. I sit down on the bed and call the number she gives me.

Hannah is sobbing as she tells me about the unexpected email she received a day earlier, in which Jonas said he felt unable to maintain a relationship while focusing on school. I can hear the disbelief and self-doubt in her voice as she speaks.

"It's not a reflection on you, Hannah," I say comfortingly. "It's just an unfortunate situation time-wise. Please don't blame yourself."

She whimpers unconvincingly.

"You can still have a great time in Europe without him," I say. "Don't let this ruin your trip. There's still so much you can see and experience for yourself."

"I'm sorry to bother you like this. I just wanted to talk to someone."

"You don't have to be sorry. I'm glad you called. I told you I would always be here, didn't I?"

After the call ends, I lie back on the bed and process the conversation. I'm giving out advice that I'm not even following myself. I've spent the past year looking for reasons to take the blame for another person's feelings, telling myself the feelings indicate I wasn't good enough.

At noon I check out of the hotel, and the same woman that checked me in leads me to the shuttle bus. Even though the airport is only a ten-minute walk away in the snow, I figure that I should make the most of the ridiculous amount of money I paid for the room. With excessive use of the footbrake, the woman warily approaches the highway junction before swearing angrily as a car pulls out in front of her.

The flight board shows delays. I sit quietly in the departure lounge and make no movement as my flight is delayed by another hour. At four o'clock, my phone starts beeping with New Year messages from England. After another thirty minutes passes, I look up at the flight board and shift restlessly in my seat. I just want to be home. Carrie has kindly offered to collect me from the airport. I don't know if she will ever truly understand how grateful I am to have met her this past year.

Finally, the airline agent tells the room they are ready to start boarding. Cold air whips my cheeks as I cross the tarmac towards the tiny plane. It only has ten or so seats inside. The plane moves slowly towards the runway, only for the pilot to announce we are turning around to do another ice check. I tap my boots on the floor, feeling like I might go mad.

As the plane approaches the runway once more and starts to pick up speed, I feel a rush of adrenaline. We launch into the air, and a sense of relief pours through me. Hopefully, Carrie won't have to wait too long.

With that thought comes a melancholy feeling. One that acknowledges that had things been different, it would have been Will collecting me from the airport. One that aches at the idea that someone and something can change so much in such a short space of time. The sore realization that I may never understand what happened.

Just under an hour later, the plane begins to descend, and I look out of the window to see the sparkling Christmas lights of Sidney. I feel a flash of déjà vu, and before I know it, my eyes are welling with tears. After a moment, I realize they are tears of pride, stemming from a sudden new outlook on the year that's been. I think of my health, my job, the friends I've made, the new places I've explored. It wasn't a year of failures; it was a year in which I tried, I persevered, and I achieved.

I start 2018 with a run to the beach and finish at the track doing interval sprints. Cold air fills my lungs as I jog towards the bend before surging forward. By the time I finish the set, I've reached the point of tasting blood, but there's something uplifting about feeling speed and power. At home, I put the most effort into cooking than I have in weeks and wash my bedsheets. As I lay the duvet over the mattress, I tell myself that this year will be better than the last.

I walk into the office the next day feeling more motivated. A fresh start with fresh energy. My desire to help others and facilitate connections has returned.

After catching up on my emails, I stand up for a break and look out of the window at people passing by. A figure crosses the road one block away. It looks like Will. There is the same tall and lean figure, the same smooth style of walk. The mourning feeling resumes as my eyes follow the figure, but I feel strangely comforted by the belief that I've seen him. Or maybe I'm just seeing things.

I turn back to my computer to see a new email from a recent graduate, thanking me for my assistance in helping him prepare for his successful job interview. I smile with fulfillment as I read the message. Then I find myself thinking about my Canadian life and how it would look if circumstances were different. With Will, my life would have more adventure, but part of me wonders if it would come at the compromise of a career that gives me purpose. As supportive as Will was, I might have always felt a need to undermine my own achievements for the sake of protecting his self-esteem.

The prospect of having seen Will lingers with me as I walk home, scanning the traffic for cars that look like his. In bed, I toss and turn, wrestling with rose-tinted glasses that still try to dwell on happier times and make excuses for behaviour. Then finally, I lie still, with a heavy acceptance that my thoughts of Will are not reciprocated, that he isn't able to be who I want him to be, that there is nothing more I can do, and that I deserve more.

I deserve more. As I reflect on the two relationships that came to an end last year, the words repeat in my head, growing firmer each time.

I tell myself that next time, I will have a relationship that is whole and equal, with a person that is present and committed. A relationship where I don't find myself questioning his feelings and looking for my faults, where I'm not pushed away either through cowardly intention or through an inability to let someone in. I'll have a partner who is willing and able to care and show affection, who is selfless and wants to actively participate in the relationship while maintaining his own interests and goals. I'll find someone who can develop himself without losing his authenticity, humility, and compassion. I'll find someone who has the graciousness and self-confidence to support my personal and professional endeavours and accomplishments. I'll find someone I can run with, not run after.

Over the weekend, I continue the healthy eating streak I've been on since returning from Kelowna. It's pouring with rain as I sit by the window writing a feature for a travel blog. It's been a while since I wrote, and I'm reminded how much I enjoy it. My mind seems to have more space to focus its attention on my interests. And yet, I can't block all consideration of Will completely. I try to quieten the caring voice that recalls him having a race scheduled on this day and wonders how he did.

There's a Tracks race scheduled next weekend, but I'm not sure if I want to do it. The possibility of seeing Will makes me reluctant. Despite the steps I'm taking in moving forward, I know there's a risk he would blank me, and such an act would humiliate me.

Connor returns home from the Maritimes that evening and shows me photos of cross-country skiing through a winter wonderland of snowy forests. When he sits down with his science journal, he seems fidgety. After a few minutes, he tosses the magazine on the coffee table with a sigh and says he has something to tell me.

I look up from my laptop. "What's up?"

"I've decided to move back home."

My eyes widen with surprise. "You're quitting your PhD?"

"I can transfer and do it from there. My supervisor confirmed."

I regard him with confusion. "So, how come you're moving?"

Connor scratches his head, and I notice a faint blush on his cheeks for the first time.

"I haven't talked about this before, but there's a girl over there. We dated a couple of years ago when we were both in Europe, but I broke things off because I wasn't ready for a relationship and, well, we didn't talk for a long time after that. She was really upset with me, understandably. But we reconnected when I went home and, truth is, I never really forgot her, and I guess she never really got over me. And so, I want to try and make it work with her."

There's a softness in his face as he talks, and the sight of it makes me feel warm inside.

"Wow. She really means a lot to you, doesn't she?" I say after a moment.

Connor smiles bashfully. "Sure does."

I look away and stare at the floor to process the news, wondering why I'm feeling flickers of sadness. I shake it off and turn to him with a supportive smile. "Well, I'm excited for you. I really hope it works out."

There's something I find admirable about his dedication to his goal, the risk he's willing to take.

I turn back to my laptop, and after a moment's thought, I open up the Tracks website and register for Sunday's race.

My alarm rings at six-thirty on Sunday. My legs feel loose and comfortable as I walk to the bus stop. With only two other passengers, the bus passes the entrance to Zoe's street. I impulsively look up it, but something tells me that I won't see Will today.

The gymnasium of the school hosting the race is packed with people in puffy jackets, and the floor squeaks with wet shoes. I stand in line waiting to check my bag. My eyes fall absent-mindedly to the floor before my ears drown out the loud chatter around me. The line moves forward slowly.

A familiar voice then catches my attention. I look up to see Zoe standing behind the counter. The sight of her makes my stomach swirl. I glance to the side, wondering if I should come back later when she isn't there. Then I glance back at the table, as if wanting to double-check it's her. She looks up, and her eyes land on my face. I stand frozen in anticipation of a hostile reception, and then I let myself breathe as her face breaks into a big smile.

"How've you been?" she asks warmly as I approach.

"Okay, thanks." My eyes leave her face with embarrassment. "Christmas was a little weird, not seeing any family."

"I bet," she says. Then she smiles encouragingly. "You're doing the 5k today?"

I nod. "We'll see how it goes."

I take a pen and scribble my name on the bag tag before holding it in my hands and looking at it hesitantly. Then I take a breath and force myself to look up with a weak smile.

"How's Will?"

Zoe's facial expression remains neutral, as if she's prepared herself for the question.

"He's doing well. He's busy getting ready for his trip in February."

My breath catches in my throat. "His trip? Where's he going? We haven't…" My voice trails off faintly.

"He's going to the States," she says brightly.

Her words hang in the air. As I absorb them, for a moment, I seem to forget where I am. Then I swallow the lump in my throat and smile.

"That's great. I'm really happy for him."

Zoe regards me quietly, and then her face wrinkles into a knowing smile of sympathy. The sight of it makes me pang inside. I say my goodbye quickly before the tears arrive.

I walk through the throng of people in a daze until I'm outside in the fresh air, alone. A fog hangs in the sky over the playing fields, but as I stand numbly processing the news, the fog slowly dissipates, and a ray of sunshine begins to pierce through. The ray grows wider and wider until the fog has completely disappeared, and I feel the warmth of the sun on my face. The part of me that wants to cry is outweighed by a feeling of happiness. A bittersweet acceptance that this is the way things should be.

I walk to the start line twenty minutes later with a fresh energy, suddenly feeling inspired. I can't pinpoint where exactly the inspiration comes from, but it gives me a sense of resolve that I haven't felt in a while.

The buzzer goes off, and I surge away from the group. Only two men are in front of me. A warning voice tells me I've gone off too fast and will struggle to maintain the pace I've set, but something inside me drives the momentum on. The voice of doubt that's lingered in my head over the past year vanishes, and my legs fly over the trail freely, uninhibited by pain. They never seem to tire as my eyes stay focused ahead, counting down markers showing me how far I've come. I'm breathing rapidly but feel in control.

I turn for home, and my legs continue to cruise along the trail, spurred on by an invisible power. Two or three men pass me, but it doesn't faze me. In this moment, nothing seems to limit me. Cheers start to sound from the side of the trail, and the claps and calls suddenly seem to signify something more than this race. They are telling me that I have persevered, that I am enough, that I am worthy. I let myself believe it, and I continue on, striding forward along the trail.

Manufactured by Amazon.ca
Bolton, ON